Sir John Vanbrugh

a reference guide

A
Reference
Guide
to
Literature

Sir John Vanbrugh

a reference guide

FRANK McCORMICK

G.K. Hall & Co.
New York

Maxwell Macmillan Canada
Toronto

Maxwell Macmillan International
New York   Oxford   Singapore   Sydney

Z
8925.15
M38
1992

G.K. Hall & Co.
Macmillan Publishing Company
866 Third Avenue
New York, NY 10022

Maxwell Macmillan Canada, Inc.
1200 Eglinton Avenue East, Suite 200
Don Mills, Ontario M3C 3N1

Macmillan, Inc. is part of the Maxwell Communication Group of Companies

Library of Congress Catalog Card Number: 92-13099

Printed in the United States of America

Printing Number
1 2 3 4 5 6 7 8 9 10

Library of Congress Cataloging-in-Publication Data

McCormick, Frank
    Sir John Vanbrugh : a reference guide / Frank McCormick ; indexed
by Frank McCormick and Janelle Carey.
      p. cm.
    Includes indexes.
    ISBN 0—8161—8990—0
    1. Vanbrugh, John, Sir, 1664-1726—Bibliography. I. Vanbrugh,
John, Sir, 1664-1726. II. Title.
Z8925.15.M38   1992
[NX547.6.V36]
016.72—dc20

92-13099
CIP

Contents

The Author

Frank McCormick is professor of English at Eastern Illinois University, where he teaches courses in the Restoration and Eighteenth Century, Literary History and Bibliography, and freshman composition. He is the author of *Sir John Vanbrugh: The Playwright as Architect* (Penn State Press, 1991) and of studies pertinent to the teaching of composition that have appeared in *Composition Chronicle, Journal of Teaching Writing, Writing Program Administration*, and elsewhere. He is currently working on *Hamlet's Progeny*, a study of *Hamlet* transformations from Shakespeare's day to the present.

Preface

With one exception of which I need to apprise the reader at once, I have sought to list in this bibliography every substantial discussion of Vanbrugh's life and his work as architect and dramatist published between 1694 and 1990. The exception pertains to reviews of performances of his plays. I have annotated such reviews when they have come to my attention through the secondary literature. I have not, however, made a systematic effort to include every review even of London performances of Vanbrugh's plays during their 284-year stage history. The reader particularly interested in nineteenth-century reviews will find useful discussion of them in Olshen (1974.11-12). Students of *The Provoked Wife* will find a generous sampling of reviews of performances of that play in Antony Coleman's edition (1982.2).

I have listed dissertations offering commentary on Vanbrugh to which I have found references in the secondary literature, as well as those listed in *Dissertation Abstracts International*. However, several Vanbrugh dissertations prepared at universities that do not report to *DAI* will likely have escaped my attention.

I must offer a caveat or two for readers whose interest is primarily in Vanbrugh the architect. In Vanbrugh's day and for a century afterward it was fashionable for ladies and gentlemen of quality to visit country houses of the sort Vanbrugh built. Often they recorded their impressions in diaries and notebooks, some of which were eventually published. Again, there are doubtless more published diaries and notebooks offering discussion of one or another of Vanbrugh's houses than I have been able to identify and annotate in the pages that follow.

For citations of *unpublished* manuscripts offering commentary on the buildings, Colvin's *Biographical Dictionary of British Architects 1660–1840* may be consulted (1980.4, Colvin's pp. 852–854). In Harris, 1979.4, the reader will find a list of studies published between 1715 and 1872 containing "illustrations" of Vanbrugh's houses, a category of publication beyond the purview of G. K. Hall's Reference Guide series.

Items pertinent to Vanbrugh's productions as comic dramatist are with rare exceptions annotated under the year of their first publication, as are (with a slightly greater number of exceptions) items pertaining to his buildings. First editions of rare items such as Benton Seeley's *Description of the Gardens of Lord Viscount Cobham, at Stow* lie scattered in a greater number of libraries than it has been possible for me to visit. In the Seeley instance and in others like it, I have placed an asterisk before the uninspected first edition, supplied bibliographical particulars gleaned from the *National Union Catalogue* or the *British Museum Catalogue of Printed Books* (or the best available alternative source), and cross-referenced the uninspected edition to the earliest subsequent edition that I have been able to inspect and annotate. An item that I have not been able to inspect in any edition is preceded by an asterisk and annotated with a citation of the source of the scant bibliographical particulars I have supplied—followed by the notation that the item is "unverified."

To a degree that will puzzle readers interested principally in reading the annotations proper, I have listed and cross-referenced a number of revised editions of works containing very brief treatment of Vanbrugh—Horace Walpole's testy paragraphs on Vanbrugh in his *Anecdotes of Painting*, for example, which appears first as 1765.1 and subsequently, with notes by editors Dallaway and Wornum respectively, as 1827.1 and 1876.1. Though neither editor of Walpole's *Anecdotes* has much that is new to say about Vanbrugh, the sheer fact of the re-introduction of Walpole's opinions *twice* into the nineteenth-century Vanbrugh conversation seemed to me to be potentially of significance to scholars wishing to trace eddies and currents in Vanbrugh's reputation. Another example of multiple listing that calls for some explanation is Disraeli's "Secret History of the Building of Blenheim" (1823.1 and 1849.1)—an essay whose ornate publication history seemed to me to require careful attention, it being the apparent fountainhead of an ensuing river of publications devoted to Vanbrugh's altercations with the Duchess of Marlborough.

A word about the indexes. There are two of them. The first—the Index of Authors and Other Sources—is principally a list of the names of authors whose works are annotated in the bibliography proper. Anonymous works are listed by title. Untitled, anonymous works are listed under the title of the journal in which they appeared. Works identified by the author's initials, or by a string of several authors' initials, or by a generalized title such as "Sir John Vanbrugh" (as is frequently the case with materials appearing in *Gentleman's Magazine* [*GM*] or in *Notes and Queries* [*N & Q*]), are listed under the title of the journal in which they appeared as well as by initials or generalized title.

A second index—an Index of Topics and Allusions—lists Vanbrugh *topoi* as well as references (chiefly) to scholars, artists, architects, friends, patrons, relations, and other figures whose connections with Vanbrugh, or whose opinions of him, are cited in the secondary literature. In this second index the reader will find references to discussions of Vanbrugh's buildings and plays, references to particular aspects of his life and work, as well as citations of a good many proper names of potential interest to the diverse community of Vanbrugh scholars.

I suspect readers of this Reference Guide who approach Vanbrugh by way of departments of English or theatre will be most surprised by the extent of the scholarship devoted to the architectural half of his career. Architectural historians, two of whom have devoted splendid chapters to Vanbrugh's achievements in the theatre, will perhaps be less surprised to find that the "Shakespeare of architects" has inspired a goodly number of books and articles attentive to his plays.

Acknowledgments

It is a pleasure to acknowledge the kind and expert help I have received over the past four years from the librarians at Eastern Illinois University's Booth Library. I am grateful as well to the libraries and librarians of the University of Illinois, whose Rare Books Room and its custodians have cheerfully supplied me with more than a hundred of the items listed in this Reference Guide. For assistance with eighty-five other items appearing in the following pages, I am much indebted to the librarians and their energetic helpers at the Library of Congress and the Folger Shakespeare Library, where I spent a particularly productive portion of the summer of 1991.

For helpful written responses to my queries concerning items in special collections at a number of other libraries I wish to express my gratitude to William L. Mitchell of the Kenneth Spencer Research Library, University of Kansas (who supplied me with a photocopy of the broadside I have annotated in 1728.1), and to Christine R. Bailey of Pennsylvania State University's Pattee Library, who supplied my earliest citation of Disraeli's "Secret History of the Building of Blenheim."

For help with other rare items, thanks are due also to Richard Oran, Public Services Librarian of the Harry Ransom Humanities Research Center of the University of Texas at Austin; to David Schoonover, Curator of Rare Books at the University Libraries of Iowa University; to Austin McLean, Curator of Special Collections of the University Libraries, University of Minnesota; and to the kind woman at the British Library who called just yesterday to tell me that the Montague Summers item that I have listed in 1921.3 appears in an untitled pamphlet pieced together many decades ago by the British Library staff.

It is a particular pleasure to express my thanks to Laurence Whistler for several pieces of helpful correspondence relating to the Whistler items annotated below—and to share with other Vanbrugh partisons Mr. Whistler's hope that the pyramid that Lord Cobham erected in Sir John Vanbrugh's memory at Stowe Gardens will one day be rebuilt at Stowe and bear once again the inscription Lord Cobham devised in his architect's memory:

Acknowledgments

"Inter plurima hortorum horum aedificia a Johanne Vanbrugh, lequite, designata, hanc pyramidem illius memoriae sacram voluit Cobham" (see 1750.1).

Introduction

I. The Plays

Jeremy Collier's decision to single out *The Relapse* and *The Provoked Wife* for extended censure in his *Short View of the Immorality and Profaneness of the English Stage* (1698.1)[1] gave both Vanbrugh's plays and their author instant notoriety. Charges of indecency would persist through the nineteenth century.[2]

His plays were, nevertheless, with few exceptions,[3] immediate hits with the theatre-going public. Three years after the first of them (*The Relapse*, 1696) had premiered, Gildon would observe in his continuation of Langbaine's *Lives and Characters of the English Dramatick Poets* that Vanbrugh's comedies had "got him the Preference to all our Modern Writers of Comedy, since [Wycherley and Etherege]" (1699.1). In 1702 the author of the anonymous *Comparison Between the Two Stages* pronounced *The Relapse* and *Aesop* two of the three "Masterpieces" that "subsisted *Drury-lane* House, the first two or three Years."[4]

Lynch (1953.4) and Kenny (1976.6) have documented the popularity of Vanbrugh's plays on the eighteenth-century stage. Kenny records that "six of them became staples in the theatrical repertory," enjoying 218 performances during the period 1715–1775—a figure that would rise to 299 were *The Provoked Husband* included in Vanbrugh's total rather than in Cibber's (see 1976.6). The response of playgoers to the 1728 premiere of the Vanbrugh/Cibber *Provoked Husband* offers vivid testimony to the relative popularity of its two authors. The audience applauded those scenes it assumed to be Vanbrugh's, hissed those it thought Cibber's.[5]

Vanbrugh's eighteenth-century admirers included Henry Fielding, who praised him for "cop[ying] Nature" and chastised those who simply "cop[ied]" Vanbrugh (1750.3)—as indeed Fielding himself had done some years earlier when he introduced into his farce *Pasquin* (1736.1) allusions to two of London theatregoers' favorite moments from Vanbrugh's plays: Lord Foppington's impoundment in Sir Tunbelly's dog kennel (*The Relapse*, IV.vi) and Sir Francis's expression of confidence in his prospects of a "Place at Court" in *The Provoked Husband*, IV.i. Samuel Johnson found Sir Francis's remarks in the latter scene so amusing that he committed them to memory (1791.1).[6]

Readers may study the "*reception*" and "*stage history*" of Vanbrugh's plays by pursuing the sources listed under those rubrics in the Index of Topics and Allusions. Purged of their randier elements, and much admired for the geniality of their humor,[7] the plays enjoyed a brisk stage life in the nineteenth century, sometimes in much altered guise, always to the disgruntlement of the chaste. Characteristic of the latter are the remarks of A. W. Ward, who in his *History of English Dramatic Literature to the Death of Queen Anne* pronounced the "morality" of *The Confederacy* to be "on Vanbrugh's usual level, which may be described as the very lowest to which English comedy has ever sunk" (see 1875.3). A reviewer of Robert Buchanan's 1890 adaptation of *The Relapse* applauded Buchanan's "Transform[ation]" of Vanbrugh's "vicious Miss Hoyden into a thoughtless, sunny, and impulsive tomboy . . ." (1890.6). For performance histories of "The Original and 'Improved' Comedies of Sir John Vanbrugh" on the nineteenth-century London stage, see Barry Olshen, 1974.11. No similarly comprehensive study of the twentieth-century stage history of Vanbrugh's plays has yet appeared.

His reputation in the earlier decades of the present century suffered under the uncomfortable perception of his comedies as "transitional" works. Palmer, who thought them "immoral," complained that Vanbrugh had pandered to the bawdier impulses of his audience while privately sympathizing with the chaster sensibility of the post–Collier era (1913.1). Perry found Vanbrugh's plays "sentimental" in their departure from the frank treatment of sexual relations of the preceding era (1925.7). Dobrée opined that they offer "no peculiar vision," hence "can add nothing either to our knowledge of life, or to our aesthetic experience" (1924.2). Mueschke and Fleisher responded in an influential article that averred (a) that the "feeling" with which Vanbrugh had endowed his characters was not sentimental but genuine; and (b) that Vanbrugh was indeed a writer of high seriousness—one who had treated rationally and sympathetically two important social issues: marital incompatibility and the unfortunate consequences for younger brothers of the law of primogeniture (1934.1).[8]

Among the studies of more recent vintage, Alan Roper's subtle exploration of the language of Vanbrugh's plays has achieved canonical status (see 1973.15), as has Arthur Huseboe's concise Twayne study of Vanbrugh's career as playwright (1976.5). Frank Patterson's analyses of the adaptations are sound and sensible (see 1966.6 and 1976.11). In 1973.1, Berkowitz offers a persuasive exposition of Vanbrugh's "subversive modifications" of the formulas of Restoration manners comedy. The present author's *Sir John Vanbrugh: The Playwright as Architect* discerns connections between the architectural and playwrighting halves of Vanbrugh's career, arguing that the plays and buildings are linked by their common concern with the imagery of the besieged citadel (1991.1).

II. The Buildings

Vanbrugh's initial reputation as an architect was shaped by party politics. The houses he designed for his Whig patrons, many of them fellow Kit-Cats, celebrated the Whig ascendancy and the myths its advocates sought to propagate—of "freedom" at home and triumph over French tyranny abroad (see Baridon, 1989.1). Early praise for the architect of Blenheim Palace tended in consequence to come from Whiggish quarters, censure from Tory ones.[9]

Partisan politics notwithstanding, by 1715 Vanbrugh had established himself as a towering figure in the British architectural community—builder of the grandest and most expensive private habitation England had yet known, intimate of Whig grandees, Comptroller of the Office of Works. A venerable fixture in the Whig establishment, he was the first man George I had seen fit to knight following his landing at Greenwich in 1714.[10] Any young man of the day who aspired to rise in architectural circles would need to address Sir John Vanbrugh in the most dulcet of tones—as did the thirty-five-year-old Colin Campbell in the prudent apostrophe he addressed to the Comptroller in his preface to the first volume of *Vitruvius Britannicus* (1715–1725.1).[11]

Campbell's efforts were of course directed toward advancing a Palladian program of building that, once established, would leave Vanbrugh's baroque palaces seeming to many observers, for the remainder of the century, to be excessively large, insufficiently attentive to the harmonies of cubes and double cubes—in a word, too "heavy."[12] Arthur Young's response to Blenheim Palace echoes that of many eighteenth-century visitors.[13] He thought it "a quarry" of "such innumerable and trifling parts, that one would think them the fragments of a rock jumbled together by an earthquake" (1768.2).[14]

The criticism to which Vanbrugh's buildings were subjected in his own day, the obloquy that fell on them in the aftermath of the Palladian revival, and the surge of praise that lifted his reputation in the last quarter of his century have been well described by Richard Boys (see 1947.1 and 1949.1). Nineteenth-century observers would find Vanbrugh's buildings "sublime," "romantic," "picturesque," rich in "imagination," evocative of England's proud history, harbingers of the Gothic revival—qualities they had been taught to admire by Vanbrugh's later-eighteenth-century champions, Robert Adam (1778.1), William Gilpin (1786.1, 1808.1), Uvedale Price (1794.1, 1810.1), and, most influentially, Sir Joshua Reynolds (1786.3, 1797.2).[15]

In our own century Laurence Whistler and Kerry Downes in particular have seen to it that Vanbrugh's achievements as architect are kept before the eyes of the fraction of the reading public that pays attention to architecture. Their minutely documented scholarship, and a good deal of other important twentieth-century scholarship, has both clarified the details of Vanbrugh's building career and rectified earlier neglect of Nicholas Hawkmoor's contributions to the building of Castle Howard and Blenheim Palace. The effusiveness of some of the nineteenth-century paeans to Vanbrugh—Sir John Soane's description of him as "the Shakespeare of Architects,"[16] for example, and Samuel Rogers's recirculation of Fox's claim that Vanbrugh was "almost as great a genius as ever lived" (1859.2)—has been replaced in our own century by a more temperate view, one that sees Vanbrugh as a "splendid amateur" whose "instant maturity" as an architect owed much to the expertise and solid draughtsmanship of his self-effacing "collaborator" Nicholas Hawksmoor.[17] The emerging consensus is tidily illustrated in H. M. Colvin's amendment of the *VANBRUGH* entry in his *Biographical Dictionary of British Architects 1660–1840*. The reference in Colvin's first edition to Vanbrugh's "highly personal" style (1954.1) is replaced in the revised edition by the assertion that his "houses must be seen as a work of collaboration" between Vanbrugh and Hawksmoor (1980.4).

The contributions of architectural and landscape historians to Vanbrugh scholarship in our own century[18] have been voluminous, with the result that we now know more about his life and the evolution of his building designs than anyone save Vanbrugh himself is likely to have known in his own day. These and other contributions to the secondary literature are listed under the *ARCHITECTURE* rubric in this volume's Index of Topics and Allusions. "Basic Works" by modern scholars are noted below.

III.   Some Basic Works

(N.B.   Some important modern studies of Vanbrugh's plays have been noted in section I above.)

Downes's new biography is essential (1987.4), as is his earlier book-length study of the architecture, with its 160 handsome photographs of the buildings and its authoritative list of Vanbrugh's architectural works and designs. (See 1977.2, pp. 277–278; cf. Downes 1987.4, pp. 515–516.) Also essential, and eminently readable as well, is Whistler's *The Imagination of Vanbrugh and His Fellow Artists* (1954.5). Beard's *The Work of John Vanbrugh* (1986.1) offers a reliable synthesis of recent scholarship on each of Vanbrugh's major buildings, as well as 125 usefully annotated illustrations. Blenheim Palace is given book-length treatment by David Green, 1950.6. Charles Saumarez Smith performs that service for Castle Howard, 1990.6.

Prospective students of the buildings might wish to begin by reading the pages devoted to Vanbrugh in Lees-Milnes's *English Country Houses: Baroque* (1970.6), in which Vanbrugh's principal houses are succinctly discussed, and illustrations are incorporated within the text. Valuable today principally for its many handsome Country Life photographs is Tipping and Hussey, *English Homes*, IV.2, *The Works of Sir John Vanbrugh and*

His School, 1699–1736 (1928.7). For descriptions and photographs of the interiors of Castle Howard, Blenheim Palace, and Grimsthorpe, see Charles Latham's *In English Homes: The Internal Character, Environment, & Adornments of Some of the Most Notable Houses of England* (1909.2).

Indispensable studies of Vanbrugh's building theory and aesthetics are those by Lang, 1965.3, and Cast, 1984.2.

H. M. Colvin's *History of the King's Works*, Volume 5 (of which Downes was one of the editors) is underconsulted (1976.1). Here is the place to learn of Vanbrugh's career at the Board of Works. For the primary documents pertaining to his career at the Works, see also Bolton and Hendry's *Wren Society* volumes, 1927.13, 1929.5, 1930.2, and 1940.4.

Wagner's *Heralds of England* (1967.6) offers authoritative discussion and assessment of Vanbrugh's career in the College of Heralds.

Concerning his career as theatre builder and impresario there are several good sources, beginning with Milhous's "New Light on Vanbrugh's Haymarket Theatre Project" (1976.10). For theatrical documents pertinent to his management of the Queen's Theatre at the Haymarket, see Thomas, ed. (1989.9). For discussion and assessment of his management practices, see Milhous and Hume's introduction and notes to their edition of Downes's *Roscius* (1987.10) and the same editors' introduction to *Vice-Chamberlain Coke's Theatrical Papers* (1982.10).

The correspondence is printed in vol. 4 of *Works* (ed. Webb, 1928.11), but many additional letters have been printed subsequently, including substantial additions in Whistler, 1954.5, and Downes, 1987.4. For a checklist of Vanbrugh's letters, their dates, and their printed sources, see Downes, 1987.4, Appendix B. For notations of several "letters not listed in Downes['s checklist]," see the "correspondence" entry under Vanbrugh's *LIFE* in the present volume's Index of Topics and Allusions.

The standard collection of the plays—printed on paper that is rapidly disintegrating—is Dobrée's edition of the *Works*, vols. 1–3 (1927.3). Michael Cordner's recent Penguin edition of the playwright's four best comedies (1989.2) offers Vanbrugh an opportunity to occupy a more conspicuous position in English and theatre curricula than the marketplace has previously permitted.

NOTES

1. Vanbrugh responded spiritedly in his *Short Vindication* (1698). For critical reaction, see the entries listed in the Index of Topics and Allusions under the rubric NONDRAMATIC WRITINGS.
2. For a sampling of the moral criticism, see the entries listed in the Index of Topics and Allusions under the rubric PLAYS, GENERAL, "criticism of [morality]." Michael Cordner, who has documented Vanbrugh's anti-clericalism in a series of recent publications, doubts that Vanbrugh "could have given such comprehensive offense to the reformers without realizing what he was doing" (see 1989.2; also 1981.4–5 and 1984.3).

3. Only *The False Friend* and *The Cuckold in Conceit* proved unsuccessful. For records of performances of the plays, consult the index of *The London Stage,* which lists, for example, eighty-seven performances of Vanbrugh's popular afterpiece *The Country House* during the period 1705–1760. Another useful source of comparative performance data is George Winchester Stone's "The Making of the Repertory," in Robert D. Hume, ed. *The London Theatre World,* 1660–1800 (Carbondale and Edwardsville: Southern Illinois University Press, 1980), pp. 181–191. Stone notes seventy-seven performances of Vanbrugh's *Pilgrim* during the period 1700–1728, seventy of *The Provoked Wife.* The former would decline in popularity as the century progressed. The Garrick years (1747–1776) saw only twelve performances of *The Pilgrim,* 134 of *The Provoked Wife.* See the *Provoked Wife* entries in the Index of Topics and Allusions for discussions of Garrick's enormously popular performances as a debrutalized Sir John Brute.

4. See 1702.1. In 1699, Gildon, the likely author of the *Comparison,* had spoken highly of *Aesop,* Part 1, of which he thought "sure, there has never been on the Stage, a Play of more general Satyr since *The Plain Dealer*" (see 1699.1). *Aesop* appears to have attracted considerable attention in its day. Concerning the versification of her poem "The Three Warnings: A Tale," Hester Thrale Piozzi reported that "this wild irregular measure is a sort of favorite with me, I learnt it in Vanbrug's *Aesop*" (see 1942.2). Huseboe thinks Vanbrugh's play "helped to popularize the anthologies of satirical fables that swarmed the book stalls around 1698, such as *Aesop at Bath, Aesop at Epsom,* and (in 1703) a collection by Bernard Mandeville, *Some Fables after . . . la Fontaine,* the forerunner of the most famous eighteenth-century collection of all, *The Fable of the Bees*"; see Huseboe (1976.5), p. 36. Commentary on *Aesop* and other of Vanbrugh's plays is cited under the WORKS/PLAYS/INDIVIDUAL PLAYS rubric in the Index of Topics and Allusions.

5. *The Provoked Husband* is Cibber's adaptation of *A Journey to London,* the play Vanbrugh had left unfinished at his death in 1726. For accounts of the 1728 premiere of *The Provoked Husband,* see Barker, 1939.2, and Woods, 1965.7. Cibber's disingenuous prologue misled the 1728 audience into assuming that the Townly scenes were Vanbrugh's creation and the "low" Wronghead scenes Cibber's. See also 1728.1, an undated broadside whose author complains that in *The Provoked Wife* Cibber had "barbarously Hack'd and Mangl'd" Vanbrugh's unfinished *Journey to London.*

6. Johnson is reported by Boswell to have "repeated, very happily, all Sir Francis's credulous account" on more than one occasion (1791.1). On the enduring popularity of *The Provoked Husband,* see 1980.6. Barry Olshen notes that the play "was performed with greater regularity" during the nineteenth century "than any other comedy of its period" (see 1974.11).

7. See, for example, 1821.1 and 1893.2.

8. Mueschke and Fleisher's article offered one of the first "thematic" approaches to comic drama. Thematic studies of playtexts proliferated through the 1970s and were widely anathematized in the aftermath of the critiques of such studies offered by Richard Levin in *New Readings vs. Old Plays: Recent Trends in the Reinterpretation of English Renaissance Drama* (1979) and Robert D. Hume in *The Development of English Drama in the Late Seventeenth Century* (1976). With respect to Vanbrugh in particular, Hume's emphasis on the "producible" aspects of playtexts is anticipated by Kronenberger, who thinks *The Confeder-*

acy Vanbrugh's "best play" because it reveals "in how great a degree he just *was* a playwright rather than a social critic or student of manners" (see 1952.3).

9. Witness, on the one hand, Kit-Cats Garth, (1715.2) and Rowe (1715.3); on the other, Tory pamphleteer Jonathan Swift (1711.2) and Abel Evans, after his falling out with the Whigs (1715.1).

10. See Thomas Hearne's notation of Vanbrugh's knighting in 1857.3. In his capacity as Clarenceux in the College of Hearalds, Vanbrugh himself had been among the party of dignitaries who had traveled to Hanover in 1706 to bestow the order of the Garter upon George I's son, the electoral prince of Brunswick-Lunenburgh and future George II. See Beltz (1841.1) and (for a detailed account of the ceremony) Downes (1987.4), pp. 318–322.

11. "Sir John Vanbrugh" himself, Campbell advised his readers, had supplied him with the "Designs of" his "Magnificent [Blenheim] Place," a palace whose "Manner [is] grand," its "Parts Noble," its "Air Majestic." So extraordinary a gift from "this worthy Gentleman" left Campbell "at a Loss, how to express my Obligations . . . for promoting my Labours in most generously assisting me with his Original Drawings. . . ." (See 1715–1725.1.)

12. Abel Evans framed his charge of "heav[iness]" so memorably (see 1780.1), and subsequent commentators have quoted the lines so incessantly, that they continue in our own day to color the popular perception of Vanbrugh's buildings.

13. For a lively catalogue of the impressions of eighteenth-century visitors to Blenheim Palace, see David Green (1950.7).

14. Swift and Pope would offer a handsome recantation of earlier criticism of Vanbrugh in their joint preface to *Miscellanies in Prose and Verse* (1727.1), but it was the earlier censure of Vanbrugh's buildings that would persist in the public mind, and apparently in Arthur Young's. Pope's disparaging account of Timon's Villa in his *Epistle to Burlington* ("a laboured quarry above ground" that "brings all Brobdignag before your thought" [1735]) would linger in the mind of many a sojourner to Blenheim Palace. Swift's witty critique of a much smaller Vanbrugh building to which he would give the name "Goose-Pie House" (1711.2) provided the stimulus to a complaint that would be frequently voiced in his own century—the complaint that the elements of Vanbrugh's building style were incongruous. (See 1765.1 for an influential early instance of this line of criticism. David Cast, in 1984.2, offers detailed discussion.)

15. See the present volume's Index of Topics and Allusions for citations of the numerous secondary works in which Reynolds's praise is quoted with approval. In the same index, under the heading BUILDINGS, TOPOI, see the citations of references to such nineteenth-century positives as "picturesqueness" and "imagination." S. Lang, in 1968.2, quotes Reynolds's and Price on Vanbrugh as a preliminary to suggesting that "Toward the end of the [18th] century [the] idea of a mixed Grecian-Gothic style is taken up in England on a conscious level . . . in part centering round a re-appraisal of Vanbrugh."

16. Soane praised Vanbrugh's buildings, apparently with some regularity, in lectures he delivered to students of the Royal Academy between 1809 and 1836. See 1929.2 and 1902.3.

17. In the Index of Topics and Allusions, see the citations of "Hawksmoor's role" listed under ARCHITECTURE, TOPOI. Goodhart-Rendel provoked a series of claims and counterclaims when he argued in 1924.3 that both Castle Howard and Blenheim Palace were "built under the supervision of Hawksmoor," and that the latter was in fact the real "author" of both buildings.

18. Vanbrugh's achievements as landscape architect and as pioneering proponent of historical preservation inspired a spate of interesting studies commencing in the 1930s. See the entries listed in the Index of Topics and Allusions under the category GARDEN DESIGN, and under the "garden" subheadings listed beneath the names of individual BUILDINGS. In the same index, see also the "Preservationist" entries listed under Vanbrugh's CAREER. David Watkin, to cite but one example of the direction some recent criticism has taken, avers in 1968.9 that the "picturesque aesthetic was invented in 1709 by Vanbrugh"—this in his memorandum of 11 June urging Woodstock Manor's preservation.

Abbreviations

A.A. Notes	*Architectural Association Notes* (not readily available in U.S. Library of Congress call number: NA12.A54)
AR	*Architectural Review*
BC	*Book Collector*
BMC	*British Museum Catalogue of Printed Books to 1965 (Compact Edition).* New York: Readex Microprint Corp., 1967.
BSEAA	*Bulletin de la Societé D'Etudes Anglo-Americaines . . .*
CahiersE	*Cahiers Elisabethains*
CLAJ	*College Language Assocation Journal*
CLife	*Country Life*
CompD	*Comparative Drama*
DAI	*Dissertation Abstracts International*
DNB	*Dictionary of National Biography*
DUJ	*Durham University Journal*
EIC	*Essays in Criticism*
ELH	*ELH*
ELN	*English Language Notes*
EM	*English Miscellaney*
GM	*Gentleman's Magazine*
HLB	*Harvard Library Bulletin*
HLQ	*Huntington Library Quarterly*

JNT	*Journal of Narrative Technique*
JSAH	*Journal of the Society of Architectural Historians*
London Stage	*London Stage, 1660–1800*
MLR	*Modern Language Review*
MP	*Modern Philology*
N & Q	*Notes and Queries*
NCTR	*Nineteenth Century Theatre Research*
NER	*New English Review*
NUC	*National Union Catalogue: Pre–1956 Imprints*
OCLC	OCLC, Inc. (originally Ohio College Library Center)
PQ	*Philological Quarterly*
PMLA	*Publications of the Modern Language Association*
RECTR	*Restoration and 18th Century Theatre Research*
RES	*Review of English Studies*
RIBA Journal	*Journal of the Royal Institute of British Architects*
Scriblerian	*Scriblerian and the Kit-Cats*
SEL	*Studies in English Literature*
SN	*Studia Neophilologica*
ThS	*Theatre Survey*
THStud	*Theatre History Studies*
TLS	*Times Literary Supplement*
TN	*Theatre Notebook*

Writings by Sir John Vanbrugh

Plays

(Parenthetical premiere date is followed
by date of first printing.)

The Relapse; or Virtue in Danger (1696), 1697.

Aesop, Part 1 (1696; adapted from Boursault), 1697.

Aesop, Part 2 (1697), 1697.

The Provoked Wife (1697), 1697.

The Country House (1698; adapted from Dancourt), 1715.

The Pilgrim (1700; adapted from Fletcher), 1700.

The False Friend (1702; adapted from Le Sage), 1702.

Squire Trelooby (1704; written in collaboration with Congreve and Walsh; adapted from Molière), not printed, but see discussion in 1928.2, 1968.7, and 1970.5.

The Confederacy (1705; adapted from Dancourt), 1705.

The Mistake (1705; adapted from Molière), 1706.

The Cuckold in Conceit (1707; perhaps by Vanbrugh, on the testimony of Cibber; adapted from Molière), not printed.

A Journey to London. [Being part of a comedy written by the late Sir John Vanbrugh, knt. and printed after his own copy: which (since his decease), has been made into an entire play, by Mr. Cibber, and call'd the Provok'd Husband . . . ; printed together with *The Provoked Husband; or A Journey to London]*, 1728.

Poetry

"To a Lady More Cruel than Fair," 1780 (see 1780.2).

Nondramatic

(Date of first verified, full printing is followed
by parenthetical citation of source.)

Mr. Van-Brugg's Proposals about Building ye new Churches, 1950 (see 1950.10).

A Short Vindication of 'The Relapse' and 'The Provoked Wife,' from Immorality and Prophaneness, 1698.

Reasons [for preserving "the Small Remains of ancient Woodstock Manour"], 1987. (Frequently—and often inaccurately—printed earlier in excerpted form. Downes, in 1987.4, pp. 347–348, prints from BL MS. Add.61353, ff.62–63 the fullest and most accurate available text.)

Sir John Vanbrugh's Justification Of what he depos'd in the Duke of Marlborough's late TRYAL, 1928 (in Webb, 1928.11, pp. 177–192).

Vanbrugh's Drawings and Buildings

DRAWINGS

Drawings by Vanbrugh in the collection at Elton Hall, Huntingdonshire, are reproduced in Howard Colvin and Maurice Craig, eds., *Architectural Drawings in the Library of Elton Hall by Sir John Vanbrugh and Sir Edward Lovett Pearce* (1964.2). Vanbrugh drawings in the Victoria and Albert Museum have not been printed collectively, though a number of them from Victoria and Albert and elsewhere are reproduced in Laurence Whistler, *The Imagination of Vanbrugh and his Fellow Architects* (1954.5) and in volumes 6, 12, and 17 of the Wren Society, London (1929.5, 1935.5, and 1940.4).

BUILDINGS

For a list of "Buildings wholly or partly executed" by Vanbrugh, see Downes, 1987.4, pp. 515–516.

Writings about Sir John Vanbrugh
1664–1726

1694

1 CARMARTHEN, MARQUIS of [Peregrine Osborne; later, 2nd Duke of Leeds]. *Journal of the Brest-Expedition*. London: Printed for Randal Taylor, pp. 13–14, 38.

Account by one of the commanders of the unsuccessful British assault on the French navy's compound at Brest includes praise of Vanbrugh's performance under fire, reporting that "Mr. *Vanbrooke* during all this Action stuck very close to me, and in a great many things, was extremely serviceable both by his advice and otherwise." (See also 1979.6.)

1698

1 COLLIER, JEREMY. *A Short View of the Immorality, and Profaneness of the English Stage*. London: Printed for S. Keble. Reprint. Edited by Benjamin Hellinger. New York and London: Garland, 1987, pp. 73, 101–103, 138–141, 180, 184, 212, 213, 214, 255–283. (Annotation and page references based on 1987 reprint.)

Includes castigation of *The Provoked Wife* and *The Relapse* for their "Jest[s] upon Religion." Cited in evidence are Berinthia's witty misapplications of Christian catch phrases, Sir John Brute's lewd impersonation of a clergyman, and Young Fashion's assertion that a clergyman can be bought with "Money, Preferment, Wine, and a Whore." In a detailed examination of *The Relapse*, the play's "Moral" is determined to be "vicious" and its dual plots ineptly crafted, the playwright having been insufficiently attentive to the "*Three Unities* of Time, Place, and Action." (See also 1704.1 and 1730.1.)

1

1699

1 LANGBAINE, GERARD, and GILDON, CHARLES. *Lives and Characters of the English Dramatick Poets*. London: Printed for Tho. Leigh and William Turner, pp. 142–145. Reprint. New York: AMS Press, 1976.

Argues that Vanbrugh's first three plays "have got him the Preference to all our Modern Writers of Comedy, since [Wycherley and Etherege]." While conceding that *Aesop*'s "Scenes are loose," the author is "sure, there has never been on the Stage, a Play of more general Satyr since *The Plain Dealer*." Defends *The Provoked Wife* against the charge of "loose[ness]" of construction, arguing that the play "teaches Husbands how they ought to expect their Wives shou'd make them a Return, if they use them as Sir *John Brute* did his." In *The Relapse* Lord Foppington is singled out for praise.

1701

1 "A True Character of the Prince of Wales's Poet, with a Discription of the New Erected Folly at White-Hall." London: Printed in the Year 1701, pp. 1–2. (Annotation based on text printed in Downes, *Sir John Vanbrugh*, pp. 527–529 [1987.4].)

Scabrous verses excoriating Vanbrugh's plays, buildings, and character. The design of his Goose-Pie House (1701) is ridiculed, asserted to be the venue of homosexual relations between its builder and "P_____" (glossed by Downes as Peregrine Bertie).

1702

1 [GILDON, CHARLES (?)]. *A Comparison Between the Two Stages*. London: Printed in the year 1702. Reprint. Princeton Studies in English, vol. 26. Edited (with introduction, notes, and index) by Staring B. Wells. Princeton, NJ: Princeton University Press; London: H. Milford; Oxford: Oxford University Press, 1942, pp. 20–21, 27, 37, 95–96. (Annotation and page references based on 1942 reprint.)

Includes scattered remarks (indexed in reprint) concerning Vanbrugh and several of his plays. Vanbrugh is denominated a "Gentleman of superior Sense" whose *Aesop* and *The Relapse* (together with Southerne's *Oroonoko*) "are Masterpieces, and subsisted *Drury-lane* House, the first two or three Years." Dryden is said to have "publickly Panegyrick'd" *The Relapse*. *The Pilgrim* is averred to have been Drury Lane's response to Betterton's planned staging of *Measure for*

Measure at Lincoln's Inn Fields. The plot of *The False Friend* is given two pages of debate, Chagrin the Critic objecting to the play's being styled "a *Comedy*, when the principal Character in the Play is kill'd."

1704

1   GILDON, CHARLES. *The Stage-Beaux Toss'd in a Blanket; or Hypocrisie Alamode.* London: Printed and sold by J. Nutt, near Stationers-Hall, pp. 28–29.

   In a comedy whose intent is to paint "a True Picture of Jerry [Collier, 1698.1] a Pretending Scourge to the English Stage," Dorimant takes "Mr. Collier" to task for discovering indecency and profanity where no other person "that ever saw or read the Play" had found it. Arguing that theatregoers are in fact vociferous in their denunciations of indecency and profanity when they encounter genuine instances of it on the stage, Dorimant cites the response of the audience to an offensive phrase uttered at the premiere of *The Relapse*: "that Expression in the *Relapse*, hinted at by the Author in his Preface, for barely having a suspicious Face, and looking a little too rudely on the Clergy, was not borne by the Audience, and left on the second Night."

2   *A Letter From several Members of the Society for Reformation of Manners. To the Most Reverend Father in God THOMAS by Divine Providence, Lord Arch-Bishop of Canterbury.* London. Annotation based on text as printed with omissions in Whistler, *Sir John Vanbrugh, Architect and Dramatist* (1938.7), p. 106. Lowe (1888.3) indicates that the *Letter* is "a four-page sheet with no title-page, dated 10th December 1704."

   Protests Vanbrugh's "Building of the Playhouse in the Hay-Market," expressing surprise that the Queen had "commit[ted] the Management of a Stage to that very Man, who Debauch'd it to a degree beyond the Looseness of all former Times . . . in the *Relapse*, *Provok'd Wife*, *False Friend*, and the rest of his Plays . . . ." Petitioners note that the Bishop of Gloucester had "recommend[ed] the Author to Punishment in the House of Lords," Vanbrugh having escaped censure only through the intervention of an unnamed "Friend."

3   [SHIPPEN, WILLIAM.] *Faction Display'd. A Poem.* London: Printed in the Year 1704, p. 13. *Reprint [says *DNB* entry for Shippen; confirmed in *NUC*]. In *A Collection of the Best English Poetry.* Vol. 1 (?). London: Printed and sold by T. Warner, 1717.

   Mock-heroic satire directed at the Whigs includes jibes at the Kit-Cat Club. One couplet is directed at Vanbrugh: "Van's Bawdy,

1705

Plotless Plays were once our Boast,/But now the Poet's in the Builder lost."

1705

1 DEFOE, DANIEL. *A Review of the Affairs of France: with Observations on Transactions at Home* 2 [Book 4], no. 26 (Thursday, May 3): 101–104. Reprint. Reproduced from the original edition with an introduction and bibliographical notes by Arthur Wellesley Secord. New York: Published for the Facsimile Text Society by Columbia University Press, 1938. Reprint. New York: AMS Press, 1965. (Annotation and page numbers based on 1965 reprint.)

   Satirical reflections on the magnificence of Vanbrugh's new theatre at the Haymarket and the motives of those peers who had contributed money toward its construction. Believes those who would "Reform the Stage" would be wise "not to Build it up, but to pull it down." Answers the "Prologue Spoken at the [theatre's] First Opening" with some verses lambasting the building, wherein "Vice's Champions, Uncontroul'd within,/Roul in the very Excrements of Sin."

2 GODOLPHIN, SIDNEY, 1st EARL OF GODOLPHIN. Treasury Warrant Appointing Vanbrugh Surveyor of Blenheim Palace. Printed in Ward (1893.3), I, lviii–lix, note and in Whistler (1938.7), p. 301. Annotation based on text printed in Whistler.

   Dated "*June* the 9th. 1705," the Lord High Treasurer's warrant appointed Vanbrugh "Surveyor of all the Works and Buildings . . . to be erected or made at Woodstock," the future site of Blenheim Palace, and "Authorize[d] and Impower[ed]" Vanbrugh "to make and sign Contracts with any Persons for Materials, And also with any Artificers or Workmen to be employ'd about the said Buildings. . . ." The warrant was placed directly in Vanbrugh's hands.

3 SWINNY [or SWINEY], OWEN. *The Quacks, or, Love's the Physician*. London: Printed for Benj. Bragg, at the Blew Ball, pp. 1, 15.

   Alluding to Vanbrugh's success in stopping the first announced performances of the play, and in having the printed version censored (see 1958.5), the prologue avers that *The Quacks* was "born with Teeth, but those in fearful doubt" ensured that "he shall not Bite." The exchange in Act II following the entrance of the Stationer "Freckles" (a farcical representation of Vanbrugh's friend, publisher, and fellow Kit-Cat Jacob Tonson) contains several scathing references to Vanbrugh. Freckles claims that he has made his ungrateful friends "an order of Poets, and manag'd the thing so gravely that out of this Body of Scriblers, have been chosen Heralds [the Earl of Carlisle had recently secured Vanbrugh's appointment as Clarenceux King at Arms],

Reformers of Manners" (an allusion to the language Queen Anne had employed in granting Vanbrugh and Congreve a license to build their theatre in the Haymarket). Several lines later Freckles avers that he has "brought [his quack physician] from Garrets to build Palaces." (See 1958.5.)

1706

1 BEDFORD, ARTHUR. *The Evil and Danger of Stage-Plays*. Printed and Sold by W. Bonny, and the Booksellers of Bristol . . . pp. 29, 31, 45, 59, 65, 88, 178, 185, 197, 198, 201–203, etc. Reprint. New York and London: Garland Publishing, 1974.

Includes frequent citation of instances of blasphemy in Vanbrugh's *The Confederacy, The Mistake, Squire Trelooby*, and in other comedies premiering at Vanbrugh's theatre at the Haymarket. Laments that the sponsors of that theatre offered "only a Pretence of *Reformation*" of the stage.

1708

1 DOWNES, JOHN. *Roscius Anglicanus, or an Historical Review of the Stage*. London: Printed by H. Playford, pp. 47–50. Reprint. Edited by Montague Summers, London: Fortune Press, 1929. Reprint. New York: Benjamin Blom, 1968. (Page numbers and annotation based on 1968 reprint.)

Includes the Drury Lane prompter's account of the unsuccessful opening season of Vanbrugh's Haymarket Theatre, commencing with the 9 April 1705 premiere of "a Foreign Opera [Greber's *Loves of Ergasto*], Perform'd by a new set of Singers, Arriv'd from *Italy*; (the worst that e're came from thence) for it lasted but 5 Days. . . ." Offers summary judgments of *The Confederacy, Squire Trelooby*, and *The Mistake*, followed by an account of Vanbrugh's August 1706 transfer of his license to Owen Swiney. (See also the annotated Milhous/Hume edition, 1987.3.)

1710

1 *SWIFT, JONATHAN. "The History of Vanbrug's House." In *A Meditation upon a Broom-Stick, And Somewhat Beside; Of the Same Author's*. . . . London: Printed for E. Curll.

Source: Swift, ed. Williams (1958.6). For annotation, see 1958.6; cf. 1711.2.

1711

1 ADDISON, JOSEPH, and STEELE, RICHARD. *The Spectator* (24 March): 94–95. Reprint. Edited by Donald F. Bond. Vol. 1. Oxford: Clarendon Press, 1965. (Page references are to vol. 1 of the 1965 reprint, on which the following annotation is based.)

The letter of 24 March 1710/1711 expresses dissatisfaction with "the mad Scene of the *Pilgrim.*" Contrasts "noble Instances of this Kind in Shakespeare" to the instance in Vanbrugh's adaptation of Fletcher's play in which "an Idiot" and his "Lust" are dramatized. That the scene was applauded by the audience of the day is suggested by the writer's request that the Spectator "animadvert frequently upon the false Taste the Town is in, with Relation to Plays as well as Operas." (Bond notes that Vanbrugh's adaptation of Fletcher's play had been "revived at Drury Lane on 30 April 1707 . . , and thereafter played frequently.")

2 *SWIFT, JONATHAN. "V———'s House[,] Built from the Ruins of Whitehall that was Burnt." In *Miscellanies in Prose and Verse.* London: Printed for John Morphew.

For annotation, see 1958.8. (See also 1701.1; cf. Swift's other verses on Vanbrugh's house in 1710.1.)

1715

1 EVANS, ABEL. "Upon the Duke of Marlborough's House at Woodstock." In *Elzevir Miscellany: Consisting of Original Poems, Translations, and Imitations by the Most Eminent Hands.* London: Printed for E. Curll, p. 33.

The speaker's interlocutor, taken on a tour of Blenheim and its park, finds the house incommodious: "'tis very fine./But where d'ye sleep, or where d'ye dine?/I find by all you have been telling,/That 'tis a House, but not a Dwelling." The poem is printed as "On Blenheim House" in 1780.1.

2 GARTH, SIR SAMUEL. *Claremont.* London: J. Tonson. Reprint. In *The Works of the English Poets, from Chaucer to Cowper . . , by Samuel Johnson, with Additional Lives,* by Alexander Chalmers. Vol. 9. London: Printed for J. Johnson [etc.], 1810, pp. 446–447. (Annotation and page references based on 1810 reprint.)

A country house poem in celebration of the seat Vanbrugh designed for the Duke of Newcastle. Lines 75–85 aver that "Nature borrows dress from Vanbrugh's art": "If, by Apollo taught, [Vanbrugh] touch the lyre,/Stones mount in columns, palaces aspire,/And rocks are animated with his fire." Adds that only the architect–poet himself "can Paint in Verse" the beauties of Claremont's park.

3 ROWE, NICHOLAS. "Reconcilement between Jacob Tonson and Mr. Congreve." In *Elzevir Miscellany: Consisting of Original Poems, Translations, and Imitations by the Most Eminent Hands.* London: Printed for E. Curll, pp. 9–10.
   For annotation, see 1720.1.

1715–1725

1 CAMPBELL, COLIN. *Vitruvius Britannicus: or, the British Architect.* 3 vols. London: [vols. 1–2] Sold by the author, John Nicholson, Andrew Bell, W. Taylor, Henry Clements, and Jos. Smith; [vol. 3] Printed and sold by the author and Joseph Smith. Reprint. New York: Benjamin Blom, 1967, 1 (Campbell, 1):5–6, plates 47–48, 55–71; 1 (Campbell, 2):2, 3, plates 31–34, 52–55; 1 (Campbell, 3):7, plates 5–6, 11–21. (Annotation and page references based on 1967 reprint, in which Campbell's three volumes are printed seriatim in vol. 1.)
   In a project designed to demonstrate that British architects since Inigo Jones had surpassed their Continental counterparts, the author includes plans, elevations, and views of Vanbrugh's Blenheim Palace, Castle Howard, Cholmondeley Hall, Eastbury Park, Grimsthorpe Castle, Kings Weston, and Seaton Delaval. Preceding each volume's plates are the author's "Explanations" of each plate. The comments on Blenheim Palace in volume one, for example, thank Vanbrugh for "most generously assisting me with his Original Drawings [of Blenheim Palace], and most carefully correcting all the Plates as they advanced."

1720

1 ROWE, NICHOLAS. "The Reconcilement between Jacob Tonson and Mr. Congreve. In Imitation of Horace, Book III, Ode IX." In *Poetical Works of Nicholas Rowe.* 2d ed. London: Printed for J. Tonson, etc., pp. 11, 49 [*sic*, pp. 11, 49 bound consecutively].
   In the poem's third verse paragraph, Vanbrugh's friend and publisher Tonson is made to say, "I'm in with Captain VANBRUGH at the present,/A most *sweet-natur'd* Gentleman, and pleasant;/He

1723

writes your Comedies, draws Schemes, and Models,/And builds Dukes Houses upon very odd Hills:/For him, so much I doat on him, that I,/If I was sure to go to Heaven, would die." First printed in 1715.3.

1723

1 JACOB, GILES. *The Poetical Register: or, the Lives and Characters of all the English Poets.* Vol. 1. London: Printed, and Sold by A. Betterworth . . , pp. 262–264. Reprint. Westmead, Farnborough, Hants., England: Gregg International, 1969. (Annotation and page references based on 1969 reprint.)

The entry for "Sir John Vanbrugh" praises the playwright as the delineator of characters who "appear more like Originals than Copies." The "Men of Wit are really so"; the "Dialogue is extremely easy, and well turn'd." Offers brief accounts of *The Relapse, The Provoked Wife*, and *Aesop*. Vindicates the "Design" of *The Provoked Wife* on the grounds that "it teaches Husbands how they ought to expect their Wives should shew a Resentment, if they use them as Sir *John Brute* did his."

1726

1 *Historical Register, Containing an Impartial Relation of All Transactions, Foreign and Domestick. With a Chronological Diary. . . .* Vol. 11, *For the Year 1726.* London: Printed and sold by R. Nutt, p. 13.

The "Chronological Diary" (at rear of volume) records the 26 March 1726 death of "Sir *John Vanbrugh,* Knt. Controller-General of his Majesty's Works, and Surveyor of his Majesty's Gardens and Waters"; former "King of Arms, by the Title of *Clarenceux*."

1727

1 SWIFT, JONATH[AN], and POPE, ALEX[ANDER]. Preface to *Miscellanies in Prose and Verse.* Vol. 1. London: Printed for Benjamin Motte, p. 9.

Includes the following recantation of the authors' earlier satire on Addison and Vanbrugh (see Swift, 1710.1 and 1711.2 and Pope, 1735.1 and 1949.7): "In regard to two Persons only, we wish our Raillery, though ever so tender, or Resentment, though ever so just, had not been indulged. We speak of Sir *John Vanbrugh,* who was a Man of

Wit, and of Honour, and of *Mr. Addison. . . .*" (In his *Imitations of Horace*, Epistle II.i [1737], Pope would write, "How Van wants grace, who never wanted wit!"—this as an instance of "how seldom ev'n the best succeed"; see ll. 286, 289 in *Poems of Alexander Pope*, ed. John Butt [1942], vol. 4, p. 219.)

1728

1 "A Full and True Account of two most horrid, barbarous, and cruel murders. . . ." [London]: Printed for J. How near Cheapside, 1 p.

    Undated broadside disparages *The Provoked Husband* on the occasion of its (10 January 1728) premiere at Drury Lane. Describes Cibber's alterations of Vanbrugh's fragmentary *Journey to London* as the murder of a "Posthumous Child"—"a fine Child," which "to all outward Appearance might have liv'd to a good old Age" had Cibber not "barbarously Hack'd and Mangl'd it in such a manner that it Dy'd on the Spot." Source of document: Kenneth Spencer Research Library, University of Kansas. In the 13 January 1728 issue of *Mist's Weekly Journal* (not seen), the same analogy is drawn using nearly identical language. (See the excerpt quoted in *The London Stage 1660–1800. Part 2. 1700–1729.* Vol. 2, p. 954 [1960].)

2 *Reflections on the Principal Characters in a late Comedy call'd The Provoked Husband. By a Private Gentleman. Dedicated to his Mistress.* London: Printed for J. Roberts, pp. 1–32 passim.

    Observes that *The Provoked Husband* has been "long the Topick of all polite Conversation." Attempts to synthesize "All the Arguments for and against it, both [Vanbrugh's] original sketch [the fragmentary *Journey to London*] and as it is form'd into an entire Play by Mr. Cibber." Claims that in printing *A Journey to London* together with *The Provoked Husband*, Cibber implicitly acknowledges that it was on Vanbrugh's "shoulders he mounted to so great a Height of Applause." Though Vanbrugh's fragment "leaves us in the dark" concerning the consequences of Lady Arabella's "Folly," her vices are said to be admirably drawn. Hence she serves as a monitory companion portrait to Vanbrugh's earlier depiction of the contemptible Sir John Brute.

1730

1 COLLIER, JEREMY. *A Short View of the Profaneness and Immorality of the English Stage.* 5th ed. London: Printed for G. Strahan

against the Royal Exchange in Cornhill . . , pp. 50–52, 54–55, 71–72, 93, 113, 136–151. Reprint. Hildesheim: Georg Olms Verlag.
A "Corrected" edition of 1698.1.

2   COLLIER, JEREMY. *A Reply to the Short Vindication of the Relapse and Provok'd Wife*. London: Printed for G. Strahan against the Royal Exchange in Cornhill . . , pp. 259–294. Reprint. Hildesheim: Georg Olms Verlag, 1969.

Rebuttal of Vanbrugh's counterattack in his *Short Vindication*. Parodies the *ad hominem* elements of the playwright's reply ("He that sees an Ulcer, or perceives an offensive Smell, is extreamly to blame in his Senses!"). In response to Vanbrugh's complaint that Collier's charges of profanity were couched in "general Terms," offers additional instances of offending passages in *The Relapse* and *The Provoked Wife*. (See also 1972.2.)

1732

1   [WEST, GILBERT]. *Stowe, the Gardens of the Right Honourable Richard Lord Viscount Cobham. Address'd to Mr. Pope*. London: Printed for L. Gilliver. Reprint. In Clarke, ed. *Descriptions of Lord Cobham's Gardens at Stowe (1700–1750)* (1990.3), pp. 39, 42, 43, 47, 49. (Annotation and page references based on 1990 reprint.)

Verse tribute to Stowe includes praise of Vanbrugh's "last design"—the "pointed Pyramid," said to be "sacred to [his] memory." Also describes two doric pavilions (attributed to Vanbrugh in a note) and Vanbrugh's "rustick" Temple of Bacchus. Described without mention of Vanbrugh's name are the "Sleeping-House" and "Nelson's airy Seat."

1733

1   VOLTAIRE, MR. DE. *Letters Concerning the English Nation*. London: Printed for C. Davis, pp. 187–188.

Remarks in Letter XIX that Vanbrugh's comedies are "more humorous" but less "ingenious" than Wycherley's. Avers that the "general Opinion is, that [Vanbrugh] is as sprightly in his Writings as he is heavy in his Buildings." Thinks it "extraordinary" that the comedy, presumably *The Provoked Wife*, he wrote while imprisoned in the Bastille contains "not a single satirical Stroke against the Country in which he had been so injuriously treated." (See also 1734.3.)

1734

1   *LANGLEY, [BATTY]. *Principles of Antient Masonry.* . . . [London]: At Parliament Stairs, Westminster.

Source: Harris, 1990.5, p. 272. Harris transcribes (from *Grub Street Journal*, no. 237, Thursday, 11 July 1734) an advertisement in which Langley's book is said to include discussion of "the different Modes or Stile of Building, according to Inigo Jones, Sir Christopher Wren, Mr. Hawksmoor, Sir John Vanbrugh, Colen Campbell, Lord Burlington, Mr. James, and Mr. Gibbs."

2   [RALPH, JAMES.] *Critical Review of the Publick Buildings, Statues, and Ornaments in and about London and Westminster.* London: Printed by C. Ackers for J. Wilford. Reprint (with "very large additions"). London: Printed for John Wallis, 1783, pp. 84, 177. (Annotation and page references based on 1783 reprint.)

Says Vanbrugh's theatre in the Haymarket "presents an execrable front to the street, and is abundantly too large or lofty for declamation." Vanbrugh's Goose-Pie House (not mentioned by name) is presumably one of "the number of little boxes that are built on the ruins of Whitehall. . . ."

3   VOLTAIRE. *Lettres Philosophiques.* Amsterdam: Chez E. Lucas, au Livre d'or. Reprint. Edited by Raymond Naves. Paris: Éditions Garnier Frères, 1962, p. 113. (Annotation and page reference based on 1962 reprint.)

French version of 1733.1.

1735

1   *POPE, ALEXANDER. Letter describing Blenheim Palace to unidentified correspondent [1717?]. In *Letters of Mr. Pope, and Several Eminent Persons. In the Years 1705, &c to 1717.* London: Printed for J. Roberts.

Source: 1956.7; unverified. For annotation, see 1956.7.

1736

1   *FIELDING, HENRY. *Pasquin. A Dramatick Satire on the Times.* . . . London: Printed for J. Watts.

Source: 1903.1. For annotation, see 1903.1.

1737

1 MORDAUNT, CHARLES, 3D EARL OF PETERBOROUGH. Letter to Alexander Pope. In *The Works of Alexander Pope, Esq.* Vol. 6. *Containing the Second Part of his Letters.* 2d ed., "corrected." London: Printed for T. Cooper, p. 211. Reprinted in *The Correspondence of Alexander Pope.* Vol. 3. *1729–1735.* Edited by George Sherburn. Oxford: At the Clarendon Press, p. 310.

In a letter that Sherburn dates "August 1732" in his 1956 ed. of Pope's *Correspondence*, the Earl of Peterborough reports his impressions of Lord Cobham's gardens at Stowe: "Immensity, and Van Brugh appear in the whole, and in every part."

1739

1 BADESLADE, J., and ROCQUE, J. *Vitruvius Brittanicus [sic], Volume the Fourth.* London: Printed for and sold by John Wilcox, George Foster, and Henry Chappelle. Plates 19–23. Reprint. New York: Benjamin Blom, 1967 [vol. 2].

Includes a "Plan and Elevation of the House, Gardens, and Park at *Claremont. . . .*"

2 *BRIDGEMAN, SARAH. *A General Plan of the Woods, Park and Gardens of Stowe, the Seat of Lord Viscount Cobham; with Several Perspective Views in the Gardens.* [London?: Bridgeman], 16 plates.
Source: *NUC.*

1740

1 CIBBER, COLLEY. *An Apology for the Life of Mr. Colley Cibber, Comedian.* London: Printed by John Watts for the author. Reprint. B. R. S. Fone, ed. Ann Arbor: University of Michigan Press, 1968, pp. 81–82, 120–122, 148–149, 151, 154, 165, 172–173, 175–178, 236, 284, 309. (Annotation and page references based on 1968 reprint.)

Among the remarks concerning Vanbrugh are the following: (1) Vanbrugh's "favourable Opinion" of Cibber encouraged the latter to "have a better [opinion] of his own acting—this after Vanbrugh "Honour[ed]" him by writing a "Sequel" [*The Relapse*] to Cibber's *Love's Last Shift*, choosing Cibber to play the role of his play's "chief Character," Lord Foppington; (2) *The Relapse* was not the "agreeable" Vanbrugh's first-written play, for "he had at that time [1696], by him, (more than) all the Scenes that were acted of the *Provok'd Wife . . .*";

(3) Vanbrugh wrote *The Relapse* "in less than three Months" to repay a debt he had contracted ("when he was but an Ensign," "at his Winter-Quarters") to Captain Thomas Skipwith, who in 1696 was principal shareholder in the United Company; (4) Lord Halifax, upon hearing "the *Provok'd Wife* read to him, in its looser Sheets, engag'd [Vanbrugh] to revise it" for production by Betterton's Lincoln's Inn Fields Company; (5) Cibber admired the rapidity of Vanbrugh's pen and the naturalness of his dialogue, which "gave [actors'] Memory less trouble" than that of any other playwright; (6) Vanbrugh's "Wit only laugh'd at" the "lashes" administered by Jeremy Collier in his *Short View*; (7) as a novice actress, Anne Oldfield went "unheeded" for nearly a year at Drury Lane until Vanbrugh, "who first recommended her, gave her the Part of *Alinda*" in his adaptation of Fletcher's *Pilgrim*; (8) Vanbrugh "had a very quick Pen, yet Mr. Congreve [Vanbrugh's partner during the first season of the Queen's Theatre venture] was too judicious a Writer to let any thing come hastily out of [Vanbrugh's] Hands"; (9) *The Confederacy* and other adaptations Vanbrugh prepared for the Queen's Theatre were hampered by the theatre's poor acoustics; (10) Vanbrugh was "prevail'd upon," prior to the 1725 revision of *The Provoked Wife*, to write a scene in which Sir John Brute masqueraded as a woman of quality as a replacement for the original scene in which Sir John had been made to "talk like a Rake, in the borrow'd Habit of a Clergyman" (cf. 1966.7 and 1982.2).

1742

1 [BOYSE, SAMUEL.] *The Triumphs of Nature; A Poem, on the Gardens at Stowe—To Mr. Pope, by a youth of 16* [title printed thus in t. of contents, June, p. 282]. Printed in installments in *GM* 12 (June, July, August):324 (June), 380–382 (July), 435–436 (August). Reprint. In Clarke, ed. *Descriptions of Lord Cobham's Gardens at Stowe (1700–1750)* (1990.3), pp. 98–99, 102–103.

Verse celebration of Stowe's gardens includes description of Vanbrugh's pyramid (a note transcribes the Latin inscription in his memory) and an apostrophe to Vanbrugh: "Nor cou'dst thou wish a more distinguish'd tomb." His "bold Rotunda" is also described.

2 [DEFOE, DANIEL.] *A Tour through the Whole Island of Great Britain. . . .* Appendix by Samuel Richardson. Vol. 3. 3d ed. London: Printed for J. Osborn [etc.], pp. 32, 271, 272, 274, 275, 276, 277, 298–299.

Includes notice of "the Duke of *Ancaster*'s pleasant seat at Grimsthorpe" in Lincolnshire. The house and park are judged to be "large and beautiful." Richardson's Appendix (reprinted in 1990.3) describes Lord Cobham's gardens at Stowe, mentioning Vanbrugh's two doric pavilions as well as his pyramid (and Cobham's inscription in his memory), Temple of Bacchus, Nelson's Seat, and Rotunda. In a section of the Appendix headed "Vol. 1, p. 301," Vanbrugh's East-bury House is briefly described.

1744

1 *SEELEY, B[ENTON]. *A Description of the Gardens of Lord Vis-count Cobham, at Stow in Buckinghamshire. . . .* Northampton: Printed by W. Dicey [etc.], 27 pp.
   Source: *NUC.* For annotation, see 1747.1.

1746

1 THOMSON, JAMES. *The Seasons.* London: A. Millar. Reprint. In *The Complete Poetical Works of James Thomson.* Edited by J. Logie Robertson. London, New York, Toronto, Melbourne: Oxford University Press, 1908, pp. 105–106, 156–157. (Annotation, page, and line references based on 1908 reprint.)
   Lines 1429–1442 in "Summer" praise Claremont's "terraced height, and Esher's groves"—this in reference to the house and grounds Vanbrugh designed for the Duke of Newcastle. Lines 652–682 in "Autumn" celebrate Eastbury and its park, designed by Vanbrugh for George Bubb Dodington.

1747

1 SEELEY, BENTON. *A Description of the Gardens of Lord Viscount Cobham, at Stow in Buckinghamshire.* 4th ed, corrected and enlarged. Northampton: Printed by W. Dicey, 26 pp. 1st ed. cited in 1744.1; many subsequent editions in 18th century, including 1745, 1746, 1747, 1748, 1749, 1750, 1752(?), 1756, 1759, 1762, and frequently thereafter.
   A guidebook for visitors to Stowe's gardens, as designed by Vanbrugh and Charles Bridgeman. Includes descriptions of several of Vanbrugh's garden buildings.

2 WHINCOP, THOMAS, [and MOTTLEY, JOHN]. *Scanderbeg; or, Love and liberty. A tragedy. . . . To which are added, A list of all the dramatic authors with some account of their lives; and of all the dra-*

matic pieces ever published in the English language, to the year 1747. [*List* putatively written by John Mottley.] London: Printed for W. Reeve, pp. 296–298.

The entry for Vanbrugh offers a biographical sketch followed by a list of his plays with notations concerning their reception. *The Relapse* and *The Provoked Wife* received "great Applause" at their premieres; *Aesop*, Pt. I had "great Success," *The False Friend* "good Success," *The Mistake* "great Success," *The Confederacy* "Applause." Vanbrugh is called "a great Genius, being not only an excellent Poet but an ingenious and skillful Architect." An account of the Haymarket Theatre's inception includes the notation that the building's "first Stone was inscribed with the Words THE LITTLE WHIG, in Honour to" the Duke of Marlborough's second daughter, the Countess of Sunderland.

1748

1 C., J. d. *Les Charmes de Stow: ou Description de La belle Maison de Plaisance de Mylord Cobham.* Londres: J. Nourse. Reprint. In Clarke, ed. *Descriptions of Lord Cobham's Gardens at Stowe (1700–1750)* (1990.3), pp. 159, 165. (Annotation and page references based on 1990 reprint.)

Includes the observation that Blenheim and Stowe comprehend "tout ce que ce riche Pays [England] a de plus brillant & de plus magnifique." Brief descriptions of three of Vanbrugh's Stowe temples— the Temple of Bacchus, the Rotunda, and the Temple of Sleep.

2 GILPIN, WILLIAM. *A Dialogue upon the Gardens of the Right Honourable the Lord Viscount Cobham, at Stow in Buckinghamshire.* London: Printed for B. Seeley. Reprint. Augustan Reprint Society, no. 176. Los Angeles: William Andrews Clark Memorial Library, 1976.

For annotation of 3d ed., see 1751.1.

1750

1 BICKHAM, GEORGE. *The Beauties of Stow: or, a Description of the Pleasant Seat, and Noble Gardens, of the Right Honourable Lord Viscount Cobham.* London: Printed by E. Owen, in Hand-Court, 67 pp. Reprint. Los Angeles: The Augustan Reprint Society, 1977.

A guidebook to the garden Vanbrugh and Bridgeman designed for Viscount Cobham in c. 1720. The text inscribed on the sixty-foot

1751

"Egyptian Pyramide," which Cobham "thought fit . . . should be erected to [Vanbrugh's] memory," is transcribed as follows: "Inter plurima hortorum horum aedificia a Johanne Vanbrugh, lequite, designata, hanc pyramidem illius memoriae sacram voluit Cobham."

2   [CHETWOOD, WILLIAM RUFUS.] *British Theatre. Containing the Lives of the English Dramatic Poets; with an Account of All Their Plays.* Dublin: Printed for Peter Wilson, pp. 127–128.

A list of Vanbrugh's plays is prefaced by a sketch of his career. Avers that he was confined in the Bastille as a "*Spy*" after "being found taking Plans of some Fortifications." There he "wrote several of his Comedies, merely for Amusement," and so charmed "several of the Nobility . . . with his Wit and Humour" that the king released him "some Days before the Sollicitation came from England."

3   FIELDING, HENRY. *The History of Tom Jones, a Foundling.* 4th ed. London: Printed for A. Millar.

For annotation, see 1973.5.

4   SEELEY, BENTON. *Views of the Temples, and other ornamental Buildings, in the Gardens at Stow.* . . . n.p. Reprint. In Clarke, ed. (1990.3), pp. 146–157. (Annotation and page references based on 1990 reprint; item not listed in *NUC* or in *BMC*. For publication history, see Clarke's headnote.)

Includes engravings by G. Vandergucht and George Vertue of the following buildings and temples in Lord Cobham's gardens at Stowe: "2 Pavilions at the Entrance to the Park," "Egyptian Pyramid," "The Temple of Bacchus," "Nelson's Seat," "The Rotunda," "The Sleeping Parlour," "The Witch House," and "The Keeper's Lodge in the Park." For discussion of evidence of Vanbrugh's hand in these temples, see Whistler, 1950.13.

1751

1   GILPIN, WILLIAM. *A Dialogue: Containing a Description of the Gardens of the Right Honourable the Lord Viscount Cobham, at Stowe in Buckinghamshire.* 3d ed. London: Printed for B. Seeley, pp. 4–5, 7.

Includes description of Stowe's pyramid with its Latin inscription to Vanbrugh, here translated, "To the Memory of Sir John Vanbrugh, by whom several of the Buildings in these Gardens were designed, Lord Cobham hath erected this Pyramid." Also describes

Vanbrugh's Rotunda, "raised upon Ionic Pillars" and "ornamented with a gilt Statue of the *Venus* of Medici." For citation of 1st ed., see 1748.2.

2 STAMPER, FRANCIS. *A Modern Character, Introduc'd In the Scenes of Vanbrugh's Aesop. As it was acted at a late private Representation of Henry the Fourth, perform'd Gratis at the little Opera-House in the Haymarket.* 3d ed. London: Printed for F. Stamper, vi. (*BMC* cites a 2d ed., 1751. No earlier ed. is listed either there or in *NUC.*)

   The preface to this adaptation of *Aesop* seeks to justify the "Impropriety of introducing" into Vanbrugh's play the "Modern Character" (Spouter) referred to in the title. In response to the protests of certain "Gentlemen . . . who were offended by some Passages, which they alone could apply," argues that "Sir John Vanbrugh himself has set such an Example throughout his whole play." (*A Modern Character* appears to have expired after the performance cited on the title page.)

3 *STAMPER, F[RANCIS]. *Sir John Vanbrugh, Dramatist.* London.
   Source: Fluchère, 1980.9; unverified. Probably a mangled citation of 1751.2 above, which is identified in *BMC* as follows: "STAMPER (F.) *Dramatist*" (the italicized "Dramatist" identifies Stamper by profession) followed by the citation "*A Modern Character* . . . London [1751]."

1753

1 Cibber, Mr. [Theophilis], and other Hands. *Lives of the Poets of Great Britain and Ireland.* Vol. 4. London: Printed for R. Griffiths, pp. 99–111.

   Avers that Vanbrugh was imprisoned for surveying the fortifications of France. Reports the information supplied in Cibber's *Apology* (1740.1) concerning the commencement of Vanbrugh's playwriting career, the conversational qualities of his dialogue, and his venture at the Haymarket. Remarks on the plays include the lament that "Many women who have beheld [*The Provoked Wife*] may have been stimulated to emulate Lady Brute in her method of revenge, without having suffered her provocation." Discerns "great force of thinking" in Aesop's reply to the country squire "who comes to complain of the bad conduct of those in power."

1754

1 [MURPHY, ARTHUR.] Remarks on *The Provoked Wife*. *The Gray's Inn Journal*, no. 96 (17 August). Reprint. In *The Gray's Inn Journal*. Vol. 2. London: Printed by W. Faden, for P. Vaillant, 1756, pp. 279–280. (Annotation and page citation based on 1756 reprint.)

Praises Vanbrugh's rendering of Sir John Brute, who "is constantly diverting us with an odd whimsical Way of Thinking, which at once serves to display his own Foibles, and entertains his Audience with a Pleasantry of which he seems . . . totally unconscious himself."

1757

1 *Review of performance of *The Provoked Wife*. *The London Chronicle*, 3–5 March.

Source: Coleman, 1982.2, pp. 25, 26, 47nn. 61, 68; unverified. Review of 3 March performance of *The Provoked Wife* at Drury Lane. Coleman cites reviewer's praise of the play's "natural dialogue," tightly knit "Fable," and plenitude of stage "Business." Notes reviewer's wish that Lady Brute had "endeavoured to reclaim" her husband "by becoming Patience and correct Behaviour on her Side."

1758

1 *Remarks on *The Provoked Wife*. *The London Chronicle*, 7 October.

Source: Coleman, 1982.2, pp. 26, 47n.66; unverified. Coleman quotes author's opinion that Vanbrugh "was wholly in the right rather to draw his women [in *The Provoked Wife*] as he has done, than by giving them opposite manners, to have made them such unmeaning things as half our modern comedies are filled with."

1759

1 "An Account of the Life and Writings of the Author." Preface to *Plays, Written by Sir John Vanbrugh*. Vol. 1. London: Printed for C. Hitch and L. Hawes . . , pp. 3–12. Reprint. London: Printed for J. Rivington, 1776.

The account of Vanbrugh's "life and writings" is principally a compilation of unacknowledged quotations from Cibber's *Apology* (1740.1).

1761

1 DYER, JOHN. *The Fleece.* In *Poems. By John Dyer, L. L. B.* London: Printed by John Hughes, pp. 146–147. Reprint. Westmead, Farnborough, Hants., England: Gregg International, 1969.

Verse celebration of Britain's sheep and wool trade records in Book III that among the products to which fleece gives rise is the "many-colour'd arras." Offered as examples are "The Duke of Marlborough's martial tapestries" in the "stately rooms" of Blenheim Palace.

1764

1 BAKER, DAVID ERSKINE. *Companion to the Playhouse.* Vol. 1. London: Printed for B. T. Becket & P. A. Dehondt [etc.], 1:E5r, G6r, R5r, S3r–v; 2:Hh2v.

Alphabetical listing of plays includes entries for Vanbrugh's *Country House* ("nearly a translation from a *French* piece"), *The False Friend* ("acted at *Dr. Lane*, with very good success"), *The Provoked Wife* (its "Moral" is defective; "all that can be deduced from it, is, that a brutish Husband deserves to be made a Cuckold"), and *The Relapse* (in which Berinthia's conversations with Loveless and Coupler's with Young Fashion are found to "convey Ideas" of excessive "Warmth and Indecency"). The "Vanbrugh" entry sketches the playwright's career, reporting that his family's origins were French and repeating the story that he was sent to the Bastille for scrutinizing French fortifications too intently. Credits Vanbrugh and Congreve with reviving the "Reputation" of the stage but regrets that neither writer was free of "Obscenity and Licentiousness." (See also 1782.1.)

1765

1 WALPOLE, HORACE. *Anecdotes of Painting in England.* Vol. 3. Strawberry Hill: Printed by Thomas Kingate, pp. 164–166.

Includes a critical portrait of Vanbrugh the architect. Cites with approval the barbs of Swift and other detractors, charging that "The style of no age, no country, appears in his works; he broke through all rule, and compensated for it by no imagination." Concludes that had Vanbrugh "borrowed from Vitruvius as happily as from Dancour[t]," two of whose comedies Vanbrugh adapted, "Inigo Jones would not be the first architect of Britain." (For later eds., see 1827.1 and 1876.1.)

19

1766

1 GWYNN, JOHN. *London and Westminster Improved*. London: Printed for the author. Sold by Mr. Dodsley [etc.]. Reprint. Westmead, Farnborough, Hants., England: Gregg International, 1969, pp. 43–45. (Annotation and page references based on 1969 reprint.)

Observes that "the offense [Vanbrugh's] wit gave to his contemporaries was amply revenged by them in criticisms on his buildings," whose "singular[ity]" rendered them vulnerable to attack. A "romantic castle builder," he is "deficient in . . . elegance and decorum," "too many . . . of his designs" being marred by "whim and caprice." The "quantity and variety" of Blenheim Palace's "parts" are nevertheless striking in their "grandeur and magnificence."

1767

1 BROWNSMITH, JOHN. *The Dramatic Time-piece: or, Perpetual Monitor*. . . . London: Printed for J. Almon, p. 69. Reprint. Louisville, Ky.: Lost Cause Press, 1961.

Includes notation of the duration of 1760s' performances of *The Provoked Wife*. Acting time for Act I was 22 minutes; for Act II, 18 minutes; Act III, 32; Act IV, 32; Act V, 39 minutes. Total acting time: 2 hours and 23 minutes.

1768

1 SWIFT, JONATHAN. Letter VIII. In *Letters, Written by the Late Jonathan Swift . . . and Several of His Friends. From the Year 1710 to 1742*. Vol 4. Edited by Deane Swift. London: Printed for C. Bathhurst, p. 82.

In a letter to Stella dated 7 November 1710, Swift writes that "Vanbrugh . . . had a long quarrel with me about those *Verses on his [Goose-Pie] House*; but we were very civil and cold. Lady *Marlborough* used to teaze him with them, which had made him angry, though he be a good-natured fellow." The letter is also printed in 1948.5.

2 YOUNG, ARTHUR. *A Six Weeks Tour, through the Southern Counties of England and Wales*. London: Printed for W. Nicoll, pp. 279–282.

Includes description of Blenheim Palace. Finds Houghton Hall "heavy" but Blenheim immeasurably more so—"a quarry" of "such innumerable and trifling parts, that one would think them the fragments of a rock jumbled together by an earthquake."

1769

1 "Genuine Anecdotes, Never Before Published, of the Late Prince of Wales, . . . Sir John Vanbrugh . . . [et al.]." *GM* 39 (February):62–63.

Anecdotes include a recapitulation of the information concerning Vanbrugh that Pope supplied to Ruffhead in 1769.2.

2 RUFFHEAD, OWEN. *Life of Alexander Pope, Esq. Compiled from Original Manuscripts; with a Critical Essay on his Writings and Genius.* London: Printed for C. Bathurst. Reprint. Hildesheim: Georg Olms Verlagbuschhandlung, 1968, p. 494. (Annotation and page citation based on 1968 reprint.)

Reports that Pope told him he had once taken Swift to task for "satiriz[ing]" Vanbrugh "severely in two or three poems" (see 1710.1 and 1711.2). Pope advised Swift that those who knew Vanbrugh personally (Swift had "not the least acquaintance with" him) knew him to be "the most easy careless writer and companion in the world." He "pretended to no high scientific knowledge in the art of building," and "wrote without much attention to critical art." To Pope's praise of Vanbrugh for capturing in his *Aesop* the "very spirit of" La Fontaine, Vanbrugh is said to have replied, "It may be so . . . , but, I protest to you, I never read Fontaine's Fables." Ruffhead's comments are repeated in 1769.1.

1770

1 BIELFELD, JACOB FRIEDRICH. *Letters of Baron Bielfeld. . . .* Translated from the German by Mr. Hooper. Vol. 4. London: Printed for J. Robson, pp. 99–101. Reprinted in part in Downes, *Vanbrugh* (1977.2). (Annotation based on portion printed in Downes, p. 275.)

Thinks Blenheim Palace "too much loaded with columns and other heavy ornaments" but admires the building's "majesty," finding it reminiscent of ancient Greek and Roman structures. Avers that Vanbrugh's son Charles had shown him "all the designs of his father. . . ."

2   GENTLEMAN, FRANCIS. *The Dramatic Censor*. Vol. 2. London: Printed for J. Bell, pp. 469–470.

Includes two paragraphs on Vanbrugh. One expresses surprise at David Garrick's revival of so indecent a play as *The Provoked Wife*. The other laments Vanbrugh's tendency to make his servant characters "smart, humorous fellows" who behave with indecorous familiarity in their interactions with their masters.

3   YOUNG, ARTHUR. *A Six Months Tour through the North of England.* . . . Vol. 1. Dublin: Printed for P. Wilson [etc.], pp. 50–52.

Includes a description of Grimsthorpe Castle. Praises the "approach" and the house's "magnificent" appearance "at first view." Describes the house's interior—its dimensions and furnishings. Cast (1984.2, p. 311n. 3) reports that in vol. 2 (p. 61 in a 1769 edition) Young describes Castle Howard as "so heavy and clumsy . . . as to be perfectly disgusting" (passage not verified in 1770 edition).

1776, 1778

1   *LICHTENBERG, GEORGE. Letters from England. In *Deutches Museum*, 1776 and 1778, addressed to the Editor, Heinrich Christian Boie.

Source: Lichtenberg, 1938.3. For annotation of the Englished letters, with commentary on *The Provoked Wife*, see 1938.3.

1777

1   "The British Theatre. Drury Lane." *London Magazine* 46 (March):126–128.

Review of Drury Lane production of *A Trip to Scarborough*, Sheridan's adaptation of Vanbrugh's *Relapse*. Notes that Sheridan's "alterations . . . were rather unfavourably received on the first and second representations"—and "justly so." Praises Vanbrugh in the face of attacks by "news-paper critics of the present day." Because he "conceived justly, drew boldly, and took nature for his guide," Vanbrugh's comedies "will be read as long as wit, humour, and character, have any estimation among us."

2   *Review of performance of Sheridan's *A Trip to Scarborough*. *The Morning Chronicle*, 25 February.

Source: Loftis, 1977.6, pp. 80–81; unverified. Loftis reports that reviewer describes Sheridan's alterations of Vanbrugh's *Relapse*. Reviewer's conclusion: "(considering the heap of indecency he had to remove), [Sheridan] achieved an Herculean task. . . ."

3 *Review of performance of Sheridan's *A Trip to Scarborough*. *The Gazetteer and New Daily Advertiser*, 28 March.
Source: Loftis, 1977.6, p. 81; unverified. Loftis notes reviewer's comment that on its third performance, Sheridan's play met a "favourable reception," despite the "modern preference for Vanbrugh."

1778

1 ADAM, ROBERT. *The Works in Architecture of Robert and James Adam, Esquires*. Vol. I. London: Printed for the Authors [etc.]. Reprint. [Paris?]: E. Thézard fils, Publisher Dourdan, 1900. Reprint. New York: Dover Publications, 1980. (Annotation based on 1900 reprint, in which most pages are unnumbered.)
The first preface (pp. 2–3 in the 1900 reprint) pronounces Vanbrugh's buildings "rough jewels of inestimable value," the work of an architect whose reputation had been unjustly maligned by "a torrent of undistinguishing prejudice and abuse." The last preface includes the judgment that "Vanbrugh understood better than either [Inigo Jones or Christopher Wren] the art of living among the great," his "particular merit" being his "commodious arrangement of compartments." Laments that his indifference to "rule" and his "passion" for magnificence left him incapable of "discerning what was truly simple, elegant, and sublime."

1780

1 EVANS, DR. [ABEL]. "On Blenheim House," "On Sir J. Vanbrugh; an Epigrammatical Epitaph," "On a Learned Device on Blenheim['s] Great Gate: 'A Huge Lion Tearing a Cock in Pieces,'" and "On the Same." In *A Select Collection of Poems: with Notes, Biographical and Historical*. Edited by John Nichols. Vol. 3. London: Printed by and for J. Nichols, pp. 161–162.
Four short satirical poems on Vanbrugh's architecture. In "On Blenheim Palace" (see 1715.1) the speaker responds to his guide's praise of Blenheim with the question, "But where d'ye sleep, or where d'ye dine?" The epitaph "On Sir J. Vanbrugh" asks "Earth" to "Lie heavy on him . . ! for he/Laid many heavy loads on thee!" "On a Learned Device on Blenheim['s] Great Gate" concludes, "Thy genius, Van, was form'd no taste to hit,/Thy castle full as lumpish as thy wit."

1782

"On the Same" avers that the Duke of Marlborough would have lost the Battle of Blenheim had he deployed his forces with as little skill as was displayed by Vanbrugh in designing the building commemorating the victory.

2 NICHOLS, J[OHN]. *Select Collection of Poems: with Notes Biographical and Historical.* Vol. 4. London: Printed by and for J. Nichols, pp. 337–340.

Vanbrugh's career as dramatist is sketched (after Cibber, 1740.1) in a lengthy note appended to his poem "To a Lady More Cruel than Fair." In the Bastille, in which he was clapped after being espied "taking a survey of [French] fortifications," Vanbrugh is said to have "amused himself by drawing rude drafts of some comedies." Avers he "lived esteemed by all his acquaintance" and "died without leaving one enemy to reproach his memory." Walpole's disparaging remarks in his *Anecdotes of Painting* (1765.1) are said to express a "party rage" that "warped his understanding."

1782

1 BAKER, DAVID ERSKINE. *Biographia Dramatica, or, a Companion to the Playhouse.* 2 vols. "New edition: Carefully corrected; greatly enlarged; and continued from 1764 to 1782." London: Printed for Mess. Rivingtons [etc.].

For annotation, see 1764.1.

1783

1 BLAIR, HUGH. *Lectures on Rhetoric and Belles Lettres.* Vol. 2. London: Printed for W. Strahan [etc.], p. 545. Reprint. Carbondale and Edwardsville: Southern Illinois University Press, 1965.

Includes a three-sentence dismissal of Vanbrugh, who, although he "has spirit, wit, and ease," is said to be "one of the most immoral of all our Comedians." *The Provoked Wife* is "full of such indecent sentiments and allusions, as ought to explode it out of all reputable society," and *The Relapse* (his only other "considerable" play) is "equally censurable."

1785

1 *SMOLLETT, T[OBIAS GEORGE]. *History of England, from the Revolution to the Death of George II.* London: n.p.

Source: *NUC.* For annotation, see 1810.2.

1786

1 GILPIN, WILLIAM. *Observations, Relative to Picturesque Beauty, Made in the Year 1772, on Several Parts of England, Particularly the Mountains and Lakes of Cumberland and Westmoreland.* London: Printed for R. Blamire.
   Source: *NUC.* For annotation of 3d ed., see 1808.1.

2 *Review of performance of *The Provoked Wife. The Morning Chronicle*, 26 October.
   Source: Coleman, 1982.2, pp. 17–18; unverified. Review of 15 October revival of *The Provoked Wife* at the Theatre Royal, Covent Garden. Coleman cites reviewer's observation that Ryder, in the part of Sir John Brute, "does not dress, nor does he deport himself so much like a gentleman as other of his most celebrated predecessors have usually done, but although his manners are rather less polished he is far from letting the spirit of the character evaporate. He gives us less of the rakish man of fashion, but more of the drunken brute than we have been accustomed to behold."

3 REYNOLDS, SIR JOSHUA. *A Discourse, Delivered to the Students of the Royal Academy on the Distribution of the Prizes, December 11, 1786, by the President.* London: Printed by Thomas Cadell.
   Source: *NUC.* For annotation, see 1797.2.

1787

1 *MAVOR, WILLIAM FORDYCE. *Blenheim, a poem. To which is added a Blenheim Guide. Inscribed to their Graces, the Duke and Duchess of Marlborough.* London: T. Cadell.
   Source. *NUC.* Apparently the first of many editions of a guidebook that beginning in 1789 would be called *New Description of Blenheim.* See 1789.2; for annotation, see 1800.1.

1789

1 BURNEY, CHARLES. *A General History of Music, from the Earliest Ages to the Present Period.* Vol. 4. London: Printed for the Author [etc.], pp. 200–201.
   Vanbrugh's initial seasons at the Queen's Theatre in the Haymarket are described in a lengthy note in which it is averred (erroneously) that the theatre opened with Dryden's *Indian Emperor.* Records the *Daily Courant*'s assertion that Vanbrugh's players returned to

1791

Lincoln's Inn Fields on 20 July (before the season's conclusion) "where they continued to act till the Queen's theatre was entirely finished." They returned to the new theatre on 30 October with a performance of Vanbrugh's *Confederacy*, an "excellent comedy" that "ran but six nights successively" despite the addition "to the entertainment" of "a dancer just arriv'd from France."

2   [MAVOR, WILLIAM FORDYCE]. *New description of Blenheim, the seat of his grace the Duke of Marlborough. To which is prefixed, Blenheim, a Poem.* "A new, and much improved ed[ition]." London: Printed for T. Cadell.
     Source: *NUC*. Revised ed. of 1787.1. Many subsequent editions and printings, including 1791 (French ed.), 1793, 1797, 1800, 1803, 1806, 1809, 1810, 1811, 1814, 1817, 1834(?), 1835, 1836, 1846. For annotation, see 1800.1.

1791

1   BOSWELL, JAMES. *The Life of Samuel Johnson.* 2 vols. London: Printed by Henry Baldwin for Charles Dilly, 1:299; 2:358.
     Includes three references to Vanbrugh. Johnson avers (1768) that Goldsmith's *Good Natured Man* is the "best comedy . . . since [Vanbrugh/Cibber's] 'The Provoked Husband.'" Elsewhere (1768) Johnson is said to have "repeated, very happily, all Sir Francis's credulous account to Manly [in *The Provoked Husband*] of his being with 'the great man,' and securing a place." Boswell affirms (1781) that Sir Joshua Reynolds's "praise" of Vanbrugh's architecture (see 1786.3) "imitate[s]" Johnson's "clear[ing]" of Sir Richard Blackmore's reputation "from the cloud of prejudice which the malignity of contemporary wits had raised around it."

1794

1   *PRICE, SIR UVEDALE. *An Essay on the Picturesque.* . . . London: J. Robson.
     Source: *NUC*. For annotation, see 1810.1.

1797

1   LEWIS, JAMES. *Original Designs in Architecture.* . . . Book II. London: Printed for the Author. Reprint. Farnborough, Hants.

England: Gregg International, 1967, p. iii. (Annotation and page reference based on 1967 reprint.)

The preface to Book II includes qualified praise of Vanbrugh, than whom "No Architect of modern times has shewn greater powers of genius and invention: witness Blenheim and his Castle Howard." But the heterogeneity of his building style is judged to have produced buildings marred by "heaviness, wildness, and extravagance"—with the result that Vanbrugh "does not hold that distinguished rank as an Architect . . . which . . . he justly deserves."

2 REYNOLDS, SIR JOSHUA. *Discourses on Art*. In *The Works of Sir Joshua Reynolds*. Edited by Edmund Malone. Vol. 1. London: Printed for T. Cadell. Reprint. Edited by Robert R. Wark. San Marino, Cal.: Huntington Library, 1959, pp. 242–244. (Annotation and page references based on 1959 reprint.)

Vanbrugh's architecture is treated in Discourse XIII (delivered in 1786 and first published in 1786.3), wherein his "imagination" is praised. His "towers and battlements" are discussed in painterly terms—as components in the composition of an "ideal Landskip." Praises his "originality of invention," his understanding of "light and shadow," his "great skill in composition," his "conduct of the background." Attributes the animus of contemporary "wits" to their ignorance of "the general ruling principles of Architecture and Painting," rules that Vanbrugh himself "understood perfectly."

1798

1 WALPOLE, HORACE, EARL OF ORFORD. "Thoughts on Comedy." In *Works of Horace Walpole*. Vol. 2. London: [no publisher indicated in *BMC*; item not listed in *NUC*]. Reprint. In *The Idea of Comedy: Essays in Prose and Verse, Ben Johnson to George Meredith*. Edited by W. K. Wimsatt. Englewood Cliffs, N.J.: Prentice-Hall, 1969, pp. 198–199. (Annotation and page references based on 1969 reprint; editor of reprint indicates in a note that the essay was "Written in 1775–1776.")

Includes praise of Vanbrugh as "the best writer of dialogue we have seen." To see his comedies is to be "entertained, not surprised or struck." One returns from his "good company" at the theatre with "neither adventures nor bon mots to repeat afterwards"—this because his "expressions are sterling . . . yet unstudied," his plots unlabored, the creations of a playwright who "has exactly hit the style, manners, and character of his contemporaries."

1799

1 KIRKMAN, JAMES THOMAS. *Memoirs of the the Life of Charles Macklin, Esq., Principally Compiled from his Own Papers and Memorandums . . . , the Whole Forming a Comprehensive but Succinct History of the Stage.* 2 vols. London: Lackington, Allen, 1:105–109, 130–132; 2:273–274.

Says Vanbrugh and Congreve in their Haymarket Theatre undertaking were "The most active" of those who in the aftermath of Collier's attack "began to form plans for recovering the stage to its original vigor, for correcting the public taste, and for restoring . . . admirable actors . . . to their due estimation." Notes the poor reception of the opera ("one of those exotic [Italian] productions") with which Vanbrugh "opened the house." Discusses the reception of the 1728 premiere of the Cibber/Vanbrugh *Provoked Husband*—attended by a "violent party" of Cibber's detractors. Thinks Macklin played the part of Sir John Brute in *The Provoked Wife* in a more "*Brut[ish]*" fashion than Vanbrugh had intended—"the author's idea" being "certainly" to have Sir John played as "a *Gentleman*."

1800

1 [MAVOR, WILLIAM.]. *New Description of Blenheim.* . . . 5th ed. London: Printed by J. Crowder, 130 pp.

Describes Blenheim's interior, exterior, and grounds; illustrations. Notes (p. 14) that when this *Description* was "first published" (1787.1) "the strictures on Vanbrugh's Architecture had been so long and so often bandied about by unreflecting prejudice, that the Author was fearful to bestow even an adequate eulogium on this noble pile." Happily, "several writers of indisputable taste" have since "stepped forward in vindication" of the writer's praise of Blenheim.

1802

1 RICHARDSON, GEORGE. *The New Vitruvius Britannicus.* Vol. 1. London: Bulmer and Co. Reprinted as vol. 3 of the three-volume edition of *Vitruvius Britannicus* published by Benjamin Blom. New York: Benjamin Blom, 1970, vol. 3, p. 18, plates LXI–LXIII. (Annotation and page references based on 1970 reprint.)

Includes "Plans and Elevations of Claremont," described as "a villa of the first class," "formerly the residence of the Duke of Newcastle, who employed the most eminent professional men, as architects, and landscape-gardeners . . , [namely] Sir John Vanbrugh, Kent, Wise, &c."

1804

1 "Mr. Urban, August 6." *GM* 74, Pt. 2 (August):137–138.

Prints a lengthy excerpt from Vanbrugh's "Justification of what he deposed in the Duchess of Marlborough's Late Tryal" (1709).

2 "Mr. Urban, May 12." *GM* 74, Pt. 1 (May):410–411.

Prints "from the *Post Boy* of March 24, 1712–1713" Vanbrugh's letter of 25 January 1712–1713 to the Mayor of Woodstock, together with an anonymous ill-wisher's notation that Vanbrugh had "met with the misfortune he deserves. . . ." In the letter Vanbrugh lamented the "continual plague and persecution [the Duke of Marlborough] has most barbarously been followed with." (Falling into Tory hands, the letter led to Vanbrugh's dismissal by the Queen from his office as Comptroller of the Board of Works.)

3 NOBLE, M. *History of the College of Arms.* London: J. Debrett. Reprint. London: Printed for T. Egerton [etc.], 1805, pp. 355–357. (Annotation and page references based on 1805 reprint.)

The account of Vanbrugh's career as herald concludes that "Sir John was improperly placed in the College"—his sponsor Lord Carlisle behaving "reprehens[ibly]" in promoting "a man totally ignorant of the profession of heraldry and genealogy." Records the family history Vanbrugh evidently supplied to the Earl of Suffolk and Bindon in support of his application for "confirmation of arms." Among the particulars supplied: a description of the family's arms and crest, the great-grandfather's flight from Flanders to England "for the enjoyment of the reformed religion," and the family's subsequent settlements in London and in Chester. Vanbrugh's architecture is pronounced "heavy in the extreme," his plays "indecent," his personality engaging.

1805

1 KNIGHT, RICHARD PAYNE. *An Analytical Inquiry into the Principles of Taste.* London: T. Payne, Mews Gate, and J. White, Fleet Street, pp. 220–221.

Discussing the proper siting of a substantial country house, the author suggests that "more consideration ought to be had of the view towards it, than of those fromwards it. . . .'' Vanbrugh is pronounced "the only architect . . . who has either planned or placed his houses" in a manner consistent with the principle of picturesque siting here advocated. Though the "views" through the windows of the principal fronts of Castle Howard and Blenheim Palace are "bad," "the situations of both houses, as objects to the surrounding scenery, are the best that could have been chosen. . . ."

1806

1 DALLAWAY, JAMES. *Observations on English Architecture, Military, Ecclesiastical, and Civil.* . . . London: Printed for J. Taylor, pp. 208–209.

Approves Reynolds's "judgment" of Blenheim (1797.2). Adds that the "numerous turrets rising pyramidally lessen the [building's] ponderosity without a diminution of the grand effect of extent and solidity. . . ." Disparages the "infinite littleness" of Castle Howard's "parts." Thinks at Grimsthorpe Vanbrugh "indulged himself in imitating Blenheim."

1808

1 GILPIN, WILLIAM. *Observations on Several Parts of England, Particularly the Mountains and Lakes of Cumberland and Westmoreland, Relative Chiefly to Picturesque Beauty, Made in the Year 1772.* Vol. 1. 3d ed. London: Printed for T. Cadell and W. Davies, pp. 26–31.

Includes a defense of Blenheim against the charge of "heaviness." Notes that the house is "a *magnificent* whole . . . invested with an air of grandeur, seldom seen in a more regular style of building." Describes the house's "situation" at the center of an "extensive park." Acknowledges that Vanbrugh becomes "ridiculous" when he "appl[ies] to small houses, a style of architecture, which could not possibly succeed, but in a large one"—this because, "In a small house, where the grandeur of a *whole* cannot be attempted, the eye is at leisure to contemplate *parts*, and meets with frequent occasions of disgust." For citation of 1st ed., see 1786.1.

2 INCHBALD, [ELIZABETH]. *The British Theatre; or, a Collection of Plays.* . . . Vol. 9. London: Printed for Longman, Hurst [etc.], pp. 3–5.

In a headnote to *The Provoked Wife* the editor notes that she has printed "the best" of the play's "wit and humour," having silently excised Vanbrugh's "rankest offenses." Takes Garrick to task for having "deliver[ed], before a mixed audience of both sexes, some of" the play's "coarse wit." Concludes that "When plays such as 'The Provoked Wife' are exhibited, it is charity to revile theatres."

3   SCOTT, [SIR] WALTER, ed. *The Works of John Dryden.* Vol. 8. London: Printed for William Miller, pp. 439–440.

In a headnote to the "Prologue, Song, Secular Masque, and Epilogue" that Dryden wrote for Vanbrugh's 1700 adaptation of Fletcher's *Pilgrim*, Scott describes Vanbrugh as "a lively comic writer" who "added some light touches of humour, to adapt [*The Pilgrim*] to the taste of the age." Relays Cibber's report (1740.1) that Vanbrugh himself "cast the parts" for the play's performance.

1809

1   MANNING, OWEN, and BRAY, WILLIAM. *History and Antiquities of the County of Surrey.* Vol. 2. London: Printed for John White by John Nichols & Son. Reprint. Classical County Histories. Edited by Jack Simmons. n.p.: EP Publishing in collaboration with Surrey County Library, 1974, p. 742. (Annotation and page reference based on 1974 reprint.)

An account of the village of Esher notes that the Earl of Clare (later Duke of Newcastle) bought Vanbrugh's "low brick house" at Esher, "made it his habitation [Vanbrugh enlarged it into Claremont House], and added a magnificent room for the entertainment of large companies when he was in Administration." The park and the house's subsequent history are briefly described.

1810

1   PRICE, UVEDALE. *Essay on the Picturesque.* London: Printed for J. Mawman, pp. 204–205, 212–217.

Opines that among "modern buildings," "no mansion of regular, finished architecture . . , has from such a number of different points, so grand an appearance as Blenheim." The apprentice architect is advised to study Blenheim's effects by drawing the building from a variety of perspectives. Batey and Lambert (1990.1) record Price's quotation of J. M. W. Turner's praise of Blenheim: "Whoever catches that view towards the close of evening, when the sun strikes the golden balls and pours his beams through the open parts, gilding every rich and brilliant ornament[,] will think he sees some enchanted palace" (vol.

1813

2, p. 254 of the 1798 ed. of Price's *Essay* is cited; unverified). For citation of first edition, see 1794.1.

2 SMOLLETT, T[OBIAS GEORGE]. *History of England, from the Revolution to the Death of George II.* Vol. 2. Edinburgh: Printed for Peter Hill and Silvester Doig, p. 460.

A note on writers of the reign of George I includes the observation that Vanbrugh "wrote with more nature and fire" than Congreve, "though with far less art and precision." For citation of first edition, see 1785.1.

1813

1 "Vanbrugh." In *Pantologia. A New Cyclopaedia, Comprehending a Complete Series of Essays, Treatises, and Systems, Alphabetically Arranged; with a General Dictionary of Arts, Sciences, and Words. . . .* Vol. 12. London: Printed for G. Kearsley [etc.], n.p.

Vanbrugh's career is given two paragraphs. He is called "an able dramatic writer." His buildings, "noted" for "heaviness," are said to include Blenheim, Claremont, the Haymarket theatre, and "the old Military Academy, in Woolwich arsenal."

1814

1 COMBE, WILLIAM. *A History of the University of Oxford, Its Colleges, Halls, and Public Buildings.* Vol. 2. London: Printed for R. Ackerman, p. 238.

Maintains that Vanbrugh designed the Clarendon Printing House. Says of that building, "huge and heavy as it is, when viewed at the end of Clarendon-street as one one of the august buildings seen from thence, the Doric portico acquires not only dignity, but picturesque effect."

2 NICHOLS, JOHN. *Literary Anecdotes of the Eighteenth Century: Comprizing Biographical Memoirs of William Bowyer, Printer, F. S. A. and Many of His Learned Friends. . . .* Vol. 8. London: Printed for the Author, by Nichols. . . . Reprint. New York: AMS Press; Kraus Reprint Corporation, 1966, p. 594. (Annotation and page citation based on 1966 reprint.)

R. Gough's letter to Tyson of 7 September 1772 urges the latter to "Look into 'Vitruvius Britannicus' for *Eastbury* house, Dorset, the work of Vanbrugh, marvellously heavy, and ill contrived without."

Adds that "there is a handsome hall open to the top, and a better suite of upper rooms than the first view promises."

1815

1 "Architectural Innovation. No. CCIV. Progress of Architecture in England." *GM* 85, Pt. 1 (May):423–424.
   Describes three buildings, each here assigned to Vanbrugh: the Kensington water tower, the Kensington Charity School, and Vanbrugh's residence at Whitehall (Goose-Pie House).

2 "Architectural Innovation. No. CCVI. Progress of Architecture in England in the Reign of Anne." *GM* 85, Pt. 2 (December):494–495.
   Praises the originality of what is presumed to be Vanbrugh's design for the "Centre of the more southern range of the West Fronts" of the Royal Hospital at Greenwich. Finds Vanbrugh's design "remarkably bold and assuming, magnificent, and highly decorated, and of a cast ['defying all precedent and order']that no one but Vanbrugh himself would have presumed at this time" to devise.

3 "Mr. Urban, Feb. 13." *GM* 85, Pt. 1 (February):202.
   An account of Yorkshire buildings includes a description of that "stupendous and magnificent mansion" Castle Howard.

4 "Review of New Publications." *GM* 85, Pt. 1 (February):144.
   Prints an excerpt from Daniel Cabanel's poem "British Scenery" (in *Poems and Imitations*, 1811) in which Blenheim Palace is described as "Proudly magnificent (the ponderous work of Vanbrugh, Architect of grand design/And princely structure). . . ." The reviewer remarks in a note that "Blenheim, though heavy, is a very majestic structure, and has more the appearance of a Palace than any I have seen in Britain."

1816

1 "Architectural Innovation. No. CCVII. Progress of Architecture in England in the Reign of Anne." *GM* 86, Pt. 1 (January):37–39.
   Describes the plans and elevations of Blenheim Palace published by Campbell in *Vitruvius Britannicus*. Finds the house "majestically designed, and well calculated to express a Nation's idea of military triumphs." Continued in 1816.2.

1817

2   "Architectural Innovation. No. CCVIII. Progress of Architecture in England in the Reign of Anne." *GM* 86, Pt. 1 (February):135–136.
   Continuation of 1816.1: description of the plans and elevations of Blenheim Palace published by Campbell in *Vitruvius Britannicus*.

3   CHALMERS, ALEXANDER. *General Biographical Dictionary*. Vol. 30. London: J. Nichols and Son, pp. 214–218. Reprint. New York: AMS Press. Kraus Reprint Co., 1969.
   A biographical sketch that in assessing Vanbrugh's comedies notes that *The Relapse* "succeeded" despite its "gross indecencies," that *Aesop* "contains much general satire and useful morality," and that *The Confederacy* was "a licentious performance," as were all of Vanbrugh's plays save Colley Cibber's rendering of *A Journey to London* as *The Provoked Husband*. Concerning the architecture, Sir Joshua Reynolds's remarks (1797.2) are called the "tribute which a painter owes to an architect who composed like a painter, and was defrauded of the due rewards of his merit by the wits of his time . . . ."

1817

1   CUMBERLAND, R[ICHARD]. "Life of Sir John Vanbrugh" and "Critique [of *The Provoked Wife*]." In *British Drama, A Collection of the Most Esteemed Dramatic Productions, with Biography of the Respective Authors; and a Critique on Each Play*. Vol. 14. London: Printed for C. Cooke, pp. [iii]–vi.
   The "Life" includes a list of Vanbrugh's preferments, noting that the "reputation" his comedies won him "was rewarded with greater advantages than usually arise from writing for the stage." Laments Vanbrugh's "obscenity." The "Critique" prefacing the text of *The Provoked Wife* praises the play's "smart" dialogue, its "abundance of whimsical situations," and its realistic portrait of the "rake" Sir John Brute. Concludes, "It was a full atonement for the licentiousness of the Provok'd Wife, that he conceived and began the Provok'd Husband." Huseboe (1976.5, pp. 134–135 and p. 162n. 2) says Cumberland reports (on "p. xx") that Vanbrugh once told George Bubb Dodington "he had sketched out some loose scenes [putatively the fragmentary *Journey to London*], which, in quantity, were enough for a comedy, but which had no plan or properties of an entire composition in them" (quotation cited by Huseboe unverified).

1818–1819

1   COXE, WILLIAM. *Memoirs of John, Duke of Marlborough; with his Original Correspondence: Collected from the Family [R]ecords at*

Blenheim. 3 vols. London: Printed for Longman, Hurst, Rees, Orme, & Brown.

Source: *NUC.* For annotation of 2d ed., see 1820.2.

1819

1 EVELYN, JOHN. *Memoirs illustrative of the Life and Writings of John Evelyn.* Vol. 3. Edited by William Bray. 2d ed. London: Printed for Henry Colburn, p. 47.

The entry for 31 May 1695 records that "Mr. Vanbrugh was made Secretary to the Commission [for building the Royal Naval Hospital at Greenwich], by my nomination of him to the Lords, which was all done that day." Though assumed by earlier commentators to refer to John Vanbrugh, the entry likely refers to Vanbrugh's cousin William Vanbrugh; see p. 201 of Downes, 1987.4. (*NUC* lists 1st ed., 1818; not examined.)

2 HAZLITT, WILLIAM. Lecture IV: "On Wycherley, Congreve, Vanbrugh, and Farquhar." In *Lectures on the English Comic Writers.* London: Taylor and Hessey. Reprint. In *Lectures on the English Poets, and the English Comic Writers.* Edited by William Carew Hazlitt. London: George Bell and Sons, 1894, pp. 92, 104–111. Reprint. New York: Doubleday, Dolphin Books, 1960. (Annotation and page numbers based on 1894 reprint.)

Remarks on Vanbrugh celebrate his "prodigious fund of comic invention and ludicrous description, bordering somewhat on caricature." His portraits of Lord Foppington and Sir John Brute are singled out for praise. The scene from *The Confederacy* in which Brass threatens Dick with exposure is quoted at length to illustrate the play's "matchless spirit of impudence."

1820

1 B., D. "The Progress of Architecture in England." *Blackwood's Magazine* 6, no. 36 (March):662–663.

A paragraph on Vanbrugh praises the "picturesque outlines" of Blenheim Palace and Castle Howard, houses "so extremely beautiful, that they may be said to be full of poetry, so singular and superb are the associations which they awaken in the minds of those who see them for the first time. . . ."

2 COXE, WILLIAM. *Memoirs of John [Churchill], Duke of Marlborough, with his Original Correspondence: Collected from the Family*

1821

Records at Blenheim. . . . 2d ed. 6 vols. London: Printed for Longman, Hurst, Rees, Orme, and Brown, 2:74; 5:349–350; 6:367.

Includes discussion of the building of Blenheim by Vanbrugh,
"who was then regarded as one of the first architects of the age."
Shows a crafty Vanbrugh attempting (unsuccessfully) to trick the
Duchess in 1710 into writing a letter "declaring that whatever might
happen [concerning funding of the project], the workers should not
suffer." Passing mention of Vanbrugh's entanglement in the workers'
Court of Exchequer suit in 1718. For citation of 1st ed., see 1818–
1819.1.

3 SPENCE, JOSEPH. *Anecdotes, Observations, and Characters, of
Books and Men. Collected from the Conversation of Mr. Pope, and
other Eminent Persons of His Time.* Edited by Samuel Weller Singer.
London: W. H. Carpenter; Edinburgh: Archibald Constable, pp. 46,
310, 338, 349. Reprint. Edited by Bonamy Dobrée. Carbondale:
Southern Illinois Press; London: Centaur Press, 1964. Reprint. Edited by James M. Osborn. Oxford: Clarendon Press, 1966.

Quotes Pope's remark that "none of our writers have a freer eas-
ier way for comedy than Etherege and Vanbrugh," and his assertion
(corroborated by Tonson) that "Garth, Vanbrugh, and Congreve, were
the three most honest hearted, real good men, of the poetical members
of the kit-cat club." "In talking over the design for a dictionary, that
might be authoritative for our English writers," Pope is said to have
named Ben Jonson, L'Estrange, Congreve, and Vanbrugh as "authorities for familiar dialogues and writings of that kind." For citation of
2d ed., see 1858.1.

1821

1 D., T. "On the Alleged Decline of Dramatic Writing." *Blackwood's
Magazine* 9, no. 51 (June):282.

Asserts that Vanbrugh's comedies, because they possess "the
greatest proportion of conjoined wit and natural character, will probably be read more than any of the comic productions of the time."
Thinks *The Provoked Wife* "a masterpiece of natural painting, easy
wit, and humorous reflection"—its pithy dialogue "not often . . .
equalled since the days of Shakespeare."

2 "Water, or Bell Tower, Kensington." *GM* 91, Pt. 1 (June):497.

Reproduces an engraving of the Kensington Water Tower (designed by Vanbrugh). Records the tower's dimensions and notes that
it was "built in the reign of Queen Anne for the purpose of supplying
the Palace of Kensington with water. . . ."

1823

1   *DISRAELI, I[SAAC]. "Secret History of the Building of Blenheim." In *A Second Series of Curiosities of Literature. . . .* Vol. 2. London: John Murray, pp. 80–99.

   Source: title page, volume no., and page reference supplied by Christine R. Bailey, Pattee Library, Pennsylvania State University (personal correspondence). For annotation, see 1849.1. This (1823) is the earliest edition of Disraeli's *Curiosities* for which there is documentation of the "Secret History" chapter. Many subsequent editions and printings (e.g., 1825, 1835, 1838, 1840, 1849, 1858, 1860, 1871, 1872, 1881). The latest edition listed in *NUC* is dated 1932. The "Secret History" chapter does *not* appear in the earliest editions of *Curiosities* (e.g., in the University of Illinois's 1791 [1st] or 1794 editions, or in Penn State's 1807 edition).

2   *NEALE, JOHN PRESTON. *Six Views of Blenheim, Oxfordshire: the Seat of His Grace the Duke of Marlborough: with an Historical Description of that Magnificent Edifice.* London: Sherwood, Jones, 24 pp.

   Source: OCLC ("7 leaves of plates"; "cover title": *An Historical Description of Blenheim with Six Views*); unverified.

1824

1   "Iver-Grove, the Seat of Lord Gambier." *Repository of Arts, Literature, Fashion, Manufactures, &c.* 3d ser. 3, no. 15 (March):126.

   Says Iver-Grove ("in the parish of Iver") "was built by Sir John [Vanbrugh] for the widow of Lord Mahon." "Though small," the house is said to illustrate Vanbrugh's "generally admitted" supremacy in the art of "forming a whole, which, when viewed at a distance, possesses a magnificent and imposing effect." Illustrated in a watercolor drawing.

1826

1   KELLY, MICHAEL. *Reminiscences of Michael Kelly, of the King's Theatre Royal Drury Lane. . . .* Vol. 2. 2d ed. London: H. Colburn, pp. 335–340.

   An appendix on "The King's Theatre; or, the Royal Italian Opera House, Haymarket" avers that Vanbrugh built his theatre for Betterton's Lincolns Inn Fields players. Retells Cibber's version (1740.1) of the theatre's early history.

2 "Reminiscences.—No. III. Richard Brinsley Sheridan, &c." *Blackwood's Magazine* 20, no. 114 (July):34.

Includes discussion of Sheridan's "strong managerial reasons" for reviving Vanbrugh's *Relapse* "under the name *A Trip to Scarborough*. Sheridan did so because "it cost him no trouble" (his alterations being minimal), because Vanbrugh's play was "well fitted for his company" (offering choice parts for all three of his premiere actresses), and because "Lord Foppington and Miss Hoyden had formerly been great favourites, and Sheridan hoped that a little pruning would restore them to favour." Expresses surprise that he would have chosen for revival a play whose merits were so dependent upon licentiousness; thinks *The Relapse* "luminous from putresence."

1827

1 DALLAWAY, JAMES. Notes to *Anecdotes of Painting in England; with Some Account of the Principal Artists*, by Horace Walpole. Vol. 3. Revised "with considerable additions by the Rev. James Dallaway." London: Printed at the Shakespeare Press, pp. 297–303.

Dallaway's annotations of Walpole's *Anecdotes* (1765.1) include the observation that Walpole does not mention that his father, Sir Robert Walpole, was one of Vanbrugh's patrons. Among the editor's other observations are these: (1) Vanbrugh "had not the slightest knowledge of heraldry, and neglected his office"; (2) at Grimsthorpe he "indulged himself in imitating Blenheim and Castle Howard"; (3) concerning the quarrels of Vanbrugh and the Duchess of Marlborough, "They were perpetually engaged in plotting and counterplotting, and as they were both wits, ingeniously tormenting each other." (Cf. 1876.1.)

1829

1 NEELE, HENRY. *Lectures of English Poetry, from the Reign of Edward the Third, to the Time of Burns and Cowper, delivered at the Russell Institution in 1827.* London: Smith, Elder.

Source: *NUC*. For annotation of 2d ed., see 1830.2.

2 Review of Henry Neele's *Literary Remains*. *GM* 99, Pt. 1 (January):42.

Quotes Neele's linkage of Swift and Vanbrugh as satirists who "do not use the vices and follies of mankind for the purpose of instruction or amusement. . . ." Thinks Swift and Vanbrugh stand "aloof from humanity, like the *Mephistophiles* of Goethe,'' making mankind's "weakness and crimes the objects of their fiend-like derision.''

1830

1 HAZLITT, WILLIAM, ed. *Conversations of James Northcote.* London: Henry Colburn and Richard Bentley, pp. 275–277.

Quotes Northcote's observation that Vanbrugh was a "black sheep" in his day because the wits envied his ablity to "build houses and write verses at the same time.'' Transcribes Northcote's praise of the ornamental chimneys at Blenheim and his claim that Vanbrugh was "the first who sunk the window frames within the walls of houses''— a "beauty which has since been adopted by act of parliament to prevent fire.'' Cites Northcote's recollection of the opinion of "Richards, the scene painter,'' that *A Journey to London* was "the best play in the language.''

2 NEELE, HENRY. *Lectures on English Poetry.* . . . 2d ed. London: Smith, Elder, pp. 149–151.

Discussion of Vanbrugh observes that whereas "Farquhar makes the sides ache,'' Vanbrugh "makes the heart ache also.'' The latter is pronounced "as appalling a Satirist as Swift''—this because Vanbrugh's "pictures are hideously'' accurate, "true to the very wrinkle.'' In his character portraits, "All the vices of humanity are treasured up,'' the "bad parts of human nature'' being "picked out and separated from the redeeming qualities. . . .'' (No examples from the plays are offered.) For citation of 1st ed., see 1829.1.

1831

1 CUNNINGHAM, ALLAN. *Lives of the Most Eminent British Painters, Sculptors and Architects.* Vol. 4. London: John Murray, pp. 253–283. Reprint. New York: J. & J. Harper, 1834.

Doubts that Vanbrugh's father was a sugar baker; repeats the "legend" that Vanbrugh was imprisoned in the Bastille for drawing French fortifications. Thinks an "air of lasciviousness . . . hovers over every scene" of *The Provoked Wife* and "hope[s] Vanbrugh's volumes are "shut for ever . . . to our countrywomen.'' Finds in the fragmentary *Journey to London* evidence that in a chaster age Vanbrugh might "have been a dramatical classic at once refined in art and blameless in morals.'' Blenheim and Castle Howard are praised for their "originality.''

1832

2 HUNTER, JOSEPH. *South Yorkshire*. Vol. 2. London: Printed for the Author by J. B. Nichols and Son. Reprint. Classical County Histories. Edited by Jack Simmons. n.p.: EP Publishing in collaboration with Sheffield City Libraries, 1974, p. 488. (Annotation and page reference based on 1974 reprint.)

A brief history of Robin Hood's well records that "In the beginning of" the eighteenth century, the Earl of Carlisle "erected a rustic dome over the well, according to a design of Sir John Vanbrugh." The covering is illustrated in an engraving.

3 Review of Cunningham, *Lives of the Most Eminent British Painters, Sculptors and Architects* (1831.1) *GM* 101, Pt. 1 (April):330.

Approves Cunningham's castigation of that "licentious dramatist" Vanbrugh. Applauds the judgment that Vanbrugh's playtexts "are forever closed to our countrymen."

1832

1 GENEST, JOHN, ed. *Some Account of the English Stage from the Restoration in 1660 to 1830*. Vol. 2. Bath: H. E. Carrington. Reprint. Burt Franklin Research & Source Work Series 93. New York: Burt Franklin, n.d. [1964?], pp. 69, 99, 111–112, 116, 133, 179, 308–309, 312–313, 321, 323, 329, 343, 352–354, 367. (Annotation and page references based on undated [1964?] reprint.)

Includes season-by-season commentary on Vanbrugh's management of the Haymarket Theatre and on each of his comedies, including cast lists for original productions, plot summaries, summary judgments, and occasional accounts of performances. Material is largely a pastiche of the language and opinions of earlier commentators, frequently Downes (1708.1) and Cibber (1740.1).

2 *PUCKLER-MUSKAU, HERMAN LUDWIG HEINRICH VON. *Tour in England, Ireland, and France in the Years 1828 and 1829*. Vol. 3. London: Effingham Wilson, Royal Exchange, p. 253.

Source: *NUC* and Batey and Lambert, 1990.1, who say (p. 122 and n.10) that *Tour* includes observations critical of Blenheim Palace; unverified.

1834

1 RICHARDSON, HENRY S. *Greenwich: Its History, Antiquities, Improvements, and Public Buildings*. London: Simpkin & Marshall and H. Richardson, pp. 88–89.

Includes a brief description of Vanbrugh Castle, "erected about the year 1717," and "Mince-pie House." Says "An arched gateway, with a lodge on each side, now standing some distance within the principal field, appears to have formed the original entrance [to 'Vanbrugh Fields'] from the Heath.''

1836

1 "Diary of a Lover of Literature." *GM*, 3d ser. 5 (January):13.

Condemns the licentiousness of *The Relapse* and *The Provoked Wife*. Thinks *Aesop* and *The False Friend* "evince . . . right moral feelings," which "were only perverted on sexual topics by the profligacy of the times."

2 EVANS, EDWARD. *Catalogue of a Collection of Engraved Portraits.* Vol. 1. London: E. Evans, p. 356.

Vanbrugh items 10658–10663 are prefaced thus: "Vanbrugh, Sir John, eminent architect and poet, erected Blenheim; Castle Howard; Kings Weston; Easton-Neston [*sic*], &c. Clarencieux King at Arms; surveyor, Greenwich Hospital; ob. Whitehall 1726; various 8vo. 6d"—followed by listings of engravings "from the Kit-Cat picture" and from "Kneller-Duncan." For annotation of vol. 2, see 1853.1.

3 "Letters of Sir John Vanbrugh to Tonson, the Bookseller." *GM*, 3d ser. 6 (July):27–29.

Prints Vanbrugh's letters to Tonson of 15 June 1703 and 13 July 1703. Glosses Vanbrugh's reference to Gregory King by noting that he was a "distinguished genealogist" who was supplanted at the College of Heralds by "a flippant wit and lumbering architect whose only claim was patronage."

4 "Letters of Sir John Vanbrugh to Tonson, the Bookseller." *GM*, 3d ser. 6 (October):374–376.

Prints Vanbrugh's letters to Tonson of 30 July 1703 and 1 July 1719.

1837

1 "Letters of Sir John Vanbrugh to Tonson, the Bookseller." *GM*, 3d ser. 7 (March):243–245.

Prints Vanbrugh's letters to Tonson of 5 November 1719 and 29 November 1719.

1838

2   "Letters of Sir John Vanbrugh to Tonson, the Bookseller." *GM*, 3d
ser. 7 (May):479–483.
      Prints Vanbrugh's letters to Tonson of 31 December 1719, 18 Feb-
ruary 1719–1720, 12 August 1725, and 25 October 1725.

1838

1   MARLBOROUGH, [SARAH JENNINGS CHURCHILL], DUCH-
ESS OF. *Private Correspondence of Sarah, Duchess of Marlborough.*
. . . Vol. 1. London: Henry Colburn, pp. 130, 140, 181, 182, 186–
187, 266, 338, 368.
      The following letters pertain to Vanbrugh and the building of
Blenheim: (1) Duke of Marlborough to Duchess of Marlborough, 1
July 1708—agrees that it is in "[Vanbrugh's] interest to have patience
till something happens which may be lasting" (presumably the be-
stowal of a knighthood); (2) Mr. Maynwaring to Duchess, July 1708—
professes to be "sorry for" Vanbrugh "because I believe he is unhappy
through his own folly," that folly being "his building the playhouse,
which certainly cost him a great deal more than was subscribed." Says
he "cannot advise" the Duchess "to do anything for [Vanbrugh] out
of [her] own estate"; (3) Duke to Duchess, 24 June 1709—discusses the
"two suites of hangings which were made at Bruxelles by Vanbrugh's
measure." Says "If Lord Treasurer and Vanbrugh approve of it," the
Duchess "may keep one of the marble blocks, so that the room where
you intend your buffet, may be well done"; (4) Duke to Duchess, 1
July 1709—"agree[s] entirely" that Vanbrugh "must be carefully observed, and not suffered to begin any new work [at Blenheim]; but to
apply all the money to the finishing what I directed before I left England"; (5) Duke to Duchess, 11 July 1709—replies to the Duchess's
"apprehensi[ons] that Mr. Vanbrugh gives me false accounts" concerning progress in the building of Blenheim. Urges her to ensure that
Vanbrugh "finish[es] what is ordered" rather than "beginning new
foundations."

1838 [–1854]

1   HUNTER, JOSEPH. "Sir John Vanbrugh." In *Chorus Vatum Angli-
canorum.* Vol. 12. Typescript of B.M. Add. MSS. 24487–24497.
Microfilm copy (positive) made by the Folger Shakespeare Library.
      A biographical sketch. Cites Le Neve's testimony (see 1873.2) that
Vanbrugh "was knighted at Greenwich house on Sunday 19th Sept.
1714 being introduced by his Grace the Duke of Marlborough." Rec-

ords the "tradition" that "the Earl of Carlisle being in debt to [Vanbrugh] made him Herald and King in one day that he might sell the places[,] which he did for 2000 [pounds]." Recalls "being told by my old friend Mr. John Milnes that having quarrelled with the Yarboroughs [his wife's relations], he [Vanbrugh] ridiculed them in Sir Francis Wronghead and his family" in *A Journey to London*. Adds that Sir Thomas Yarborough "indeed was twice returned member for the borough of Pontefract viz. in 1685 and 1688 and the servant in the play [*A Journey to London*] is made to speak of the Humber as near the residence of the Wronghead family."

1839

1 "Letter of Sir John Vanbrugh." *GM,* 3d ser. 11 (February):149–150.
   Prints Vanbrugh's letter to Edward Southwell of 23 October 1713 relating to the chimneys at Kings Weston.

2 QUÉRARD, J. M. *La France Littéraire, ou Dictionnaire Bibliographique.* Vol. 10. Paris: Firmin Didot. Reprint. Paris: G. P. Maisonneuve & Larose, Éditeurs, 1964. (Annotation and page reference based on 1964 reprint.)
   Entry for Vanbrugh indicates that he is the author of a five-act English comedy, published in 1761 and 1783, entitled *Mari (le) poussé à bout, ou le Voyage de Londres*, completed by Cibber (i.e., *The Provoked Husband*).

3 THOMSON, MRS. A. T. *Memoirs of Sarah Duchess of Marlborough, and the Court of Queen Anne.* Vol. 2. London: Henry Colburn, pp. 443–460.
   Includes an account of the building of Blenheim Palace and the disagreements that arose between Vanbrugh and the Duchess of Marlborough during its erection. Observes that the Duchess "took a considerable share in the management of the works, combating stoutly against the extravagances and impositions of Sir John Vanbrugh in detail, though she was wholly unable to check the gross amount of his charges."

1840

1 HUNT, LEIGH. "John Vanbrugh." In *The Dramatic Works of Wycherley, Congreve, Vanbrugh, and Farquhar.* London: Edward Moxon, pp. xlvii–lvi.
   A biographical sketch written without certain knowledge of the dates or the fact of Vanbrugh's imprisonment in France, and drawing

heavily for its account of Vanbrugh's theatrical activities on Cibber's remarks in the *Apology.* Sir Joshua Reynolds's comments on the imaginativeness of Vanbrugh's architecture are adduced by way of demonstrating the "secret reason and proportion . . . at the bottom" of his work both as dramatist and architect.

1841

1 BELTZ, GEORGE FREDERICK. *Memorials of the Order of the Garter from its Foundation to the Present Time.* London: William Pickering, pp. cxxiii–cxxiv.

Records Vanbrugh's role in investing with the Garter the electoral prince of Brunswick-Lunenburgh, the future George II. The investiture was conducted at Hanover, on 11 and 13 June 1706, with Clarenceux Vanbrugh presiding in place of the ailing Garter, Henry St. George.

2 BRAYLEY, EDWARD WEDLAKE. *A Topographical History of Surrey.* Vol. 2. London: Tilt and Bogue, pp. 440–441, 449.

Observes that "after a long season of sarcastic reproach," Vanbrugh's reputation as an architect is "at length beginning to be held in due estimation"—this by way of introduction to a brief account of Vanbrugh's conversion of his (Chargate) house at Esher into the Duke of Newcastle's Claremont House. For annotation of later edition, see 1879.1.

3 MACAULAY, THOMAS BABINGTON. "Comic Dramatists of the Restoration." *Edinburgh Review* 72 (January):490–528. (Pages discussing Vanbrugh are noted in reprint citation.) Reprinted in *Miscellaneous Works of Lord Macaulay.* Edited by Lady Trevelyan. Vol. 3. New York: Harper & Brothers, 1866, pp. 129, 139. (Annotation based on 1866 reprint.)

Review of Hunt (1840.1) is devoted principally to the achievements of Wycherley and Congreve. Mentions Vanbrugh to make the point that Jeremy Collier, in his *Short View,* "does not sufficiently distinguish between the dramatists and the persons of the drama." In response to Collier's "blam[ing]" of Vanbrugh "for putting into Lord Foppington's mouth some contemptuous expressions respecting the church service," opines that Vanbrugh "could not better express reverence than by making Lord Foppington express contempt."

1842

1 *GWILT, JOSEPH. *Encyclopedia of Architecture.* London: Longman, Brown, Green, & Longmans.
For annotation, see 1845.1. Later editions: 1867.1; 1899.4.

2 LEWIS, SAMUEL. *Topographical Dictionary of England, Comprising the Several Counties, Cities, Boroughs . . . with Historical and Statistical Descriptions.* 5th ed. Vol. 3. London: S. Lewis, p. 310.
Asserts that Vanbrugh designed (and the Howard family commissioned) the town hall in Morpeth, Northumberland. The hall is described as "a plain structure of hewn stone, with a piazza and turrets, erected in 1714."

1843

1 CHAMBERS, ROBERT, ed. "Sir John Vanbrugh." In *Cyclopaedia of English Literature.* . . . Vol. 1. Edinburgh: William and Robert Chambers, pp. 597–598. (Later editions are usually entitled *Chambers's Cyclopaedia of English Literature*—e.g., the undated "new edition" edited by David Patrick and J. Liddell Geddie. London: W. & R. Chambers. The appraisal remains as in the 1843 edition.)
The "Vanbrugh" entry speculates about the playwright's early life, notes that Blenheim and Castle Howard "have outlived the *Provoked Wife* and the *Relapse*" (both "highly popular once"), and prints two samples of Vanbrugh's comic style: (1) an excerpt from the revised scene in *The Provoked Wife* (IV.iii) in which Sir John Brute, masquerading as a woman of quality, converses with a JP; and (2) the concluding parable (final five stanzas) of *Aesop, Part II.* The "lively ease" of Vanbrugh's "dialogue" is praised and illustrated with quotation of Lord Foppington's final remarks to his brother at the conclusion of *The Relapse.* Though "dashed with the most unblushing licentiousnesss," Vanbrugh's plays are praised for their "vivacity," their utter freedom from "hypocrisy" being their "most genial feature." (In the undated "new edition" cited above, a reproduction of J. Faber's engraving of J. Richardson's 1725 portrait of Vanbrugh is substituted for the reproduction of Vanbrugh's "Autograph and seal" appearing in the 1843 ed.)

2 HALLAM, HENRY. *Introduction to the Literature of Europe.* Vol. 3. London: John Murray, pp. 504, 518.
Thinks "the best parts" of *The Provoked Husband* are Vanbrugh's. In the depiction of Amanda in *The Relapse*, discerns "the

45

first homage the theatre had paid, since the Restoration, to female chastity." Applauds Vanbrugh's "endeavour to expose the grossness of the older [Caroline] generation" in his depiction of Sir John Brute.

1845

1 GWILT, JOSEPH. *Gwilt's Encyclopaedia of Architecture*. No. 4 of *A Series of Encyclopaedias and Dictionaries, forming Special and Independent Works, edited by Writers Distinguished in the Various Departments*. London: Printed for Longman, Brown, Green, & Longmans, pp. 215–217.

Credits Sir Joshua Reynolds (1797.2) with raising the public estimate of "the thitherto condemned works of the extraordinary architect" Vanbrugh. Offers a brief sketch of Vanbrugh's career, devoting several sentences apiece to description of Castle Howard, Blenheim, Eastbury, Kings Weston (where the "grouping of the chimneys" has perhaps never been "equaled"), and Grimsthorpe (where Vanbrugh "indulged himself in an imitation of Blenheim and Castle Howard"). For other editions, see 1842.1, 1867.1, and 1899.4.

1848

1 BLISS, PHILIP, ed. *Athenae Oxonienses, an Exact History of Writers and Bishops Who have Had Their Education in the University of Oxford. Containing the Life of Wood*, by Anthony [à] Wood. Oxford: Printed by T. Combe, p. 48n.

Editor's gloss of Wood's remarks on the advent of a coffee house near Oxford University in 1651 includes an attribution of two later houses to Vanbrugh: one in Oxford "in New Inn Hall Lane, now occupied by Mr. Walsh"; the other "in St. Aldates, near Folly bridge, pulled down some twenty years since." No other particulars are supplied.

2 HUNT, LEIGH. *The Town; Its Memorable Characters and Events*. Vol. 2, *St. Paul's to St. James's*. London: Smith, Elder, and Co., pp. 210–212.

In a brief discussion of Vanbrugh, contemporary ridicule of his architecture is attributed to Tory malice. Sir Joshua Reynolds's encomium (1797.2) is quoted at length.

1849

1   DISRAELI, ISAAC. *Curiosities of Literature.* Vol. 3. 14th ed. London: Edward Moxon, pp. 113–122. Frequent reprints throughout the century.

A chapter entitled "Secret History of the Building of Blenheim" records that Vanbrugh "contrived to obtain" from Lord Godolphin a warrant in which he had himself denominated "*Surveyor* [of Blenheim Palace], *with power of contracting on the behalf of the Duke of Marlborough*"—and did so without the Duke's knowledge. When the Treasury, following the death of Queen Anne, stopped payment on the building, the guileful Vanbrugh "contrive[d] how to make the duke the great debtor," whereupon the Duchess "contrived a counterplot to turn the debts on Vanbrugh." Ends by reporting that Vanbrugh was "born in the Bastille" (a literal reading of metaphorical language Vanbrugh employed in his 25 October 1725 letter to Tonson; *Works*, IV, p. 170; 1928.11). (See also 1823.1, the earliest edition I have located in which the "Secret History" chapter appears.)

2   M., B. "Vanbrugh's London Improvements." *N & Q*, 1st ser. 1, no. 9 (December):142.

Cites a reference in the *London Journal* of 16 March 1722/1723 to Vanbrugh's "scheme for new paving the cities of London and Westminster." Author asks if readers can offer "a reference to any detailed plan, from Sir John, for the general improvement of the metropolis."

3   *MACAULAY, THOMAS BABINGTON. *History of England from the Accession of James II.* London: Printed for Longman, Brown, Green, & Longmans.

Source. *NUC.* Margaret Cruickshank (in *Thomas Babington Macaulay.* Boston: Twayne, 1978, p. 165) avers that "The first two volumes . . . appeared in 1848." *NUC* and *BMC* list no 1848 edition, however. For annotation, see 1873.3.

1851

1   *IBBOTSON, HENRY. *The Visitor's Guide to Castle Howard.* Ganthorpe.

Source: Saumarez Smith, 1990.6, p. 215; unverified.

2   O., O. "Sheridan and Vanbrugh." *N & Q*, 1st ser. 4, no. 89 (July):24.

Expresses surprise that Vanbrugh's *Relapse* is printed (with "No comment . . . or any mention of Vanbrugh") in Sheridan's *Dramatic Works*, wherein the play bears the title *A Trip to Scarborough*.

1853

1 EVANS, EDWARD. *Catalogue of a Collection of Engraved Portraits.*
Vol. 2. London: E. Evans, p. 396.
Item 22290 lists the following engraved portrait of "poet" Van-
brugh: "fol. mez. *proof before letters*, scarce, 21s. Kneller-Faber."
For annotation of engraved Vanbrugh portraits listed in vol. 1, see
1836.2.

2 GARLICHITHE. "Sir John Vanbrugh (Vol. viii, p. 65)." *N & Q*, 1st
ser. 8, no. 198 (August):160.
Advises Vanbrugh scholars to search for Vanbrugh's place of birth
in Chester's parochial register "in or about" the year 1762.

3 HOSKING, WILLIAM. "Architecture." In *Encyclopaedia Britannica.* 8th ed. Vol. 3. Boston: Little, Brown, p. 455.
Vanbrugh's buildings are said to be "distinguished by massiveness
unsuited to the ['Italian'] style in which he built," a style "more
suited" to "ecclesiastical" than to "secular" uses. A "painter's architect," he had a better understanding of light and shadow than of "proportion and detail" (as did Michelangelo, whose "faults" he shares).
A headnote indicates that this article was "first written" in 1830.

4 HUGHES, T. "Sir John Vanbrugh." *N & Q*, 1st ser. 7, no. 191
(June):619.
A query requesting documentation of the birthplace and birth date
of the "eminent architect and poet of the last century" Sir John Vanbrugh.

5 HUGHES, T. "Sir John Vanbrugh (Vol. viii, pp. 65, 160)." *N & Q*,
1st ser. 8, no. 201 (September):232–233.
Notes absence of John Vanbrugh's name from the registers of the
Holy Trinity Church, Chester, where the "baptisms or burials of seven
sons and six daughters of Mr. Giles Vanbrugh" were recorded.

6 RIMBAULT, EDWARD F. "Sir John Vanbrugh (Vol. viii, pp. 65, 160,
232)." *N & Q*, 1st ser. 8, no. 206 (October):352.
From the 1759 preface to Vanbrugh's plays (1759.1), quotes testimony that Vanbrugh's forebears were merchants in Antwerp, driven
to England by religious persecution. Quotes from *Chambers' Cyclopaedia of English Literature* (1843.1) the assertion that Vanbrugh's father was a sugar baker, that his son John was probably not born either
in the Bastille or in the parish of St. Stephen's, Walbrook, and the

statement that "It is certain he was in France at the age of nineteen, and remained there some years."

7 S., N. W. "Sir John Vanbrugh (Vol. viii, p. 65 &c.)" *N & Q*, 1st ser. 8, no. 211 (November):480.

From *An Account of the Life and Death of Mr. Matthew Henry*, quotes testimony that in Chester, Vanbrugh's father, Giles, was "in communion with the Church of England," though he also attended the Dissenter Matthew Henry's "week-day lectures, and always treated him with great and serious respect."

8 "Sir John Vanbrugh (Vol. vii, p. 619.)" *N & Q*, 1st ser. 8, no. 194 (July):65.

Reports that the "Duke of Alva's persecution drove" Vanbrugh's grandfather to England and that Giles Vanbrugh, "the son of this refugee, resided in Chester, became rich by trade, and married the youngest daughter of Sir Dudley Carleton, by whom he had eight sons, of whom Sir John Vanbrugh was the second."

1855

1 SCOTT, SIR WALTER. "Drama." In *Encyclopaedia Britannica*. 8th ed. Vol. 8. Boston: Little, Brown, pp. 162–163.

Vanbrugh and Farquhar are pronounced "inferior to Congreve in real wit," but "perhaps his equals in the composition of acting plays." The comedies of Vanbrugh and Farquhar are said to offer "portraits of ordinary life."

1856

1 CUNNINGHAM, PETER. "Sir John Vanbrugh." *N & Q*, 2d ser. 1 (January):7–8.

Transcribes the burial records of members of the Vanbrugh family at St. Stephen's, Walbrook. Also records the names of brothers and sisters mentioned in Vanbrugh's will.

2 HUGHES, T. "Sir John Vanbrugh." *N & Q*, 2d ser. 1, no. 6 (February):116–117.

Avers that Vanbrugh's father Giles was a "sugar-baker" in Chester (but see Downes's caveat in 1987.4). Transcribes baptism records of the fourteen Vanbrugh offspring and suggests that young John Vanbrugh attended the "King's School, then a seminary of the highest repute." Also prints an abstract of Giles Vanbrugh's will "direct[ing] the whole of his real estate, &c, to be sold . . . , and the proceeds to be divided into fourteen parts, two of which he gave to his eldest son John. . . ."

1857

1 "Bliss's 'Reliquiae Hearniane.'" *GM*, 4th ser. 2 (October):420.
   Glosses Hearne's reference to Vanbrugh as "a silly fellow, who is the architect at Woodstock" (1857.3) by noting that Vanbrugh "was more knave than fool; at least, his extortionate demands on the building of Blenheim would lead one to think so."

2 D., H. C. "Vanbrugh Family." *N & Q*, 2d ser. 4, no. 88 (September):187.
   Transcribes the burial records of Charles Vanbrugh (1721), Lady (Henrietta Maria) Vanbrugh (1776, "relict of the celebrated Sir John Vanbrugh"), and Edward Vanbrugh (1802, "an immediate descendant of the celebrated Sir John V").

3 HEARNE, THOMAS. *Reliquiae Hearnianae.* Edited by Philip Bliss. Vol. 1. Oxford: Printed for the Editor, pp. 317, 374–375.
   Entry for 25 September 1714 includes the notation that "The first K[nigh]t. that King George made is one Vanbrugh, a silly Fellow, who is the Architect at Woodstock." The entry for 29 May 1717 records a visit to Woodstock. Blenheim Palace is described as "a grand, but a sad, irregular, confused Piece of Work." The Jacobite author identifies Vanbrugh as "The Architect (if a Blockhead may deserve that Name). . . ." For other eds., see 1869.1 and 1966.4.

4 *The Illustrated Hand-Book to Castle Howard, the Yorkshire Seat of the Right Hon. the Earl of Carlisle.* Malton, England.
   Source: Smith, 1990.8, p. 215; unverified.

5 LUTTRELL, NARCISSUS. *A Brief Historical Relation of State Affairs from September 1678 to April 1714.* Vol. 2. Oxford: Oxford University Press, pp. 355, 387.
   Two entries pertain to Vanbrugh's imprisonment in France. The entry for Thursday, 11 February 1691–1692 begins with the notation, "Last letters from France say, 3 English gentlemen, Mr. Vanbrook, Mr. Goddard, and Mr. North, were clapt up in the Bastile, suspected to be spyes." The entry for 15 March 1691–1692 includes the notation,

1860

"French merchants were the other day sent to the Tower, to be used as Mr. North and Mr. Vanbroke are in the Bastile."

6 RILEY, HENRY T. "Sir John Vanbrugh (1st S.vii.619; viii *passim* 2nd S.i.7.116)." *N & Q*, 2d ser. 3, no. 57 (January):95.
   Notes Disraeli's (1849.1) report that Vanbrugh was "born in the Bastille." Thinks it "just possible, however," that Vanbrugh used the phrase figuratively.

1858

1 SPENCE, JOSEPH. *Anecdotes, Observations, and Characters, of Books and Men. Collected from the Conversation of Mr. Pope, and other Eminent Persons of His Time.* 2d ed. Edited by Samuel Weller Singer. London: John Russell Smith, pp. 34–35, 235n., 257, 265.
   For annotation, see 1820.3.

1859

1 DAVIS, HENRY GEORGE. *Memorials of the Hamlet of Knightsbridge.* Edited by Charles Davis. London: J. Russell Smith, pp. 83–84.
   After recording the 19 June 1721 death of Charles Vanbrugh, notes that Charles was "Most probably . . . brother of the celebrated architect and dramatist, Sir John Vanbrugh."

2 ROGERS, SAMUEL. *Recollections.* London: Longman, Brown, p. 32.
   Among the recollections is Charles James Fox's assertion that Vanbrugh was "almost as great a genius as ever lived." Also records Fox's positive impressions of Vanbrugh's *The Provoked Wife* and *The Confederacy.*

1860

1 ASHPITEL, ARTHUR. "Vanbrugh." *Encyclopaedia Britannica.* Vol. 21. 8th ed. Boston: Little, Brown, & Co., pp. 515–519.
   Pioneering sketch of the career of the "talented, warm-hearted, and prosperous" Vanbrugh. Speculates about the early years in Chester and the causes of his imprisonment in the Bastille. Notices the plays, the career as herald, theatre manager, architect. Praises Castle

1861

Howard's avoidance of both the contemporary error of excessive balance and the subsequent nineteenth-century error of studied irregularity. Endorsing Uvedale Price's praise of Blenheim, ascribes the malice of "rival wits" to "envy."

2 CARLYLE, ALEXANDER. *The Autobiography of the Rev. Dr Alexander Carlyle, Minister of Inveresk, Containing Memorials of the Men and Events of His Time.* Edinburgh and London: William Blackwood and Sons, p. 364.

Includes an account of the Carlyle party's visit to Blenheim in 1753. The chapel, "though much cried down by the Tory wits of Queen Anne's reign," is adjudged "magnificent," and "Our companion James Adam," who had toured Italy's grandest palaces, pronounced that Blenheim Palace "ill deserved the aspersions laid upon it." Says Adam singled out the building's "movement" for particular praise. The 1910.1 revised ed. repeats this account verbatim.

3 "The Genius of Vanbrugh: Blenheim." *Builder*, 21 July, pp. 460–461.

Citing the authority of Cunningham (1831.1) and Gwilt (1842.1), pronounces Vanbrugh's detractors to be slaves to precedent, denouncers of originality. Praises Blenheim's "various perspectives" for their "power to delight" and its architect for the "exuberance of his imagination."

4 WHARTON, GRACE AND PHILIP. *Queens of Society.* New York: Harper & Brothers, 40–41.

A brief account of Vanbrugh calls *The Relapse* and *The Provoked Wife* "at once witty and immoral." Avers that at the Haymarket Theatre, he "assisted Betterton as manager." Claims it is "To his [Vanbrugh's] fantastic taste we owe St. John's Church, Westminster." A paragraph on his quarrel with the Duchess of Marlborough seeks "to do him justice" by noting that he "wished to restore the ['picturesque'] old Manor House of Woodstock."

1861

1 DIXON, W. HEPWORTH. "Kimbolton Castle." *Athenaeum*, 19 January, pp. 83–86.

Praises architect Vanbrugh's "fire, his daring, his picturesqueness, his solidity and grandeur," suggesting that contemporary coffee-house detractors were prompted by "envy." Prints five of Vanbrugh's

1707–1708 letters to the Earl of Manchester. In the letters Vanbrugh describes his Haymarket Theatre affairs and his plans for rebuilding Manchester's Kimbolton Castle.

2   RIMBAULT, EDWARD F. "Was Sir John Vanbrugh a Musician?" *N & Q*, 2d ser. 11 (April):326–327.

Seeks to disentangle the careers of Sir John Vanbrugh and his contemporary "Mr. [George] Vanbrugh," whom the *Dictionary of Musicians* (1824) describes as "a professor of music, resident in London. . . ." Concludes that "Lysander, a Cantata, Now first published [apparently privately, by George Vanbrugh, Rector of Aughton], October, 1813" is mistakenly ascribed to John Vanbrugh on its title page. The latter "was not the composer of *Lysander*, nor, as far as we know, of any other piece of music."

3   ROBINSON, CHARLES BEST. *History of the Priory and Peculiar of Snaith, in the County of York*. London: Simpkin, Marshall; York: E. H. Pickering, p. 77.

Includes a paragraph in which Henrietta Maria Yarburgh's [or Yarborough's] marriage to Vanbrugh is recorded and the death of the pair's son Charles in 1745 following the battle of Tournay is noted. Blenheim and Castle Howard are called Vanbrugh's "best known works." Duncombe Park and Robin Hood's Well ("near Doncaster") are said to have been built "from his design."

1862

1   "Correspondance de Londres." *Revue Britannique* 1 (January):491.

Denies *Athenaeum*'s allegation (1862.4) that Voltaire's *le Comte de Boursoufle*, recently performed at the Odéon, is a plagiarized version of Vanbrugh's *Relapse*. Acknowledges similarities in spirit but not in phrasing, noting that Vanbrugh's *Relapse* was itself derived from Cibber's *Love's Last Shift* and Sheridan's *Trip to Scarborough* from *The Relapse*.

2   *FERGUSSON, JAMES. *History of the Modern Styles of Architecture*. London: J. Murray. (*NUC* lists a 2d ed. of 1877 and a 3d ed. of 1891.)

For annotation, see 1899.3.

1863

3 GATSCHENBERGER, STEPHAN. *Geschichte der Englischen Liter-atur.* Vol. 3. Wien: Markgraf, pp. 209–210.

   A brief account of Vanbrugh expresses uncertainty whether he was born in the Bastille or in London. Describes him as the architect of Blenheim and Castle Howard and Comptroller of the Office of Works. A list of his comedies is prefaced by the assertion that they are marked by lightness of dialogue and unaffected humor.

4 "Voltaire's Newly-Discovered Comedy." *Athenaeum*, 8 February, p. 192.

   Pronounces that *le Comte de Boursoufle*, purportedly written by Voltaire and currently being performed at the Odéon in Paris, is an unacknowledged adaptation of Vanbrugh's *Relapse* "from beginning to end." (See 1862.1.)

1863

1 *TAYLOR, TOM. "The Great Actors of 1775." *Victoria Magazine* 1 (May–October).

   Source: Coleman, 1982.2, p. 46n. 42, reports that Taylor published portions of Lichtenberg's account (see 1938.3) of Garrick's performance as Sir John Brute; unverified.

1864

1 MONTAGU, CHARLES, FIRST DUKE OF MANCHESTER. *Court and Society from Elizabeth to Anne: Edited from the Papers at Kimbolton.* Vol. 2. London: Hurst and Blackett, pp. 53–57, 60, 224–227, 288–289, 317, 323, 354, 377.

   Prints and comments on a number of Vanbrugh's letters to his friend and patron the Earl of Manchester, principally concerning Vanbrugh's opera affairs at the Haymarket Theatre and his rebuilding of Kimbolton House. Suggests that the sneers of Pope and Swift were rooted in "envy" at the success of an artist who was "at once the rival of Congreve and Wren." Praises the "splendour and originality" of Castle Howard and Blenheim.

2 PAPWORTH, WYATT. "Sir John Vanbrugh." *N & Q*, 3d ser. 5 (June):498.

   Query: are there "any drawings known to have been made" by Vanbrugh?

1866

1 B., D.; S., W. H.; A., A., et al. "Sir John Vanbrugh's Plays (3rd S.x.9)." *N & Q*, 3d ser. 20 (July):52–53.

Five readers' responses to Payne's (1866.2) request for help with the meanings of phrases from Vanbrugh's *Confederacy*, *The Mistake*, and *A Journey to London*.

2 PAYNE, CORNELIUS JUN. "Sir John Vanbrugh's Plays." *N & Q*, 3d ser. 10 (July):9.

A lexicographer's query concerning the meanings of six phrases in Vanbrugh's plays: "rising of the lights" (*Confederacy*, I); "he scolds one Rubbers" (*Confederacy*, II); "a crooked stick" (*Confederacy*, III); "a Scotch pair of boots" (*Mistake*, I); "to keep your back hand" (*Mistake*, V); "Norfolk-nog" (*Journey to London*, I). (See 1866.2 and 1866.3.)

3 SPEED, J. "Sir John Vanbrugh's Plays: 'A Crooked Stick' (3rd S.x.9,52,99)." *N & Q*, 3d ser. 10 (September):197.

In response to query in 1866.2, explains that "a crooked stick" (*The Confederacy*, III) is an "Exchequer tally"—a notched stick formerly used "as a receipt for money paid into the Exchequer."

1867

1 GWILT, JOSEPH. *The Encyclopedia of Architecture, Historical, Theoretical, and Practical.* Revised with alterations and considerable additions by Wyatt Papworth. London: Longmans, Green, pp. 216–217. Reprint. New York: Bonanza Books, 1982.

Estimate of Vanbrugh remains as in 1845.1.

2 H., C. "Hannah Lightfoot (3rd S.xi.219)." *N & Q*, 3d ser. 11 (March):245.

Includes the information that the respondent had once visited a physician named "Potts, who lived at Blackheath, in a house called Vanbrugh Castle . . . built by Sir John Vanbrugh, for himself . . ."; it was for "many years" the residence of "George III's beautiful Quakeress, Hanna Lightfoot."

1869

1 HEARNE, THOMAS. *Reliquiae Hearniane.* Edited by Philip Bliss. 2d ed., enlarged. London: J. R. Smith, 1869.

For annotation, see 1857.3.

1872

2 *ZINCK, AUGUST GEORG LUDVIG. *Congreve, Vanbrugh og Sheridan. En Skildring til Belysning af de sociale Forhold og dot aaudelige Liv i England fra Carl den Andens Tid og til henimod den franske Revolution.* Kjobenhavn: C. A. Reitzels.
Source: *BMC.*

1872

1 CLARKE, CHARLES COWDEN. "On the Comic Writers of England. X.—Vanburgh [*sic*] and Farquhar." *GM* 232, n.s. 8 (January–June):39–49.
Endorses Hazlitt's praise of Lord Foppington in *The Relapse* (1819.2). Admires the rendering of Miss Hoyden but thinks her "perhaps" too closely modeled after Congreve's Miss Prue in *Love for Love.* Thinks Vanbrugh "redeemed the married female" from the "opprobrium" to which she had been subjected by his "predecessors." In *The Provoked Wife,* Sir John Brute is pronounced a "monster-curiosity"; the play's other characters (excepting Lady Brute, who "tells her own tale clearly and well") are judged to be "little better than common stock from the dramatic warehouse." Thinks *The Confederacy* Vanbrugh's "most entertaining" comedy. Thinks Vanbrugh's comic language "inelegant—even at times false," but praises the playwright's "constant flow of mirth, good humour, invention of situation, and humorous painting." A two-paragraph account of the architecture assigns to Vanbrugh "the several designs of St. John's, Westminster," the design of St. Mary Woolnoth's by the old Post Office, and the "principal church at Greenwich, and that at Limehouse."

2 P., W. "Sir John Vanbrugh." *N & Q,* 4th ser. 9, no. 234 (June):499–500.
Offers a conjectural chronology of Vanbrugh's career.

3 T., G. D. "Sir John Vanbrugh (4th S.ix.490)." *N & Q,* 4th ser. 10 (July):17–18.
Cites the testimony of Robinson (1861.3) that Vanbrugh married Henrietta Maria Yarburgh at St. Lawrence, York, on 14 January 1718/1719. Records Hunter's testimony (1831.2) that Vanbrugh designed the canopy for Robin Hood's Well, near Duncaster, and "furnished the design for Duncombe Park."

1873

1   "The Family of the First Countess of Coventry: and the Matrimonial Relations of Gregory King, Lancaster Herald." *Herald and Genealogist* 7:112–114.

Quotes from Gregory King's 1710 letter to Harley (later Earl of Oxford) protesting Vanbrugh's appointment as Clarencieux in 1704 (a position to which King had expected to be appointed). Rues the further injustice that would be done to "some of our Society" who "have spent the Prime of their days . . . qualifying themselves for" office in the College of Heralds if the unqualified Vanbrugh were now appointed Garter.

2   [LE NEVE, PETER.] *Le Neve's Pedigrees of the Knights Made by King Charles II., King James II., King William III. and Queen Mary, King William Alone, and Queen Anne.* Edited by George W. Marshall. Publications of the Harleian Society 3. London: Michell and Hughes, pp. 511–512.

Reports Vanbrugh's knighting "at Greenwich house [S]unday 19th of September 1714 introduced by his grace the Duke of Marleburgh." Describes the Vanbrugh family's coat of arms, quoting John Baptist Gramay's notation in *Antiquitys of West Flanders* that in 1383 John Van Brugghe was one of "severall eminent Knights" holding the praetorship of Ypres. Adds that Gyles Vanbrugh (Sir John's grandfather) "fled from flanders in the Duke D'Alvas p'secution." Includes a family tree.

3   MACAULAY, THOMAS BABINGTON.   *The History of England from the Accession of James II.* Vol. 1. Philadelphia: Lippincott, pp. 287–288.

The "conversation" of the fops who in the 1680s congregated in houses "near St. James Park" is said to have been conducted "in that dialect which, long after it had ceased to be spoken in fashionable circles, continued, in the mouth of Lord Foppington, to excite the mirth of theatres." The "chief peculiarity" of Lord Foppington's dialect "was that, in a large class of words, the O was pronounced like A" (e.g., "stork" being pronounced "stark"). The reader is advised to "See Vanbrugh's *Relapse.*" For citation of earlier ed., see 1849.3.

4   MARSHALL, EDWARD.   *Early History of Woodstock Manor and its Environs.* . . . Oxford and London: James Parker, pp. 262–263.

Says Blenheim was "completed" in 1715. Refers readers to Disraeli's "Secret History of the Building of Blenheim" (1849.1) for discussion of the "serious differences" that arose between Vanbrugh and

1875

1   MACREADY, WILLIAM CHARLES. *Macready's Reminiscences, and Selections from his Diaries and Letters.* Edited by Sir Frederick Pollock. New York: Macmillan, p. 361.

  Diary entry dated 21 December 1835 includes the following observation: "Read 'The False Friend' of Vanbrugh—a play in which I fancied there was a contradiction to Pope's assertion that 'Man [Van] never wanted wit.' I could not discover it."

2   WALFORD, EDWARD. *Old and New London: A Narrative of Its History, Its People, and Its Places.* 6 vols. London, Paris, and New York: Cassell Petter & Galpin, pp. 3:332; 4:209, 212; 5:130; 6:230–231.

  Briefly describes Vanbrugh's Goose-Pie House. Notes Swift's ridicule (1710.1) and Reynolds's encomium (1797.2), which is quoted at length, as well as Rowe's lines of praise (1715.3). Discusses the inception of Vanbrugh's Haymarket Theatre, describing it as a "dull plain building, not unlike a Quaker's meeting-house." Ascribes Kensington Charity School to Vanbrugh. Brief description of Vanbrugh Castle and Mince-Pie House in Greenwich.

3   WARD, ADOLPHUS WILLIAM. *A History of English Dramatic Literature to the Death of Queen Anne.* Vol. 2. London: Macmillan, pp. 589–592.

  Offers summary judgments of Vanbrugh's original plays and adaptations. Lord Foppington is "the best fop ever brought on the stage," but *The Relapse* itself is a "recklessly immoral production." The "realism" of *The Provoked Wife* is praised, the "morality" of *The Confederacy* pronounced to be "on Vanbrugh's usual level, which may be described as the very lowest to which English comedy has ever sunk." Note 3 (pp. 591–592) cites testimony to a Yorkshire tradition identifying Sir Francis Headpiece (in *A Journey to London*) with "Sir Thomas Yarborough, twice M.P. for Pontefract, whose granddaughter was married to Vanbrugh."

1876

1   WORNUM, RALPH N. Notes to *Anecdotes of Painting in England; with Some Account of the Principal Artists. . . . With Additions by the Rev. James Dallaway,* by Horace Walpole. "A new edition,

revised, with additional notes by Ralph N. Wornum." Vol. 2. London: Chatto and Windus, pp. 254–257. Reprint. New York: Arno, 1969.

Wornum's only addition to Dallaway's notes on Vanbrugh (1827.1) is the notation that the latter's father, "Giles Vanbrugh, was the son of a Flemish Protestant, who fled from the persecutions of the Duke of Alva." (See 1765.1.)

1877

1 RAVAISSON, FRANÇOIS, ed. *Archives de la Bastille; documents inédits recueillis et publiés par François Ravaison.* Vol. 9. Paris: A. Durand et Pedone-Lauriel. Reprint. Geneva: Slatkine-Megariotis Reprints, 1975, pp. 338–342. (Annotation and page numbers based on 1975 reprint.)

Prints French officials' correspondence relating to Vanbrugh's imprisonment at Calais, Vincennes, and the Bastille during the period 1688–1692. Correspondence is summarized in Appendix B of Downes, 1977.2.

1878

1 BOASE, GEORGE CLEMENT, and COURTNEY, WILLIAM PRIDEAUX. *Bibliotheca Cornubiensis. A Catalogue of the Writings, Both Manuscript and Printed, of Cornishmen, and of Works Relating to the County of Cornwall.* . . . Vol. 11, *P–Z.* London: Longmans, Green, p. 820.

The entry for Vanbrugh lists, as written "by the late John Vanbrugh," *The Cornish Squire,* "printed for J. Watts," 1734.

2 DE GRISY, A. *Histoire de la Comédie Anglaise au Dix-Septième Siècle.* Paris: Didier, pp. 259–275.

A chapter on Vanbrugh includes a biographical sketch and an account of his principal productions as dramatist and architect. Concludes that Vanbrugh was an "homme complet" whose rather cold ("froid") architecture evinced a gothic sensibility and whose plays contributed to the triumph of "idées genéreuses."

3 [NORCLIFFE, C. B.] "Additions to Le Neve's Knights." *Genealogist* 2:237–240.

Reports the provisions of the wills made by John Vanbrugh and his wife Henrietta and recounts the life and death of the Vanbrughs' son Charles. The latter died in the Battle of Fontenoy at the age of twenty-six.

1879

4 SMITH, JOHN CHALONER. *British Mezzotinto Portraits.* . . . Part 1. *Engravers: Adams to Faber.* London: Henry Sotheran, p. 435.

Item 358 describes J. Richardson's 1725 engraving of Vanbrugh as follows: "T.Q.L., standing, directed toward front, facing and looking towards right, wig, flowered morning gown, collar and medal, right hand on hip, left elbow on pedestal to right, hand holding plan, lettered *Blenheim*."

1879

1 BRAYLEY, EDWARD WEDLAKE. *Topographical History of Surrey.* Revised and edited by Edward Walford. Vol. 2. London: J. S. Virtue, p. 237.

Attributes to Vanbrugh a house at Kingston-upon-Thames in Surrey. The house is described as "a residence of peculiar structure," "of brick, and strongly built," with a "stack of chimneys form[ing] a turret in the centre of the roof," "one of the latest productions of Sir John Vanbrugh." For annotation of 1st ed., see 1841.2.

1881

1 BELJAME, ALEXANDRE. *Le Public et les Hommes de Lettres en Angleterre au Dix-Huitième Siècle, 1660–1744.* Paris: Librairie Hachette.

For annotation, see 1897.1.

2 ASHTON, JOHN. *Social Life in the Reign of Queen Anne.* 2 vols. London: Chatto & Windus, 1:61–62; 2:50.

As an illustration of the bias against "any originality" in architecture in Queen Anne's day, quotes a lengthy excerpt from Swift's satirical "History of Vanbrugh's [Goose-Pie] House" (1710.1). Elsewhere quotes the final couplet from Evans's "Lie heavy on him" epitaph (1780.1). Concludes that though he was not Wren's equal, Vanbrugh's "two best works, Blenheim and Castle Howard, testify" to his "good taste and scientific knowledge."

1883

1 CRAWFURD, OSWALD. *English Comic Dramatists.* London: Kegan Paul, pp. 84–105.

Prints one scene each from *A Journey to London* and *The Relapse*, and portions of three scenes from *The Confederacy.* A one-page headnote claims Vanbrugh possessed "the rare and great merit that he wrote to be acted, not to be read." He is judged to be "more civilized and human in his satire" than is Wycherley. Though less witty than Congreve, his plays have "greater natural flow and natural ease." He goes "farther afield for his plots than his contemporaries, and brings more than mere fine ladies and gentlemen on to the stage." Praises Lord Foppington, whose "part . . . was as famous in its day as Lord Dundreary in ours."

1886

1   *ADAMS, WILLIAM HENRY DAVENPORT. *Good Queen Anne; or Men and Manners, Life and Letters in England's Augustan Age.* Vol. 1. London: Remington & Co., pp. 50–51.

Sources: *NUC* and Coleman, 1982.2, pp. 28, 48 n.77; unverified. Coleman cites author's opinion that although *The Provoked Wife* is "a masterpiece of the comic drama," Vanbrugh's "indecorum of . . . language" and "suggestiveness of . . . situations . . . shock and confuse us."

2   HASTED, EDWARD. *Hasted's History of Kent, Corrected, Enlarged, and Continued to the Present Time. . . . Part I. The Hundred of Blackheath.* Edited by Henry H. Drake. London: Mitchell and Hughes, p. 78.

Includes description of two of Vanbrugh's houses in his Greenwich compound: one "on Maize Hill called Bastille House [i.e., Vanbrugh Castle] said to be a model of the Bastille"; another "in Vanbrugh Fields . . . called the Mince-Pie House." A footnote briefly describes his career as architect and herald (he advanced "Through pleasing the Earl of Carlisle . . . in the design for Castle Howard"). Blenheim and "the Mansion House, London" are said to be "Among his chief architectural works." Concerning the Greenwich compound, avers that "Vanbrugh built 4 houses under lease granted by the Biddulphs in 1717." Notes that the entrance arch bears the date 1714. Claims the "two houses south of this arch were built in 1719 for the Duchess of Bolton (Polly Peacham) and Sir James Thornhill."

3   "King's Weston House, near Bristol." *Gloucestershire Notes and Queries* 3, Pt. 30 (April):359–360.

Reprints from *Old-Worlde Gleanings*, no. 83, Vanbrugh's 23 October 1713 letter to Edward Southwell concerning the chimneys at Kings Weston. Also reprints a response from *Old-World Gleanings*, no. 85, in which Sholto Vere Hare records his ownership of the original of the letter here reprinted.

1887

1   BEDE, CUTHBERT. "Sir John Vanbrugh's Designs for Rebuilding Grimsthorpe Castle." *N & Q*, 7th ser. 4 (July):47.

Reports purchase of loose book leaves containing three engraved elevations of Grimsthorpe and a fourth engraving of Vanbrugh's plan for Grimsthorpe's "principal floor." Observes that "the imposing north front was the only portion of Vanbrugh's design that was carried out, and it includes the largest entrance hall in the kingdom." The four purchased plates are "from the 'third vol.' of some work"; asks if readers can identify the title of that work (probably Campbell, *Vitruvius Britannicus*, 1715-1725.1).

2   FITZGERALD, PERCY. "The Drury Lane Managers. From Killigrew to Augustus Harris. Part IV." *Theatre*, n.s. 9 (May):262-263.

A paragraph on Vanbrugh asserts that his name is properly spelled "Vanbrugge." Says his plays, "of course, are leavened with the grossness of the time," but thinks his *Vindication* makes it "quite evident that he sincerely believed" Collier's attack was "unjust." The "innocent fashion" in which he defended his comedies in the *Vindication* is said to anticipate Charles Lamb's line of reasoning in his essay "On the Artificial Comedy of the Last Century."

3   P., C.; SCARLETT, B. F.; and DREDGE, J. INGLE. "Sir John Vanbrugh (7th S.iv.28)." *N & Q*, 7th ser. 4 (August):113.

Three successive notes: (1) C. P. reports that Vanburgh is said (in the biographical account prefacing the 1759 edition of his plays, 1759.7) to have been buried in the church of St. Stephen, Walbrook; also advises readers of the "very good biography of Sir John Vanbrugh in the 'Encyclopaedia Britannica, eighth edition'"; (2) Scarlett reports that a portrait of Vanbrugh appears in Walpole's *Anecdotes of Painting* (1765.1) and opines that Vanbrugh "may have been buried in Greenwich"; Dredge likewise points readers to the Vanbrugh portrait in Walpole's *Anecdotes*.

4   STUKELEY, WILLIAM, and GALE, ROGER and SAMUEL. *The Family Memoirs of the Rev. William Stukeley, M.D. and the Antiquarian and other Correspondence of William Stukeley, Roger & Samuel*

Gale, etc. Vol. 3. Publications of the Surtees Society. Vol. 80. London: Whittaker; Edinburgh: William Blackwood, p. 373.

Includes brief description of the covering "erected by the Lord Carlisle" (and designed by Vanbrugh, though his name is not mentioned) over Robin Hood's Well, "a pretty ornament to the [Roman] road" in Doncaster.

5   VYVYAN, EDWARD R. "Sir John Vanbrugh." *N & Q*, 7th ser. 4 (July):28–29

Asks for help regarding the "correct" spelling of Vanbrugh's name, birthplace, location of his house in "Scotland Yard," place of burial, and extant portraits of Vanbrugh.

1888

1   BINGHAM [DENIS ARTHUR]. *The Bastille.* Vol. 1. New York: Scribner and Welford, pp. 443–450.

Quotes Disraeli's (1849.1) speculations concerning Vanbrugh's experiences in France. Thinks Vanbrugh Castle—here called "Bastille House"—resembles the Bastille "both externally and internally." To "clear up the mystery" concerning Vanbrugh's remark about "finish[ing] my days in an English [Bastille] as I began them in a French one," quotes (from Ravaisson, 1877.1) the Bastille documents pertinent to Vanbrugh's confinement there in 1692.

2   GOSSE, EDMUND. *Life of William Congreve.* London: W. Scott; New York: T. Whittaker.

For annotation, see 1924.4.

3   LOWE, ROBERT W. *Bibliographical Account of English Theatrical Literature from the Earliest Times to the Present Day.* London: John C. Nimmo, pp. 348–349.

The following works are listed in the "Vanbrugh" entry: (1) *Short Vindication* (glossed "Vanbrugh's comedies were especially indecent, and were singled out for censure justly by Jeremy Collier"); (2) *A Letter from Several Members of the Society for Reformation of Manners* . . . (1704.2, glossed "an attack on Vanbrugh protesting against his being appointed manager of the new theatre in the Haymarket, on account of the notorious indecency and profanity of his plays"); (3) *A Journey to London*; (4) *Reflections on the Principal Characters in the Provoked Husband* (1728.2).

1889

1 AITKEN, GEORGE A. *The Life of Richard Steele.* 2 vols. London: Wm. Isbister. Reprint. New York: Greenwood Press, 1968, 1:61, 99, 146–147; 2:57–58n., 239.

Notes the inclusion of Vanbrugh's name on a list of "contributors" to *Commendatory Verses, on the Author of the Two Arthurs.* Quotes from two of Vanbrugh's letters to Tonson concerning the Kit-Cat Club. Quotes Steele's celebratory remarks on Vanbrugh in his prologue to Vanbrugh's *The Mistake* (1705). Cites an entry signed by Clarenceux Vanbrugh in the Heralds College Partition Book indicating that Steele had been knighted by the king. Also quotes from Vanbrugh's 18 February 1719/1720 letter to Tonson concerning "talk" that Steele's outspoken attack on the ministry would result in his expulsion from the House of Commons.

2 MARTIN, BENJAMIN ELLIS. *Old Chelsea: A Summer-Day's Stroll.* London: T. Fisher Unwin, pp. 82–83.

Includes brief discussion of Walpole House—"built by Sir John Vanbrugh," "grand in its day, grand still in its mutilation" (having been pressed into service as an old soldiers' hospital). Thinks the dining room remains "one of the most impressive relics of by-gone grandeur in all London."

1890

1 AILESBURY, THOMAS, 2ND EARL OF. *Memoirs of Thomas, Earl of Ailesbury Written by Himself.* 2 vols. Westminster: Nichols & Sons. Printed for the Roxburghe Club, 1:309; 2:586–587.

Includes the English Jacobite's (ca. 1730?) account of the terms of the exchange of French and English prisoners he proposed in 1692 to Secretary of State Nottingham. Among the prisoners released in the exchange was Vanbrugh, here described as "the famous poet since, who composed in the Bastille his most ingenious play 'The Provoked Wife.'" Elsewhere recounts a conversation with the Duke of Marlborough in which the author speculated that the Duke had chosen Vanbrugh as his builder at Blenheim "because he is a professed Whig." Concerning Blenheim Ailesbury records his opinion that it is "like one mass of stone, without taste or relish."

2 BRIGG, WILLIAM, ed. *The Register Book of the Parish of St. Nicholas Acons, London, 1539–1812.* Leeds: Walker and Laycock, pp. 31–33.

Transcribes the 14 October 1659 record of the birth (October 6) of Giles Vanbrugh to Giles and Elizabeth Vanbrugh. The 24 January

1891

1663/1664 birth of John Vanburgh ("the celebrated Sir John Vanbrugh") to Giles and Elizabeth notes that John was "christned in the
house by M^r. John Meriton." Also recorded is a 20 February 1661/
1662 notation of the birth (on February 14) of Dorothe Vanbrugh to
Giles and Elizabeth Vanbrugh.

3 "Letters of Sir John Vanbrugh. I." *Athenaeum* II, no. 3279 (September):289–291.
   Prints sixteen letters Vanbrugh wrote to the Duke of Newcastle
and the Duchess of Marlborough between 1715 and 1723. Subjects
include Vanbrugh's work on Newcastle's Claremont House and Nottingham Castle and Vanbrugh's efforts to negotiate a marriage between Newcastle and the Duchess of Marlborough's granddaughter
Henrietta Godolphin.

4 "Letters of Sir John Vanbrugh. II." *Athenaeum* II, no. 3280 (September):321–322.
   Prints without commentary a number of Vanbrugh's letters to the
Duke of Newcastle of 1718–1719 (all printed subsequently in 1928.11).
Subjects include Vanbrugh's marriage to Henrietta Yarburgh, the progress of his work on Newcastle's Nottingham Castle, and protest against
the planned demolition of an ancient gateway in Westminster.

5 *LOVEDAY, JOHN. *Diary of a Tour in 1732 through Parts of England, Wales, Ireland and Scotland. . . .* Edinburgh: Privately printed
for the Roxburghe Club.
   Source: *NUC.* Evidently includes a detailed account of Castle
Howard, from which Markham (1984.6, pp. 136–137) quotes Loveday's conclusion that the house "altogether pleases me more than any I
have yet seen."

6 "Miss Tomboy." *Theatre* 15, 1 May, pp. 256–258.
   Reviews a performance of Robert Buchanan's *Miss Tomboy*, a
three-act adaptation of Vanbrugh's *Relapse*. Includes a brief performance history of Vanbrugh's play. Says Buchanan's version "has done
away completely with the objectionable characters, and the intrigue of
Loveless and Berinthia." Applauds Buchanan's "Transform[ation]"
of Vanbrugh's "vicious Miss Hoyden into a thoughtless, sunny, and
impulsive tomboy. . . ."

1891

1 ALLIBONE, S. AUSTIN. *A Critical Dictionary of English Literature
and British and American Authors, Living and Deceased, from the*

1891

Earliest Accounts to the Latter Half of the Nineteenth Century. Vol. 3. Philadelphia: Lippincott, pp. 2508–2509.

Biographical sketch draws information from preface to the 1759 edition of Vanbrugh's plays (1759.1). Lists the plays and premiere dates. Quotes the judgments of Blair (1783.1), Hazlitt (1819.2), Hallam (1843.2), and others concerning both plays and buildings. Brief bibliography.

2 Historical Manuscripts Commission. Twelfth Report, Appendix, Part IX. The Manuscripts of the Duke of Beaufort, K. G., the Earl of Donoughmore, and Others. London: H. M. Stationery Office, p. 97.

Among the documents printed is a missive of 21 March 1703/1704 in which "W. Walsh" advises an unnamed correspondent of the Lord Marshall's intention to install John Vanbrugh as Clarenceux King of Arms. Reports that Gregory King, to whom the Lord Marshall had refused to grant the place, "persuaded some other heralds to join with him in a petition against the Lord Marshall" (Vanbrugh's friend and patron the Earl of Carlisle). The Council "unanimously" rejected King's petition.

3 LOWE, ROBERT W. *Thomas Betterton.* London: Kegan Paul, pp. 154, 158–159, 175.

Cites the testimony of *Comparison between the Two Stages* (1702.1) concerning Vanbrugh's "powerful contribution to the success of Drury Lane." Summarizes the charges leveled by Collier against Congreve and Vanbrugh, "the principal purveyors of indecency" on the stage of their day, on whom Collier's "bolt fell with crushing effect." Claims Vanbrugh built his Haymarket Theatre to "obviate" the "disadvantage" of the small size of Betterton's Lincoln's Inn Fields Theatre in its competition with Drury Lane.

4 WHEATLEY, HENRY B. *London Past and Present: Its History, Associations, and Traditions. Based upon the Handbook of London by the Late Peter Cunningham.* 3 vols. London: John Murray; New York: Scribner & Welford, 2:199, 208–210; 3:225, 311, 506.

Includes brief description of Vanbrugh's Haymarket Theatre. In a list of "Celebrated Officers of the [Heralds] College," includes "Sir John Vanbrugh, the poet, Clarenceux." Notes that Vanbrugh lived in a house he "designed . . . and built [Goose-Pie House] out of the ruins of Whitehall." In a description of St. Stephen's, Walbrook, observes that Vanbrugh, "the architect and wit, was buried (1726) in the family vault of the Vanbrughs in the north aisle."

1892

1 BEAVER, ALFRED. *Memorials of Old Chelsea: A New History of the Village of Palaces.* London: Elliot Stock, p. 288.

Thinks Vanbrugh's letter to Robert Walpole of 27 October 1725 "probably refers to" the "summer-house and garden house" Vanbrugh designed for Walpole in Chelsea. (The letter is not cited in Downes's list of Vanbrugh's published letters in *Sir John Vanbrugh*, Appendix B, 1987.4.)

1892[-1904]

1 DALTON, CHARLES, ed. *English Army Lists and Commission Registers, 1661-1714.* 6 vols. London: Francis Edwards. Reprint. 1960, 2:67, 3:409-410, 4:147, 5:99. (Annotation and page numbers based on 1960 reprint.)

Transcribes records of Vanbrugh's military commissions. The 1696 commission of "Jno. Brooke" as captain in the "2nd MARINE REGT." (4:147) is glossed (n.1) as follows: "Afterwards the celebrated Sr. Jno. *Vanbrugh*, Knt. Appointed Capt. in the Earl of Huntingdon's Regt. of Foot 10 Mar. 1702." 3:409-410 reprints 1894.2 and 1894.4.

1893

1 HISTORICAL MANUSCRIPTS COMMISSION. *Thirteenth Report, Appendix, Part II. The Manuscripts of his Grace the Duke of Portland, Preserved at Welbeck Abbey.* Vol. 2. London: Printed for H. M. Stationery Office, p. 185.

Includes a transcript of Vanbrugh's 8 May 1704 "Agreement to allow the Duke of Newcastle, in consideration of the payment by him of a sum of one hundred guineas, free entrance to the theatre intended to be built in the Haymarket, and certain other privileges." The agreement was "Witnessed by William Congreve and another."

2 "Sir John Vanbrugh" (review of Ward, *Sir John Vanbrugh*, 1893.3). *Saturday Review* 75, no. 1,950 (March):268-270.

Records the outlines of Vanbrugh's career as presented by Ward (1893.3). Praises the tight structure and "extraordinary realism" of Vanbrugh's plays—qualities that make him "the pleasantest of the late seventeenth-century comic dramatists to read and remember." Among the adaptations, singles out *The Mistake* for praise. Regrets *The Pilgrim* not printed in Ward's collection. Notes that Vanbrugh's Goose-Pie House "is still extant, though doomed to immediate destruction."

3 WARD, W.C., ed. Introduction to *Sir John Vanbrugh*. Vol. 1. London: Lawrence & Bullen, pp. ix–lxxviii.

Pioneering study depicts Vanbrugh as a man of "gaiety and good humour." Surveys the Collier stage controversy, conceding the justice of Collier's criticisms of Vanbrugh's plays for lack of unity (e.g., *The Relapse*'s two plots are "very slightly connected"), but approving Vanbrugh's deft defense of passages Collier had called immoral or profane. The account of his buildings focuses on the Blenheim episode.

1894

1 BIRRELL, AUGUSTINE. "Sir John Vanbrugh." (Source of original publication not identified; table of contents in *Collected Essays* indicates "1893" as essay's original publication date.) In *The Collected Essays and Addresses*. Vol. 1. New York: Scribner's, 1894, pp. 107–112; reprinted London: Elliot Stock, 1899; London and Toronto: J. M. Dent, 1922; Freeport, N.Y.: Books for Libraries Press, 1968.

A brief and appreciative sketch of Vanbrugh's career. Proposes that *The Provoked Wife* (II.i.172–182) adumbrates a "Philosophy of Clothes" similar to that of Swift in *A Tale of a Tub* (1704) and of Thomas Carlyle in *Sartor Resartus* (1833–1834). Vanbrugh's "Style" is argued to be the progenitor of Sheridan's, Vanbrugh's repartees having "more brains, if less sparkle."

2 DALTON, CHARLES. "Sir John Vanbrugh." *Athenaeum*, no. 3488 (1 September):299. Reprinted in 1892 [–1904].1.

Reply to 1894.4, offering speculations concerning Vanbrugh's military career and calling attention to the notation in *English Army Lists* 2:67 (1892 [–1904].1) that Vanbrugh "left the Earl of Huntingdon's Regt. in 1896." Comments that "after the Revolution . . . John Vanbrugh [appears to have] re-entered the army as an Ensign in Col. Wm Beveridge's Regiment of Foot (14th Foot)."

3 KNIGHT, JOSEPH. *David Garrick*. London: Kegan Paul, pp. 79, 321.

Includes discussion of eighteenth-century performances of the part of Sir John Brute (in *The Provoked Wife*)—"one of the great parts of Cibber, whose conception was derived from Betterton." Cibber's performance as Sir John is compared to that of Garrick, who "in the more boisterous passages was triumphantly riotous, keeping the spectators in continual glee."

4 "Sir John Vanbrugh" *Athenaeum*, no. 3486 (18 August): 234. Reprinted in 1892.1.

Clarifies several documents concerning Vanbrugh's military career transcribed in *English Army Lists* (1892 [-1904].1) and cites an additional document: Vanbrugh's 1702 petition for back pay owed him and his servant for his period of service in the Second Marine Regiment between "April 1st, 1696 and September 20th, 1698." Other documents printed and discussed pertain to Vanbrugh's imprisonment in the Bastille and his tenure at the Board of Works.

1895

1 HIPWELL, DANIEL. "Sir John Vanbrugh, Knt. (Died 1726), Dramatic Poet and Architect." *N & Q*, 8th ser. 7 (March):166.

Notes that Vanbrugh's "baptism is recorded in the parish register of St. Nicholas Acons, London, under date Jan. 24, 1663/4."

2 HIPWELL, DANIEL. "Sir John Vanbrugh, Knt. (8th S.vii.166)." *N & Q*, 8th ser. 7 (March):258.

Suggests that Charles Vanbrugh "of the parish of St. Martin-in-the-Fields, Middlesex" was "probably" John Vanbrugh's brother.

3 LOFTIE, W. J. *Whitehall: Historical and Architectural Notes.* The Portfolio: Monographs on Artistic Subjects with Many Illustrations, Published Monthly, No. 16 (April). London: Seeley, p. 74.

Prints (without identifying it as such) an engraving of Vanbrugh's Goose-Pie House dated 1807. Vanbrugh's name is mentioned in neither the text nor the engraving (captioned "View in Privy Garden. From an Engraving by J. Malcolm").

4 ROBINS, EDWARD. *Echoes of the Playhouse: Reminiscences of Some Past Glories of the English Stage.* New York and London: Putnam's, 98–99, 105, 106, 118, 120, 131, 132.

Calls Vanbrugh's *The Provoked Wife* one of those "long-since-forgotten plays of early eighteenth century celebrity," which if revived would appear "stupid . . . and horribly archaic." Lady Brute's "conniv[ing] at the ruin of her niece" is deplored, Garrick's performance as Sir John noted. Vanbrugh and Congreve are cited as co-directors of the Haymarket Theatre, a venue for "Italian opera." Brief mention of *The Relapse* and of Vanbrugh's role in furthering the career of "Nance" (Anne) Oldfield.

1896

5 SWAEN, A. E. H., and KNIGHT, JOSEPH. "Vanbrugh: Mrs. Rogers: Mrs. Cross: Mrs. Verbruggen." *N & Q*, 8th ser. 8 (June):509
   Swaen's query solicits information concerning the careers of actresses Rogers, Cross, and Verbruggen and premiere dates for Vanbrugh's *Relapse, The Provoked Wife, The Mistake,* and *The Country House.* Knight's response supplies information concerning the actresses culled from Genests's *Account of the English Stage* (1832.1) and offers premiere dates for *The Mistake, The Confederacy,* and *The Country House.*

1896

1 *BENSE, J. F. Review of Swaen's Mermaid edition of Vanbrugh's plays, *Sir John Vanbrugh* (1896.3). *Nederlandsche Spectator,* pp. 329–330.
   Source: Heldt, 1922–1923.1; unverified.

2 HUNT, LEIGH. "Sir John Vanbrugh." In *Sir John Vanbrugh.* Edited by A. E. H. Swaen [or Swain]. Mermaid Series. London: Unwin; New York: Scribner's, pp. 19–52.
   Reprinted from 1840.1.

3 SWAEN [or SWAIN], A. E. H., ed. Preface, Bibliography of Vanbrugh's Works, Genealogical Table, & Bibliographical Notice to *Sir John Vanbrugh.* London: Unwin; New York: Scribner's, pp. 7–18. Reprint. London: Ernest Benn; New York: A. A. Wyn, 1949.
   The Preface declares Vanbrugh's comedies to be "less witty but more humorous" than Congreve's, and "more natural than either Congreve's or Wycherley's." A Genealogical Table lists the Vanbrugh family tree but not that of Vanbrugh's mother, Henrietta Maria Yarburgh, and her influential Carleton connections (see Downes 1977.2). The Biographical Notice preceding the reprinting of Leigh Hunt's sketch of Vanbrugh's career (1840.1) offers an "account of discoveries made since that essay was written."

1897

1 BELJAME, ALEXANDRE. *Le Public et les Hommes de Lettres en Angleterre au Dix-Huitième Siècle, 1660–1744.* 2d ed. Paris: Librairie Hachette, pp. 225–338 passim.
   Revised ed. (index added) of 1881.1. In a chapter ("Joseph Addision") devoted to changes in the status of English writers following

the Revolution of 1688, Vanbrugh receives passing mention as an officer, Kit-Cat, recipient of patronage, and central figure in the Collier controversy.

2   BLOMFIELD, REGINALD. *A History of Renaissance Architecture in England, 1500–1800.* 2 vols. London: George Bell, 1:50, 181; 2:197–200, 201, 202, 206, 208, 214, 221, 285, 286, 288, 292, 300.

Surveying Vanbrugh's reputation as an architect, observes that his buildings "met with merciless ridicule from all the critics of the time." Sir Joshua Reynolds is said to be his sole champion, but the picturesque effects for which Reynolds praised him are judged to be Vanbrugh's "weak point"—testaments to his "want of training," one consequence of which was his subordination of "comfort" to "exterior architecture." Discussion of his major buildings from Castle Howard to Grimsthorpe sees Vanbrugh "steadily advancing in mastery of his art," Grimsthorpe being "a well-arranged and convenient house." His faults are said to be lack of "taste" and an "ambition for size" that "rapidly grew into mania"; his strengths, "passionate appreciation of the abstract qualities of architecture." Elsewhere, Vanbrugh's hand in alterations of Audley End and in the planning of Greenwich Hospital is noted. Oulton Hall and the "general idea" of the Clarendon Press Building are attributed to him. Archer is called a "pupil" of Vanbrugh, as is Hawksmoor.

3   *Historical Manuscripts Commission. Fifteenth Report, Appendix, Part VI. The Manuscripts of the Earl of Carlisle, Preserved at Castle Howard.* London: H. M. Stationery Office, pp. 28, 29, 30–33, 34, 36–37, 38–39, 41–42, 55.

Prints Vanbrugh's letters to Carlisle bearing the following dates: 2 Feb. 1720/1721, 7 Feb. 1721, 18 Feb. 1721, 28 Feb. 1720/1721, 25 March 1721, 22 April 1721, 16 Nov. 1721, 6 April 1722, 5 May 1722, 10 May 1722, and 19 July 1722. All but the letter of 28 February 1720/ 1721—concerning the South Sea scandal—are reprinted in *Works*, IV, 1928.11; the 28 February letter does not appear in Downes's list of Vanbrugh's letters ["Appendix B," 1987.4]. Also prints a 9 May 1721 letter from Lady E. Lechmore informing Carlisle that Vanbrugh is "frighted about" having sent Carlisle a "printed paper" justifying his conduct in the continuing Blenheim litigation—"frighted" because "he has made himself liable to severe punishment, by being guilty of a breach of the House of Lords, in printing a libel upon a peer [the Duke of Marlborough] while a case is depending before them in judgment. . . ." Also prints Lady A. Irwin's 18 January 1729 letter to Carlisle expressing her certainty that she will be "well entertained"

1898

at the evening's performance of "Sir John's Provoked Husband. . . ."

1898

1   DAMETZ, MAX. *John Vanbrughs Leben und Werke.* Wien and Leipzig: Wilhelm Braumöller, 206 pp. Reprint. New York: Johnson, 1964.

Twenty-three pages on the architecture are largely devoted to the Blenheim episode (as mediated by Disraeli, 1849.1). The bulk of the book addresses Vanbrugh's achievement as a comic dramatist in the tradition of Molière. Discussions of each of Vanbrugh's original works and adaptations begin with plot summary and conclude with brief remarks on characterization.

2   GOSSE, EDMUND. *A Short History of Modern English Literature.* Short Histories of the Literatures of the World, 3. London: William Heinemann, p. 192.

Vanbrugh is said to possess "great fire and vigour of redundant fancy" but to have "no style at all," "simply throw[ing] his characters at one another's heads, and leav[ing] them to fight it out as they will."

3   SWAEN, A. E. H. Review of Dametz's *John Vanbrugh's Leben und Werke* (1898.1). *Englische Studien* 25:450–453.

Corrects a number of Dametz's citations and takes issue with several points of interpretation. For example, thinks Coupler (in *The Relapse*) a "pursy old man, fulsome in his familiarities"—this in response to Dametz's observation that Coupler is "nicht scharf gezeichnet." Wishes Dametz had noted that *The Confederacy* is "entirely englished," betraying "not a sign of its French origin."

1899

1   "Blenheim Palace, Oxfordshire, the Seat of the Duke of Marlborough." *CLife* 5, no. 126 (June):688–692.

Praises the "breadth of conception and character" of Vanbrugh's Blenheim Palace while acknowledging the building to be "exceedingly heavy and monotonous in effect." The interior's "many splendid apartments" are noted and the gardens of "the greatest of English country seats" are praised and illustrated with photographs.

1899

2   "'Dictionary of National Biography': Notes and Corrections. (Continued from 9th S.iii.204.)" *N & Q*, 9th ser. 4 (July):4.

As an addendum to the *DNB* account of Vanbrugh, notes that "[Thomas] Tickell praises his work at Blenheim in prologue to Addison's 'Rosamond,' *Works*, 1726, i.90."

3   FERGUSSON, JAMES. *History of the Modern Styles of Architecture*. Vol. 2. 3d ed. New York: Dodd, Mead, pp. 53–58.

Vanbrugh's "lofty aspiration after grandeur and eternity" is averred to have given rise at Blenheim, Castle Howard, Seaton Delaval, and Grimsthorpe to "gloomy grandeur, coupled with something that looks very like pretentious vulgarity." For citation of 1st ed., see 1862.2.

4   *GWILT, JOSEPH. *The Encyclopedia of Architecture, Historical, Theoretical, and Practical*. Revised with alterations and considerable additions by Wyatt Papworth. "New impression" (of 1867.1?). London, New York [etc.]: Longman, Green.

For annotation, see 1845.1.

5   "King's Weston, Gloucester, the Seat of Mr. R. Napier Miles." *CLife* 6, no. 149 (November):592–97.

Describes Kings Weston's gardens, "formed about the year 1711." The building's west front and the gardens are illustrated in photographs. Vanbrugh's name is not mentioned.

6   POWYS, CAROLINE [GIRLE]. *Passages from the Diaries of Mrs. Philip Lybbe Powys of Hardwick House, Oxon. A.D. 1756 to 1808.* Edited by Emily J. Cleminson. London, New York, and Bombay: Longmans, Green, pp. 62–63.

Briefly describes and records the dimensions of Eastbury House: "The building, as you see thro' a fine lawn, may be styl'd an elegant fabrick; 'tis of stone, extending in length 570 feet, of which the main body of the house takes up only 144; the rest is arcades and offices. Having ascended a grand flight of steps, you come under a Doric portico, whose pediment extends 62 feet, with pillars 46 feet high; from thence you enter a noble hall, adorn'd by statues and busts. . . ."

7   WARD, ADOLPHUS WILLIAM. *A History of English Dramatic Literature to the Death of Queen Anne*. Vol. 3. 2d ed. London and New York: Macmillan, pp. 477–481.

For annotation, see 1875.3.

1901

1 HARLEY, LORD [EDWARD], 2ND EARL OF OXFORD. "Journeys in England, by Lord Harley, afterwards the second Earl of Oxford. II. A Journey through Hertfordshire, Lincolnshire, and Notts to the Northern Counties and Scotland. [1725]." In *Report on the Manuscripts of His Grace the Duke of Portland, K. G., Preserved at Welbeck Abbey.* Edited by the Historical Manuscripts Commission. Vol. 6. London: Printed for H. M. Stationery Office, p. 90.

Includes Lord Harley's description of "a famous spring called Robin Hood's Well, with a new stone building, that covers it over raised at the expense of the Earl of Carlisle, under the peculiar direction of Sir John Vanbrugh."

2 STRATFORD, DR. WILLIAM. Letter [1710] to Edward, afterwards Lord, Harley 2nd Earl of Oxford. In *Report on the Manuscripts of His Grace the Duke of Portland, K. G., Preserved at Welbeck Abbey.* Edited by the Historical Manuscripts Commission. Vol. 7. London: Printed for H. M. Stationery Office, pp. 3, 19–20.

Prints a letter of 13 July 1710 in which William Stratford advises Edward Harley that "Van Brug passed through this place on Tuesday and dined with George Clark." Reports that Vanbrugh told his dinner companions that the consensus was "there would be no new Parliament, that all differences were made up, and that Lord Halifax had been very instrumental in reconciling the contending parties." Concludes, "You see what opinion they have of us, when they think this will pass upon us from poor Van." Also prints a letter of 4 October 1710 reporting that "all who were at work at Blenheim . . . were discharged yesterday by Vanbrugh" at the request of the Duchess of Marlborough. An "uproar in the town" followed. Believes "the coming frost and wet will ruin all that has been done this summer" at Blenheim.

1902

1 CHUBB, JOHN B. "Sir John Vanbrugh." *A. A. Notes* 17, no. 181 (March):47.

Thinks Hawksmooor, not Vanbrugh, designed "Greenwich Church" (St. Alphege), whose "details of woodwork . . . are precisely similar to corresponding work at St. George's, Bloomsbury, and St. Mary Wollnoth." (See also 1902.2, 1902.4, and 1902.5.)

2 DINWIDDY, T. NORMAN. "Vanbrugh and Greenwich Church." *A. A. Notes* 17, no. 187 (September):143.

Response to 1902.1 reports that although St. Alphege, Greenwich, is "by some attributed to Nicholas Hawksmoor, local tradition associates it with John James."

3 LOVEGROVE, GILBERT H. "The Life, Work, and Influence of Sir John Vanbrugh." [Architectural Association Prize Essay for 1901; printed in installments, "slightly condensed for publication."] *A. A. Notes* 17 (January–December):5–6, 20–22, 55–56, 68–69, 76, 99–101, 116–119, 132–133. *Reprint. London: Pewtress, 1902, 38 pp.

Finds resemblances between Vanbrugh's decorum-violating building designs and the "license," "extravagence," and "[im]purity" of his comic drama. Describes and evaluates Castle Howard, Kneller Hall, the Clarendon Printing Office (Oxford), Claremont, Blenheim, Kings Weston, Eastbury, Vanbrugh Castle, Vanbrugh (Mince-Pie) House, the Stowe temples, Seaton Delaval, and Grimsthorpe. Thinks Vanbrugh's designs are "direct descendents of those of Wren," with the addition of Gothic elements and an "unbridled freshness." The effect is "pleasing from a distance," disappointing on closer inspection—at which point the "coarseness of the detail" and the violation of decorum become apparent. Claims that only Reynolds (1797.2) and Sir John Soane (through his lectures; see, e.g., 1929.2) have spoken vigorously in praise of Vanbrugh's architecture.

4 M. (*sic*). "Vanbrugh and Greenwich Church." *A. A. Notes* 17, no. 183 (May):79.

Response to 1902.1 notes that Reginald Blomfield (in 1897.2?) "attributes St. Alphege, Greenwich, to Hawksmoor, 1711–1718."

5 ROBERTS, ALFRED. "Vanbrugh and Greenwich Church." *A. A. Notes* 17, no. 182 (April):64.

Supports Chubb's (1902.1) contention that Hawksmoor rather than Vanbrugh designed St. Alphege Church, Greenwich. Notes that an "old print" of the church bears the inscription "designed by N. Hawksmoor."

1902–1903

1 TITHERINGTON, R. H. "The Architect of Blenheim." *Munsey's Magazine* 28 (October–March):448–452.

A survey of Vanbrugh's architectural career that paints a picture of an affable man with few enemies save the Duchess of Marlborough.

1903

1 FIELDING, HENRY. *Pasquin. A Dramatick Satire on the Times.
. . .* In *The Complete Works of Henry Fielding, Esq.
With an Essay on the Life, Genius and Achievement of the Author. Plays and Poems in Five Volumes.* Edited by William Ernest Henley. Reprint. New York: Barnes & Noble, 1967, vol. 4, p. 222. (Annotation and page reference based on 1967 reprint.)

In *Pasquin* V.i, Fustian speaks with exasperated irony of theatre-goers who become "tired with the dull works of Shakespeare, Jonson, Vanbrugh, and others. . . ." Wonders "how it was possible for any creature of human understanding, after having been diverted for three hours with the productions of a great genius, to sit for three more" watching pantomimists "playing . . . juggling tricks. . . ." For citation of 1st ed., see 1736.1; cf. 1750.3.

2 "Grimsthorpe Castle, Lincolnshire, the Seat of the Earl of Ancaster." *CLife* 14, no. 346 (August):272–277.

Finds the north front Vanbrugh designed for Grimsthorpe (c. 1720) "very characteristic of his ponderous and sombre style"—and evocative of Evans's epitaph.

1904

1 "Castle Howard, Yorkshire, the Seat of the Earl of Carlisle." *CLife* 15, no. 371 (February):234–242.

Encomiastic description of "the greatest of the classic mansions in Yorkshire." Concentrates on the interior, illustrated with numerous photographs.

2 OGLESBY, ROBERT P. "Sir John Vanbrugh: Architect and Dramatist." *RIBA Journal*, 3d ser. 11, pp. 213–220.

Surveys Vanbrugh's career, focusing on the architecture. Castle Howard's plan is called "a blending of Palladian and Elizabethan." Its interior is described in detail. Clarendon Building, Oxford, is adjudged a joint Vanbrugh/Hawksmoor invention, Seaton Delaval a "medieval wolf ill concealed in a sheep's clothing of Palladian refinement." Kings Weston is said to show the defects of Vanbrugh's indiscriminate application of large scale to small buildings. The Blenheim project is given extended treatment. Also mentioned are Grimsthorpe, the garden buildings at Stowe, Fleurs (Floors) Castle in Roxburgshire, Kneller House in Hounslow, and Greenwich Hospital's "King William's block."

3 WALPOLE, HORACE. *The Letters of Horace Walpole.* Edited by Paget Toynbee. Vol. 3. *1771–1774.* Oxford: Clarendon Press, pp. 193–194.

Letter to George Augustus Selwyn of 12 August 1772 offers an enthusiastic account of Walpole's "first vision" of Castle Howard. Calls the house and grounds "sublime": "a palace, a town, a fortified city. . . ." Reports he had "heard" that on one occasion Vanbrugh and Sir Thomas Robinson "stood swearing and spitting at one another" (this presumably an altercation over Vanbrugh's plans for completing the house; in the 1750s Robinson would be engaged by his brother-in-law Carlisle to complete Castle Howard's west side in Palladian style).

1906

1 "The Fountain at Castle Howard." *CLife* 20, no. 509 (October):492–494.

Castle Howard is termed "the greatest . . . of all the Yorkshire houses," "a magnificent example of the classic style, as we see it in England."

1907

1 LOVEGROVE, GILBERT H. "Recent Demolitions in Blackheath." *London Topographical Record* 4:23–26.

Describes and illustrates with photographs and plans two of Vanbrugh's houses on Maze Hill in Blackheath—Vanbrugh Castle and Vanbrugh House (alternatively called, *pace* Lovegrove, "Mince-Pie House"). Notes that "a subterranean passage" had been thought to connect the two houses, but "recent excavations . . . have failed to discover any proof of the connection." (See Downes, 1976.2, for corrections of several of Lovegrove's speculations.)

2 WATERHOUSE, OSBORN. "The Development of Sentimental Comedy as Seen in Vanbrugh's *Aesop* and in the Plays of Cibber and Steele." *Anglia* 30:155–158.

Proposes that the "first signs" of the "sentimentalizing of the comedy of manners" are discernible in Vanbrugh's *Aesop*, Part 1 (1696). The play's "sentimental" elements—which Vanbrugh inherited from his source, Boursault's *Les Fables d'Ésope*—are averred to be the "love-plot and all those tender and pathetic incidents which grow out of" Learchus's efforts to persuade his daughter to marry the aged philosopher Aesop rather than the young man she loves.

1909

1   GOTCH, J. ALFRED. *The Growth of the English House: A Short History of its Architectural Development from 1100 to 1800.* London: B. T. Batsford; New York: Scribner's, pp. 242-244.

Thinks "no architect of the time succeeded better" than Vanbrugh "in pleasing the passer-by with his stately buildings." Regrettably, however, Vanbrugh paid insufficient attention either to the private or the public functions his clients were obliged to perform inside the buildings. Seaton Delaval and Castle Howard are cited as evidence that "the early eighteenth century built for show rather than for use."

2   LATHAM, CHARLES. *In English Homes: The Internal Character, Environment, & Adornments of Some of the Most Notable Houses of England.* 3d ed. 3 vols. London: Country Life; New York: Scribner's, 1:59-64, 233-242; 3:281-301. (*NUC* lists no 1st edition. There the initial entry for this item offers the following publication information: "London: Offices of Country Life and G. Newnes; New York: Scribner's 1904-09 [with notation 'Vol. II, 2d ed.'].'' *BMC* lists only a 3-vol. "London, 1904-09" edition.)

Includes detailed accounts of the interiors of Grimsthorpe and Castle Howard (vol. 1) and of Blenheim Palace (vol. 3); many photographs. Judgments include praise of Blenheim's internal corridors for giving "ready access and private entry to almost every apartment." Opines that the "general grouping" of Blenheim's "manifold and elaborately-ordered buildings round three sides of the immense forecourt is the most satisfactory and impressive thing of its kind that we have in England."

3   S[ECCOMBE], T[HOMAS]. "Vanbrugh." In *DNB*. Vol. 20. Edited by Sidney Lee. London: Smith, Elder, pp. 86-94. Reprint. Vol. 20. Edited by Sir Leslie Stephen and Sir Sidney Lee. London: Oxford University Press, 1921-1922.

A sketch of Vanbrugh's career, some particulars of which have been corrected by subsequent scholarship. Summary judgments include the observation that Vanbrugh "was probably the most enlightened of the early patrons of opera in England." Concerning Blenheim Palace, suggests that "The last thing the architect had in mind was the personal comfort of his clients. Provided he made his effect, he was satisfied." Many parenthetical citations of earlier biographical and critical materials no longer much consulted.

4 T. [*sic*]. "Blenheim Palace–I. Oxfordshire, the Seat of the Duke of Marlborough, K. G." *CLife* 25, no. 647 (May):786–798.

Discusses and illustrates Blenheim's exterior. Thinks the structure's "megalomaniac" proportions reflect the architect's desire to "produce novel forms and effects wherewith to . . . make the house the only one of its kind"—one in which "Monumental masses of masonry enclose or cover spaces that serve no possible purpose."

5 T. [*sic*]. "Blenheim Palace–II. Oxfordshire, the Seat of the Duke of Marlborough, K. G." *CLife* 25, no. 648 (June):834–843.

Discusses and offers photographic illustrations of Blenheim's interior.

1909 [–1916]

1 WESLEY, JOHN. *Journal of the Rev. John Wesley, A. M. Enlarged from Original MSS., with Notes from Unpublished Diaries.* . . . Edited by Nehemiah Curnock. "Standard Edition." Vol. 6. London: Charles H. Kelly, pp. 257–258.

Concerning a 1779 tour of Lord Cobham's gardens at Stowe, complains that "the buildings, called Temples, are most miserable, many of them both within and without." Thinks "Sir John Vanbrugh's [temple unspecified] is an ugly, clumsy lump, hardly fit for a gentleman's stable." Notes that "One of the stateliest monuments is taken down—the Egyptian Pyramid" (designed by Vanbrugh).

1910

1 CARLYLE, ALEXANDER. *The Autobiography of Dr. Alexander Carlyle of Inveresk, 1722–1805.* "New edition." London and Edinburgh: T. N. Foulis, p. 381.

For annotation, see 1860.2.

2 Miles, D. H. *The Influence of Molière on Restoration Comedy.* New York: Columbia University Press, pp. 209–215. Reprint. New York: Octagon, 1971.

Concludes that Vanbrugh "exhibited curiously little study of models, but everywhere displayed a full reliance on his native sense of the humorous and the dramatically effective." He is judged to be "closer to the comedy of manners as Etherege introduced it . . . than any other writer of the period," his "presentation of manners" being "completely lacking in the sympathy with life and the insight into character that distinguished Molière."

1912

1 CROISSANT, DE WITT C. *Studies in the Work of Colley Cibber.* Bulletin of the University of Kansas, Humanistic Studies, vol. 1, no. 1. Lawrence: University of Kansas Press, pp. 26, 55–56.

Notes several of Cibber's departures in *The Provoked Husband* (1728) from its source, Vanbrugh's unfinished *Journey to London.* Cibber "somewhat softened the characters of Vanbrugh's Lord and Lady Loverule" when he transformed them into Lord and Lady Townly. "[W]ith its undeserved happy ending," Cibber's play is "a typical sentimental comedy" possessing "a very decided inferiority to Vanbrugh's play, even in its unfinished and imperfect state."

2 LONDON COUNTY COUNCIL. *Survey of London.* Vol. 3. *The Parish of St. Giles-in-the-Fields. (Part I.) Lincoln's Inn Fields.* Edited by Sir Laurence Gomme and Philip Norman. London: London County Council, pp. 110–113.

Section "XXI.—Nos. 66 and 67, Lincoln's Inn Fields (Newcastle House)" offers a building history of a house that in 1705 "passed into the possession of the Dukes of Newcastle." Cites Vanbrugh's brief mention of his plans for altering the house in his letters to Newcastle of "Autumn 1714 or early 1715" and 27 November 1716 (see *Works,* vol. 4, pp. 61 and 88, 1928.11).

3 NUNN, F. W. "The Illustrations [of Vanbrugh's 'Nunnery' and Vanbrugh Castle]." *Transactions of the Greenwich Antiquarian Society* 1, no. 3:102 [not numbered] + 6 pp.

Six pages of unnumbered plates, including a plan, an elevation, and six photographs of Vanbrugh's "Nunnery" (in Blackheath, Greenwich) on the eve of its demolition in 1911. (Nunn erroneously identifies the building as "Mince Pie House.") Also prints plans of Vanbrugh Castle's basement, ground floor, first and second floors, and roof—plans "prepared by Mr. Dunn" shortly before Alexander Duckham's "restorations and alterations" of c. 1907.

4 WHIBLEY, CHARLES. "The Restoration Drama. II." In *Cambridge History of English Literature.* Edited by A. W. Ward and A. R. Waller. Vol. 8, *The Age of Dryden.* New York: Putnam's; Cambridge: Cambridge University Press, pp. 182–185.

Vanbrugh is described as "delight[ing] in farce" and possessing a "talent of caricature," writing "as he talked, without reflection and with great good humour." Describes *The Relapse* as "two plays spliced into one." Offers appreciative comments on Lord Foppington,

Sir Tunbelly, and Hoyden (the "immortal three"). Sir John Brute in *The Provoked Wife* is said to have inspired English novelists, his last incarnation being Sir Pitt Crawley in *Vanity Fair*. Vanbrugh's "happy fragment" *A Journey to London* is praised as a "picture of manners" from which Fielding and Smollett borrowed.

1913

1 PALMER, JOHN. *The Comedy of Manners*. London: George Bell, pp. 201–241. Reprint. New York: Russell, 1962.

A preliminary sketch of Vanbrugh's career quotes liberally from his correspondence and finds him to be a "mischievous, tolerant, and kind man of humour." His plays are seen as transitional, their bawdy Restoration elements uneasily "leavened with an element of feeling"— this a consequence of his having idly embraced Restoration comic conventions "that he could not honestly employ" in the altered moral climate of his own day. He is praised for his humor and his insight, qualities that shine brightly in his renderings of Sir John Brute and Lady Fancyfull.

1914

1 MACLEAN, CHARLES. "The Lord Chamberlain and Opera in London, 1700–1740." *Proceedings of the [Royal] Musical Association* 40 (January):37–71.

Early report on the contents of Vice-Chamberlain Coke's papers, intermittently bearing on Vanbrugh's affairs at the Haymarket Theatre. Largely superseded by 1982.10.

2 NETTLETON, GEORGE HENRY. *English Drama of the Restoration and Eighteenth Century*. New York: Macmillan.

For annotation, see 1921.2.

1918

1 GOTCH, J. ALFRED. *The English Home from Charles I to George IV: Its Architecture, Decoration, and Garden Design*. London: B. T. Batsford, pp. 216–229.

The pronouncements concerning Vanbrugh's buildings include the following: his are some of the "most ponderous houses ever built in

England''; Castle Howard's interior corridors are ''too many,'' the rooms too small, their ceilings too high; Blenheim is ''overwhelmed by its own size''; the ''omission of pilasters'' in the alterations of Kimbolton ''would have had more point if there had been anything preserved of the ancient castle beyond its name.'' Concludes that despite their flaws, Vanbrugh's houses ''may be taken as the finest manifestation of the spirit of the age in house-building; the exaltation of social grandeur. . . .''

1921

1 LAWRENCE, W. J. "The Early Years of the First English Opera House." *Musical Quarterly* 7:104–112, 117.

Claims Vanbrugh intended his theatre at the Haymarket to be a "habitat" for Betterton's Lincoln's Inn Fields Company. Reproduces Capon's 1783 drawing of the theatre's front. Concerning the theatre's operation under Vanbrugh's management, cites the testimony of Cibber (1740.1), Downes (1708.1), Burney (1789.1), Genest (1832.1), and Kelly (1826.1).

2 NETTLETON, GEORGE HENRY. *English Drama of the Restoration and Eighteenth Century (1642–1780).* New York: Macmillan. (Reprint of 1914.2?) Reprint. 1923, 1928, 1932. Reprint. New York: Cooper Square, 1968, pp. 132–136, 301–302. (Annotation and page numbers based on 1968 reprint.)

Citing Abel Evans's lines on the heaviness of Vanbrugh's architecture, the author argues that "In character painting, too, [Vanbrugh] shows at times a certain Flemish heaviness, a following of the 'fleshly school' of Rubens"—as witness his portraits of Sir Tunbelly Clumsy and Sir John Brute. In "character construction" Vanbrugh excels Etherege and Congreve, his plots being "skillfully built, easily followed, and productive of excellent stage situations." For citation of 1st ed., see 1914.2.

3 SUMMERS, MONTAGUE. *"The Provok'd Wife.* Theatrical History." In untitled pamphlet pieced together by British Library; photocopy examined, pp. 9–12(?).

Characterizes audience response to premiere of *The Provoked Wife* as "immediate and overwhelming." Finds "no good reason to doubt" Cibber's assertion that Vanbrugh's altered scenes were first performed in 1726. Thinks the 1706 "alterations were probably nothing more than the introduction of a new song for Treble, and new catches for the drinking scene" (cf. 1966.7 and 1982.2). Records dates and cast lists of eighteenth-century performances. Concludes, "Having enjoyed a well-deserved popularity of over a hundred years 'The Provok'd Wife' at last waned in general favour, and after the first decade of the nineteenth century it soon entirely disappears from the bills." Assents to Fox's opinion that the play "entitles Vanbrugh to be called 'almost as great a genius as ever lived.'"

1922

1   BOLTON, ARTHUR T. *The Architecture of Robert & James Adam (1758-1794).* Vol. 1. London: Country Life; New York: Scribner's, pp. 9, 45, 63, 65, 76, 79, 131, 140, 216, 219, 221, 225. Reprint. Woodbridge: Antique Collectors' Club, 1985.

Includes brief discussion of Vanbrugh's alterations of Kimbolton, noting that in his work there Vanbrugh "respected" the suites that Catherine of Aragon had occupied from 1533 until her death in 1536. Assumes Vanbrugh altered Compton Verney (an attribution Downes has rejected [1977.2]). Cites Robert Adam's belief that "Vanbrugh understood better than either [Inigo Jones or Wren] the art of living among the great" (1778.1) and avers that Reynolds in his praise of Vanbrugh in his thirteenth discourse was "merely following Adam's earlier lead" (1797.2). Includes Vanbrugh in list of five "greatest" British architects, but laments that his works are "crowned with barbarisms and absurdities, and so borne down with their own preposterous weight, that none but the discerning can separate their merits from their defects."

2   NICOLL, ALLARDYCE. "Italian Opera in England. The First Five Years." *Anglia* 46, n.s. 34:257–281.

Includes conjectures (clarified by subsequent scholarship, especially 1976.10, 1982.10, and 1987.10) concerning the operas and plays performed in the initial seasons at Vanbrugh's Haymarket Theatre.

1922–1923

1   HELDT, W. "A Chronological and Critical Review of the Appreciation and Condemnation of the Comic Dramatists of the Restoration and Orange Periods." *Neophilologus* 8:[Pt. 1]:49, 55; [Pt. 2]:111, 115–16.

Includes a defense of Vanbrugh's *Relapse* against Jeremy Collier's charges of implausibility and profanity. Cites Hazlitt's judgment that Vanbrugh's "morality 'sits very loose upon him'" (1819.2) and Hunt's observation that Vanbrugh's language is "'not over-nice in its decorums'" (1840.1). Notes de Grisy's praise of *A Journey to London* (1878.2); approves Dametz's remarks on the "improbability" of *The Relapse* (1898.1); reproves Bense (1896.1) for failing to recognize the "knowledge of the female heart" displayed by Vanbrugh in his portrayal of Lady Brute in *The Provoked Wife*.

1923

1 ARCHER, WILLIAM. *The Old Drama and the New: An Essay in Re-Valuation*. Boston: Small, Maynard, pp. 196–199.

Thinks Vanbrugh's *Relapse* and *Provoked Wife* have "less wit and more humor" than the comedies of his Restoration predecessors. Though the two plots of *The Relapse* are "wholly unconnected," they are "absolutely clear," and the "nastiness" of several "very nauseous passages . . . is not so ingrained as in Wycherley and Congreve." *The Provoked Wife*, however, is "one of the most malodorous plays of the time." *A Journey to London*, had he finished it, "might have proved his best play."

2 COLVILLE, KENNETH NEWTON. "Sir John Vanbrugh." In *Fame's Twilight: Studies of Nine Men of Letters*. London: P. Allen & Co.; Boston: Small, Maynard ("printed in Czecho-Slovakia"), pp. 185–212. Reprint. Essay Index Reprint Series. Freeport, N.Y.: Books for Libraries Press, 1970.

In a book devoted to the resurrection of authors who "looked giants to their own contemporaries" but whose fame is currently diminished, a chapter is devoted to Vanbrugh (one of the "masters of English Comedy," "[i]f the fingers of the second hand are to be" counted). Vanbrugh's "reverence" as an architect for the "product of earlier ages" is noted. As a dramatist he is judged to be more successful in his depictions of men than of women. Concerning the putative indecency of his comedies, the author cites Loveless's "frank seduction" of Berinthia in *The Relapse* (IV.iii), arguing that here and elsewhere in his plays the viewer who finds Vanbrugh offensive testifies by his response that the playwright has shown seduction to be "an offensive act."

3 HUSSEY, CHRISTOPHER. "Seaton Delaval—I. Northumberland, the Property of Lord Hastings." *CLife* 54, no. 1405 (December):800–808.

Thinks Seaton's "vast entrance court" evocative of the landscapes of Lorraine and Rosa and of Dryden's tragedies, but finds little common ground between Vanbrugh's "racy" plays and his "romantic architecture." Attributes to his travels and incarceration in France the "strange combination of French, Italian and castellated styles" discernible in his buildings. Posits as an influence on Seaton Delaval the "semi-Gothic style of the Smythsons." Examines Vanbrugh's correspondence for the light it sheds on the progress of his plans for Seaton, whose interior and exterior are described and illustrated with photographs.

4 HUSSEY, CHRISTOPHER. "Seaton Delaval—II. Northumberland, the Property of Lord Hastings." *CLife* 54, no. 1406 (December):860–868.

Handsome photographs of Seaton Delaval accompany an article principally devoted to the genealogy of the Delaval family.

5 NICOLL, ALLARDYCE. *A History of Restoration Drama 1660–1700*. Cambridge: At the University Press, pp. 232–233. 2d ed. revised, 1928; 3d ed. revised, 1940; 4th ed. revised 1952. (Issued as vol. I of *A History of English Drama 1660–1900*. Cambridge: Cambridge University Press, 1952.)

Avers that though "wantonly indecent," Vanbrugh injected "sensibility" and "feeling" into his comedies, thereby serving, "along with others, to hasten the break-away of comedy from the Etheregian model." Revised editions offer no alterations of the 1923 appraisal.

1924

1 BARMAN, CHRISTIAN. *Sir John Vanbrugh*. New York: Scribner's, 61 pp.

An impressionistic sketch principally of Vanbrugh's architectural career. Speaks of the "instant maturity" of Castle Howard, describes the quarrel with the Duchess of Marlborough, and praises the stateliness and "movement" of Blenheim Palace. Thirty-one photographs.

2 DOBRÉE, BONAMY. *Restoration Comedy, 1660–1720*. London: Oxford University Press, pp. 151–161. Reprint. 1938, 1946, 1951.

Suggests that because Vanbrugh "had no peculiar vision," his plays "can add nothing either to our knowledge of life, or to our aesthetic experience." In *The Relapse*, for example, Vanbrugh's "interest" lies not in the "'problem play' of Loveless, Amanda, and Berinthia . . , but in the story of Tom Fashion outwitting his brother. . . ." Moreover, the self-consciousness of Vanbrugh's adulterous characters "sometimes" results in an "air of lasciviousness which

1924

destroys the comic''—as witness Berinthia's surrender to Loveless in *The Relapse*. Preferring to "adapt" old plays rather than create new ones, Vanbrugh even in his few original plays is derivative, "borrow[ing] freely" without improving on the originals—a point the author illustrates by placing several of Vanbrugh's "commonplace" passages beside the "vivid" passages from Congreve from which he is averred to have borrowed. Vanbrugh's Lord Foppington and his "pseudo-Elizabethan portrayals"—Sir Tunbelly Clumsy and Sir John Brute—are praised, as is the flair for "domestic scenes" manifest in *A Journey to London*.

3 GOODHART-RENDEL, H. S. *Nicholas Hawksmoor*. London: Ernest Benn, pp. 10, 13–14.

Thinks Hawksmoor, rather than the novice Vanbrugh, is the "author" of Castle Howard and Blenheim. The former was "built under the supervision of Hawksmoor" (this on the evidence of the building's "great technical skill"). The latter was "begun under Hawksmoor's supervision, and . . . finished by him in sole charge of the building." Vanbrugh's contribution to these and his other buildings was his "boldness of idea" and "power of picturesque composition." That "the presentation of an idea and the realisation of a composition were . . . never fully within his grasp" is said to be evident in the deficiencies of "classical greatness" manifest in the houses Vanbrugh executed independently of Hawksmoor (e.g., Grimsthorpe, Oulton Hall, Kimbolton, and Lumley Castle).

4 GOSSE, EDMUND. *Life of William Congreve*. "The edition of 1888[.2] revised and enlarged." New York: Scribner's; London: William Heinemann, pp. 104–106, 135–137.

Pronounces Vanbrugh "one of the merriest and most ingenious of comic writers" and "one of the most ribald." Avers that Collier in his *Short View* "was more blind to the artistic merit of Vanbrugh than to that of any other playwright." There is brief treatment of Vanbrugh's reply in his *Vindication* and fuller discussion of the problematical Walsh/Congreve/Vanbrugh collaboration, *Squire Trelooby*.

5 HUSSEY, CHRISTOPHER. "Grimsthorpe Castle—I. Lincolnshire, the Seat of the Earl of Ancaster." *CLife* 55, P. 2, no. 1423 (April):572–579.

Emphasizes Grimsthorpe's castellar elements. Proposes that Vanbrugh's imprisonment in France gave him a "Bastille complex . . , so that architecture with him became for ever after associated with fortresses." Thinks the "insipid" Palladian garden front illustrated in

Campbell's *Vitruvius Britannicus* was pieced together from the ailing Vanbrugh's sketches, it being "unlikely that Vanbrugh made out detailed elevations for [Grimsthorpe's] fronts or a complete plan."

6 HUSSEY, CHRISTOPHER. "Grimsthorpe Castle–II. Lincolnshire, the Seat of the Earl of Ancaster." *CLife* 55, no. 1424 (April):614–621.

Discusses the hall Vanbrugh designed for Grimsthorpe, noting a similarity between the hall's screen of three arches and the screen he designed for Audley End. Compares the two-tiered arcading of the walls of Grimsthorpe's hall to that at Seaton Delaval. Also describes and illustrates with photographs Grimsthorpe's chapel and state dining room.

7 KRUTCH, JOSEPH WOOD. *Comedy and Conscience after the Restoration.* New York: Columbia University Press, pp. 108–110, 124–126, 187–188. Reprint, 1949, with additional bibliographical material and index. (Page references and annotation based on 1949 reprint.)

Includes intermittent commentary on the contemporary reception of Vanbrugh's plays. Cites Collier's remarks (1698.1) on Vanbrugh's violation of the "rules" and his improbabilities of plot in *The Relapse* and *The Provoked Wife.* Here Collier is judged to have seen "an opportunity to weaken the position of the enemy by attacking a matter indifferent to himself yet important to the writer." Concerning Collier's charge that in *The Relapse* Vanbrugh put "the prize in the wrong hand," notes that Foppington "is a heartless and brainless ass, and certainly deserves a prize as little as does his brother." Nor in fact is Hoyden "a prize." Thinks Vanbrugh's reply to Collier's charges of immorality and profaneness "more successful" than Congreve's—this because Vanbrugh documented Collier's "inability to recognize satire" or to distinguish the opinions of the dramatist from those of his characters. Also notes the opposition of Defoe and the Society for the Reformation of Manners to Vanbrugh's undertaking at the Haymarket.

8 RICHARDSON, A[LBERT] E[DWARD], and GILL, C[HARLES] LOVETT. *Regional Architecture of the West of England.* London: Ernest Benn, pp. 2, 9, 51, 89, 95, 173.

Thinks it likely that Vanbrugh designed "the original gun wharf" in the dockyard at Devonport, and "certain" that he designed "the brick house for the Commissioner" that stands "within an enclosing wall above the original yard."

1925

1 ARUNDELL, DENNIS. "'The Gordian Knot Untied' [Pt. 1]." *TLS*, 4 June, p. 384.

Proposes that William Walsh was the author of the unprinted comedy *The Gordian Knot Untied* (1691). Drawing on the hint supplied by the play's title, suggests that *Gordian Knot* was an early version of the Walsh/Congreve/Vanbrugh collaboration, *Squire Trelooby* (1704). See also 1925.2 and 1925.5.

2 ARUNDELL, DENNIS. "'The Gordian Knot Untied' [Pt. 2]" *TLS*, 18 June, p. 416.

Reaffirms the suggestion offered in 1925.1 that "*The Gordian Knot Untied* was a version of *Trelooby*.

3 BERNBAUM, ERNEST. *The Drama of Sensibility: A Sketch of the History of English Sentimental Comedy and Domestic Tragedy, 1696–1780*. Cambridge, Mass.: Harvard University Press, pp. 77–79, 137–138.

Cites Vanbrugh's remark in his *Short Vindication of "The Relapse" and "The Provok'd Wife"* . . . (1698) concerning "the frailty of mankind" by way of illustrating Vanbrugh's aversion to sentimentalist notions of human perfectability. Argues that Vanbrugh's "purpose" in *The Relapse*, V, iv, 42–190, was "to cast a doubt upon the perfection of Amanda and upon the perfectability of Loveless."

4 DOBRÉE, BONAMY. "The Architect of Blenheim (Sir John Vanbrugh)" and Appendices I ("Godolphin's Warrant to Vanbrugh") and II ("Mrs. Yarburgh"). In *Essays in Biography 1680–1726*. London: Oxford University Press, pp. 57–195, 349–350. Reprint. Essay Index Reprint Series. Freeport, N.Y.: Books for Libraries Press, 1967.

Portrays Vanbrugh as a man "too simple-hearted for his time." His quarrel with the Duchess of Marlborough over the building of Blenheim is given extended treatment.

5 LAWRENCE, W. J. "'The Gordian Knot Untied.'" *TLS*, 11 June, p. 400.

Doubts that *The Gordian Knot Untied* (1925.1) bears any connection to *Squire Trelooby*.

6 NICOLL, ALLARDYCE. *A History of Early Eighteenth-Century Drama 1700–1750*. Cambridge: Cambridge University Press, pp. 128–139, 144–145, 150–153, 284–285, 288–289. 2d ed., 1929; 3d ed. 1952.

(Issued as vol. 2 of *A History of English Drama 1660-1900*. Cambridge: At the University Press, 1952.)

Offers season-by-season frequency counts (now superseded by *The London Stage*, 1960 [-1968].1) of performances of Vanbrugh's plays during the period 1700-1750. Summary judgments of *The False Friend, The Confederacy, The Mistake, Squire Trelooby, The Country House*, and *A Journey to London* conclude with the observation that "On the whole, Vanbrugh's work may . . . be held disappointing"— this because "Most of it is based on French comedy, and only too often it degenerates into the realm of farce." Several documents pertinent to his management of the Haymarket Theatre are printed in Appendix B. (The appraisal of Vanbrugh is unaltered in revised editions.)

7 PERRY, HENRY TEN EYCK. *The Comic Spirit in Restoration Drama: Studies in the Comedy of Etherege, Wycherley, Congreve, Vanbrugh, and Farquhar.* New Haven: Yale University Press, pp. 82—106. Reprint. New York: Russell & Russell, 1962.

Argues that "by compromising with public taste [Vanbrugh] produced a great deal of very mediocre work, strongly tinged with the taint of sentimentality." A case in point is *The False Friend*, whose heroine Vanbrugh made even more virtuous than had his source, Le Sage's *Le Traitre Puni.* Vanbrugh excels in his rendering of such rustics as Sir Tunbelly Clumsy, whose inclusion in his cast of characters both widened the social ken of comedy and blurred the "fixity of purpose" that had governed comedy of the preceding decades.

8 WEBB, GEOFFREY. "Sir John Vanbrugh." *Burlington Magazine* 47, no. 272 (November):222-227.

An appreciation of the "frankly Gothic" qualities of the three houses Vanbrugh built atop Maze Hill in Greenwich—Vanbrugh Castle, Vanbrugh House (alternatively known as Mince-Pie House), and the Nunnery (here mistakenly referred to as "Mince-Pie House"). Cites Vanbrugh's reference to Hugh May's pseudo-medieval alterations of Windsor Castle as "the only hint as to real precedent for Vanbrugh's Gothicisms." For amplification and correction of several of Webb's surmises, see Downes (1976.2).

1926

1 "Architecture: Sir John Vanbrugh." *Nation & Athenaeum* 38 (March):893-94.

Horace Walpole's mention of rival architects Vanbrugh and Sir Thomas Robinson "spitting and swearing" in a heated exchange at

1926

Castle Howard is set against the background of the debate between old and new schools of English architecture in Vanbrugh's day. The "baroque" and "Gothic" qualities of Vanbrugh's buildings are alleged to have provoked the efforts of Colin Campbell and the third Earl of Burlington to return English architecture to the principles of Palladio and of Inigo Jones. Vanbrugh's remarks on the necessity of giving Kimbolton Castle "something of the Castle air" are cited as evidence of his being "a Romantic born out of due season." His "Romanticism" is then linked to the particularly "Elizabethan quality" of "the best comic 'humours' of his plays"—a "boisterous quality" apparent as well in some of the "broad effects . . . to be found in his architecture."

2   BOLTON, ARTHUR T. "The Completion of Greenwich Hospital (1702-1715) [Pt. 1]." *Architects' Journal* 63, no. 1640 (23 June):842–846.

Prints and discusses several plans for the completion of Greenwich Hospital. The 1702 plan reproduced as Figure One is ascribed to Vanbrugh, principally on the basis of an inscription appearing under the date 1702 on the base of a stone pedestal in a corner of the drawing. The author interprets the inscription's cryptic "B.S.L" as an abbreviation for "Pro Bono Publico et Salus Legum." (See also 1926.3.)

3   BOLTON, ARTHUR T. "The Completion of Greenwich Hospital (1702-1715) [Pt. 2]." *Architects' Journal* 63, no. 1641 (30 June):874–878.

Includes discussion of the 1702 plan for the completion of Greenwich Hospital as printed in 1926.2. Prints and assigns to Vanbrugh several other drawings, presumably elaborations of elements appearing in the 1702 plan. Among the drawings are a sketch of a "great portico with wide supporting masses and a high podium" and another of a "central feature rising above the internal dome of the [Greenwich] chapel." The 1702 scheme is judged "a remarkable *tour de force* only comparable with Bernini's forecourt of St. Peter's."

4   BOLTON, ARTHUR T. "Sir John Vanbrugh." *RIBA Journal* 3d ser. 33 (April):338–339.

A bicentennial tribute to architect Vanbrugh. Glossing Swift's satirical lines on the sudden turn of "Van's genius" to architecture, suggests that a glance at the "College of Nations, opposite the Louvre" in Paris and a persual of Palladio while imprisoned in the Bastille—together with Wren's "concurrence" and Hawksmoor's "draughtsmanship"—supplied all the stimulus Vanbrugh required in his maiden effort at Castle Howard. Discerns the influence of Blenheim's "massive nonchalance" on Sir John Soane's "official report for a palace for the Duke of Wellington after Waterloo" and in his "Royal Palace design of 1821."

5 EDWARDS, A. TRYSTAN. "Sir John Vanbrugh: A Critical Note." *Architect and Building News* 115, no. 2988 (March):253-257.

Bicentenary praise of Vanbrugh, who commenced his architectural career "with a maturity of mind which enabled him to grasp in a few months technicalities of building which untutored youth takes years to apprehend. . . ." The portrait of Vanbrugh attributed to Closperman is reproduced, as are several of Campbell's *Vitruvius Britannicus* engravings of Castle Howard, Eastbury, and Kings Weston. Those buildings are discussed as instances of Vanbrugh's gift for introducing into his designs a "maximum of variety . . . consistent with order and symmetry." The "coherence" he succeeded in giving his "enormous" buildings suggests he might have designed "magnificent civic centers" had he been given the opportunity.

6 ESDAILE, ARUNDELL. "Sir John Vanbrugh: Some New Historical Facts." *Architect and Building News* 115, no. 2988 (March):258-261.

Quotes from Bubb Doddington's 9 August 1753 letter to Dr. Thomas Hunt, thanking him for his "entertaining story about Sir John Vanbrugh and the Bastille." Hunt appears to have found his "entertaining story" in a letter sent to him from Paris by his friend Gregory Sharpe. The fact that a story about Vanbrugh's imprisonment in the Bastille should have been circulating in Paris three decades after Vanbrugh's death is said to offer evidence of the strong impression Vanbrugh's "personal charm" left on the French.

7 SPRAGUE, ARTHUR COLBY. *Beaumont and Fletcher on the Restoration Stage.* Cambridge, Mass.: Harvard University Press, pp. 89-93, 244-248. Reprint. New York: Benjamin Blom, 1965.

Discusses the April 1700 production of Vanbrugh's adaptation of Fletcher's *Pilgrim*. Proposes April 29 as the premiere date, lists the cast, and cites testimony concerning performances in 1703, 1704, and 1706. Offers detailed analysis of Vanbrugh's alterations of the Fletcher original, concluding that "Vanbrugh's positive contributions are not many" (cf. 1981.4).

1927

1 BOLTON, ARTHUR T. "Sir John Vanbrugh's Design for the Completion of Greenwich Hospital." *Builder* 132, Pt. 1, no. 4379 (January):9.

Surmises that King William "very early recognized the genius of Vanbrugh" and brought him "into the Office of Works as a possible successor" to Wren. The latter, occupied with St. Paul's and with his duties at the Privy Council, Treasury, and Board of Works, is averred to have delegated the completion of Greenwich Hospital to Vanbrugh and Hawksmoor, with the result that at some point between 1702 and 1712 Vanbrugh prepared some fragmentary drawings for the project. (See also 1929.5.)

2 CAZAMIAN, LOUIS. *A History of English Literature.* Vol. 2. *Modern Times.* New York: Macmillan, pp. 74–75.

Praises the "realism" of Vanbrugh's comedies, which, "when they are reviewed with other works," enable us "to form a probable opinion of what the truth [concerning contemporary "manners"] really was." "[B]ehind" Vanbrugh's "verve," discerns "pessimism of intelligence," "moral sincerity," "satire upon the new ideal of sentimentalism . . . outlined by Cibber," the "joy of a builder who constructs a play of solid workmanship, and who in it—one hardly knows how—joins two plots in one." *The Relapse* and *The Provoked Wife* are cited in evidence.

3 DOBRÉE, BONAMY. Introduction to the plays. In *The Complete Works of Sir John Vanbrugh.* Vol. 1. London: Nonesuch Press, pp. xi–xxxiii.

Surveys Vanbrugh's career and assesses his achievement as playwright. Concludes that though "only second rate, perhaps," Honest Van "towers over" his eighteenth-century successors "by virtue of his sheer vitality," "his keen enjoyment of the bustle of the world." By way of illustration, a robust passage from *The Relapse* is juxtaposed against the parallel passage in Sheridan's "superficial, ill-phrased, metallic" *Trip to Scarborough.*

4 HUSSEY, CHRISTOPHER. "Eastbury Park, Dorset." *CLife* 62, no. 1598 (September):330–337.

Thinks Vanbrugh, "in mixing Roman massiveness and Gothic castellation" in his design for Eastbury House, "had in mind the picturesque architecture painted by Pannini and Gaspar." Uses contemporary accounts by visitors, Campbell's *Vitruvius* plan, and two paintings of Eastbury as it stood in 1760 to reconstruct the house on which George Dodington and his nephew and heir George Bubb had expended 140,000 pounds by the time of its completion in 1738. Only the west wing and office court survive today. Material is incorporated into 1928.7.

5 HUSSEY, CHRISTOPHER. "Kings Weston, Gloucestershire, the Seat of Mr. P. Napier-Miles." *CLife* 61, no. 1580 (April):680–687.

Describes Vanbrugh's alterations to Kings Weston. Doubts that any of the drawings in the house's folio volume entitled "Designs, by Sir John Vanbrugh" were produced by Vanbrugh. Discusses and illustrates with photographs the entrance front, eastern façade, arcaded chimneys, hall, staircases, banqueting loggia, and statues and garden houses. (Material is incorporated into 1928.7.)

6 HUSSEY, CHRISTOPHER. *The Picturesque: Studies in A Point of View.* London & New York: Putnam's, pp. 190–193, 198, 202.

Cites testimony to the picturesque aspects of Vanbrugh's architecture offered by Robert Adam (1778.1), Uvedale Price (1810.1), and Joshua Reynolds (1797.2). Defines the "picturesque conception of architecture" on which Reynolds's appreciation of Vanbrugh is based as one that "gives to dramatic massing, the handling of light and shade, and the wedding of a building to its landscape by the architectural treatment of the foreground, greater importance than to clear logic of design or nicety of detail."

7 SUMMERS, MONTAGUE, ed. Introduction to *The Complete Works of Thomas Shadwell.* Vol. 1. London: Fortune Press, p. ccv.

Thinks the presence of the "sentimental character" Lady Brute "goes far to balance the riot of the more deboshed [*sic*] scenes" in that "rollicking" comedy *The Provoked Wife.* Recalls Sir Edmund Gosse's comment, following a 1919 performance of the play at King's Hall, Covent Garden, that the actress Margaret Halsten succeeded in bringing out "the tenderness and sentiment which Vanbrugh introduced for those who had the wit to see it into the character of Lady Brute."

8 TIPPING, H. AVRAY. "Castle Howard–I, Yorkshire, the Seat of the Hon. Geoffrey Howard." *CLife* 61, no. 1585 (June):884–893.

A preliminary biographical sketch examines the chain of events leading to Vanbrugh's surprising capture of his first big commission as architect. Success with *The Relapse* and *The Provoked Wife* won admission to the Kit-Cat Club. Its members included the Earl of Carlisle, whom Vanbrugh "so impressed . . . with his views on architecture" that Carlisle awarded him the Castle Howard commission in preference to Wren or Talman. The Vanbrugh-Hawksmoor-Carlisle correspondence is examined for the light it sheds on the building's early development. (Material is incorporated into 1928.7.)

1927

9 TIPPING, H. AVRAY. "Castle Howard–II, Yorkshire, the Seat of the Hon. Geoffrey Howard." *CLife* 61, no. 1586 (June):948–957.

Discusses and illustrates with photographs Castle Howard's interior. The "Dramatic and picturesque" corridors, with their "almost endless vistas at every turn," are pronounced unprecedented—the product of Vanbrugh's inspiration unaided by his "second fiddle" Hawksmoor, to whom he left the "details" of his rooms. Surmises that the limited floor space Vanbrugh allotted to the hall, stairways, and corridors is a consequence of his "efforts to balance" his "ideas of grandeur with the client's requirements and purse." The resultant "compromise" produces an effect of "sumptuous gaiety," an expression of "Baroque style at its best." (Material incorporated into 1928.7.)

10 TIPPING, H. AVRAY. "Castle Howard–III, Yorkshire, the Seat of the Hon. Geoffrey Howard." *CLife* 61, no. 1588 (June):1022–1030.

Vanbrugh's correspondence with the Earl of Carlisle is examined for the light it sheds on the progress of his plans for Castle Howard. Beginning in 1724, Vanbrugh urged his patron to let him proceed with the west wing. Carlisle elected instead to spend his funds on the outworks—with the result that the west wing was not begun until 1753, and followed a plan very different from that devised by Vanbrugh. Cites the testimony of the fifth Duke of Rutland that Thomas Robinson's "erection of this [west] wing was merely the commencement of a plan of a very extensive nature," his plan being "not to complete" Vanbrugh's work but to "replace much of it by his own." The straitened finances of the fourth earl of Carlisle's successor appear to have "prevented this destruction." (Material incorporated into 1928.7.)

11 TIPPING, H. AVRAY. "The Outworks of Castle Howard, Yorkshire–I. The Seat of the Hon. Geoffrey Howard." *CLife* 62, no. 1594 (August):200–208.

Describes and illustrates the exterior and interior of Vanbrugh's temple, the several park and garden gateways, and other of his outworks at Castle Howard. Notes the "touch of dramatic romanticism" he gave to Wray Wood—which he treated as an "ordered wilderness, Nature being rendered more 'polite' by the introduction of alleys and architecture." (Material incorporated into 1928.7.)

12 TIPPING, H. AVRAY. "The Outworks of Castle Howard, Yorkshire–II. The Seat of the Hon. Geoffrey Howard." *CLife* 62, no. 1595 (August):230–237.

Describes and illustrates the obelisk, entrance archway, and park walls and bastions Vanbrugh designed for Castle Howard. (Material incorporated into 1928.7.)

13   WREN SOCIETY, LONDON. *The Fourth Volume of the Wren Society. 1927. Hampton Court Palace 1689–1702. Original Wren Drawings from the Sir John Soane's Museum and All Souls Collections.* Edited by Arthur Thomas Bolton and Harry Duncan Hendry. Oxford: Printed for the Wren Society at the University Press, pp. 74–75.

Includes a transcription of a "Treasury order" of 22 July 1699 granting Vanbrugh "leave . . . to build himself a lodging in Whitehall, upon ground where Mr Vice Chamberlain's stood before the ffire [*sic*]." Also transcribes Christopher Wren's (undated) petition objecting to the order and William Lowndes's reply reaffirming permission for Vanbrugh "(by his own workmen) to build the said lodgings upon the said ground. . . ."

1928

1   HAGUE, RENÉ. "Sir John Vanbrugh." Review of *The Complete Works of Sir John Vanbrugh.* Edited by Bonamy Dobrée and Geoffrey Webb. 4 vols. London: Nonesuch Press, 1927–1928 (1927.3 and 1928.11). *London Mercury* 18 (August):395–402.

Chides Palmer (1913.1) for taking the wickedness of Vanbrugh's comedies (as did Jeremy Collier) "seriously," a mistake akin to "confusing a joke with a sermon." Vanbrugh is said to have had two modes of writing: (1) "frank burlesque" and (2) hasty transcription of "the sort of conversation that was accepted as amusing in the clubs and drawing rooms of the day." His mixture of the two modes results in a sometimes awkward medley of critical comedy and farce. In the comic rendering of altercations between husbands and wives, however, Vanbrugh has no equal.

2   HODGES, JOHN C. "The Authorship of *Squire Trelooby*." *RES* 4, no. 10 (October):404–413.

In his preface to the printed *Squire Trelooby*, which appeared three months after the 1704 premiere of the Walsh/Congreve/Vanbrugh play of the same name, John Ozell asserts that he had appropriated the title, the names of the characters, the prologue and epilogue, and the list of performers appearing in the staged version. He acknowledges the translation of the play proper (from Molière's *Monsieur de Pourceaugnac*) to be his own. Because (a) Congreve himself disowned the printed *Squire Trelooby*, (b) the same *Squire Trelooby* is reprinted in Ozell's translation of the complete Molière in 1714, and (c) Vanbrugh's friend Tonson would himself almost certainly have undertaken the printing of any published version of the Walsh/Congreve/Vanbrugh play, Hodges concludes that the printed *Squire*

1928

> *Trelooby* (included in the third volume of Summers's 1923 edition of Congreve's *Complete Works*) does *not* represent the text produced by Walsh, Congreve, and Vanburgh (cf. 1968.7 and 1970.5).

3 MORTIMER, RAYMOND. Review of *The Complete Works of Sir John Vanbrugh* (1927.3 and 1928.11). *Nation & Athenaeum* 43 (April):48–49.

Corrects Dobrée's gloss of Lord Foppington's "mis en chartré," proposing that Vanbrugh intended (but misspelled) *châtré*—that is, "castrated." The reviewer judges Vanbrugh's letters to be "dull," the liveliest of them (those to Tonson) "express[ing] little save good humour." Similar limitations are discerned in the plays, though the architecture is found to be expressive of "a most romantic imagination."

4 PORTER, ALAN. "Too Much Restoration." Review of *The Complete Works of Sir John Vanbrugh* (1927.3 and 1928.11). *Spectator* 140 (March):375, 377.

Criticism of the "indecency" and "viciousness" of "Restoration" drama is followed by admiration of "the way in which [Vanbrugh] threw off his works, as if with one hand." In reading the letters the reviewer is struck by Vanbrugh's "courage and tenacity" in the face of difficulties, particularly in his struggle with the Duchess of Marlborough over the building of Blenheim Palace.

5 SHANKS, EDWARD. "Sir John Vanbrugh." Review of *The Complete Works of Sir John Vanbrugh* (1927.3 and 1928.11). *Saturday Review* [London] 145 (March):258.

Praises Dobrée and Webb for their restraint in estimating Vanbrugh's accomplishment and suggests that his "unaffected self-revelations" in his letters show him "at his best." Though "He was not a great dramatist, nor yet was he in the first flight of British architects," his comedies are "healthily vigorous, and his buildings are a part of English history" written "in brick and stone."

6 "Sir John Vanbrugh." Review of *The Complete Works of Sir John Vanbrugh* (1927.3 and 1928.11). *New Statesman* 31, no. 788 (June):298.

Offers a brief assessment of Vanbrugh's achievement. Though he "lacks some of the wit and polish of Congreve, and some of the vigor . . . of Wycherley," he possesses a compensating geniality, common sense, and intelligence. "[T]he Trollope of our dramatists," he paints accurately and engagingly the lives of gentlemen of his day, and he possesses "the unique distinction of being" simultaneously one of his century's best dramatists as well as one of its best architects.

7 TIPPING, H. AVRAY, and HUSSEY, CHRISTOPHER. *English Homes. Period IV—Vol. II. The Work of Sir John Vanbrugh and his School, 1699-1736.* London: Country Life; New York: Scribner's, 396 pp.

Discussion (illustrated by many photographs) of each of Vanbrugh's major houses and of a number of other houses of the day designed in the Vanbrugh manner—Frampton Court in Gloucestershire, for example, a specimen of "'The Vanbrugh School' of architecture." Hawksmoor is judged to have been not a "mere assistant" to Vanbrugh but a "coadjutor" in his earlier projects (cf. 1924.3 and 1926.4). The "partnership" is averred to have come about after Christopher Wren, observing "the qualities and defects of these two men," encouraged what he perceived to be their potential for "great success in combination"—with the result that at Castle Howard "we cannot precisely differentiate between Vanbrugh's and Hawksmoor's contributions." (Incorporates material included in 1927.4, 1927.5, 1927.8, 1927.9, 1927.10, 1927.11, 1927.12.)

8 "Vanbrugh's Plays and Letters." Review of *The Complete Works of Sir John Vanbrugh* (1927.3 and 1928.11). *TLS.* 19 April, p. 287.

Not an original writer (most of his plays being adaptations), Vanbrugh "shows the interest of an intelligent observer rather than the constructive imagination of an artist," rendering the events of his comedies "with the detached interest of a man who has standards other than the temporary and trivial standards of his world." Cited in evidence are Heartfree's efforts to reason Lady Fancyfull out of her affectations (*The Provoked Wife*) and Aesop's efforts to reason with the country gentleman who believes he and his relations are capable of governing the "town" (*Aesop* II).

9 VAUGHAN, HERBERT S. "Vanbrugh Family." *N & Q* 155 (August):117.

A request for information concerning the whereabouts of Sir Joshua Reynolds's 1743/1744 portrait of Vanbrugh's brother Philip, who "died as Commissioner at Plymouth in 1753."

10 WALPOLE, HORACE. *Journals of Visits to County Seats, &c.* Prefatory note by Paget Toynbee. In *Sixteenth Volume of the Walpole Society, 1927-1928.* Oxford: At the University Press, p. 33.

Includes Walpole's account of a visit to Audley End in 1762. Reports that Vanbrugh "advised the pulling down the outer court, which consisted of two colonades with marble columns, & building the present ugly brick walls. . . ." Vanbrugh "designed too the modern screen & flights of steps at one end of the hall."

1929

11 WEBB, GEOFFREY. Introduction to the letters. In *The Complete Works of Sir John Vanbrugh*. Vol. 4. London: Nonesuch Press, pp. ix–xl.

Surveys Vanbrugh's career as builder and garden designer. Praises the internal arrangements of his large-scale houses for their suitability both for "magnificent ceremonial occassions" and for the necessarily elaborate "ritual of [their occupants'] daily lives." Castle Howard is judged to be "immature and tentative," Seaton Delaval to be Vanbrugh's "finest and most complete achievement."

1929

1 BATESON, F. W. *English Comic Drama, 1700–1750*. Oxford: At the Clarendon Press, p. 35. Reprint. New York: Russell & Russell, 1963.

In a chapter devoted to Colley Cibber's plays, observes that *The Provoked Husband* "is based on and incorporates Vanbrugh's brilliant fragment, *[A] Journey to London*." Thinks the play's "most successful scenes are not Cibber's."

2 SOANE, SIR JOHN. *Lectures on Architecture. As delivered to the students of the Royal Academy from 1809 to 1836 in Two Courses of Six Lectures each*. Edited by Arthur T. Bolton. Sir John Soane's Museum. No. 14. London: Printed by Jordan-Gaskell, pp. 89–90.

Lecture 5 notes that though innocent of "classical correctness," Vanbrugh's buildings are "full of character, and his outlines rich and varied." His Goose-Pie House reveals his capacity to make "small things interesting." The design of Blenheim Palace, his best work, is "analogous" to the Duke of Marlborough's "warlike genius." Vanbrugh's "bold flights of irregular fancy" qualify him as "the Shakespeare of Architects."

3 THORNDIKE, ASHLEY H. *English Comedy*. New York: Macmillan, pp. 328–334.

Thinks the most "diverting" scenes in *The Relapse* are those involving Young Fashion and Lord Foppington in the underplot. The conversations in *The Provoked Wife* are judged to be "always sprightly," "never protracted into a tiresome succession of epigrams without incident." The description of the Headpiece family's arrival in London in *A Journey to London* is compared to "a chapter in Smollett or a print by Hogarth in its realism and humour."

4 VAUGHAN, HERBERT S. "Some Vanbrugh Problems." *N & Q*, 13th ser. 157 (July):62.

The "problems" are these: (1) why was the Vanbrugh family's eldest son, John, left only one share in his father's will? (2) Was the

Dudley Vanbrugh who killed Colonel Beveridge in 1692 indeed John Vanbrugh's brother? (3) Should the "Kendrick" Vanbrugh cited in *Notes and Queries* 2S.vi.116 (unverified) be corrected to "Hendrik"?

5   WREN SOCIETY, LONDON. *The Sixth Volume of the Wren Society. 1929. The Royal Hospital for Seamen at Greenwich 1694-1728. Original Drawings by Sir Christopher Wren, Sir John Vanbrugh, Nicholas Hawksmoor, John James.* Edited by Arthur Thomas Bolton and Harry Duncan Hendry. Oxford: Printed for the Wren Society at the University Press, pp. 11-14, 28-29, 44-58, 69-75, 86-92 (incl. plates xxxvi-xli), 99-101.

Includes discussion of Vanbrugh's design for the completion of Greenwich Hospital. Transcribes records of his attendance at Boards of Works directors' meetings, prints his "Estimate to finish" the hospital, and documents his examination of hospital account books. (There are several notations that the committee was "to meet at Sir J. Vanbrugh's house in Whitehall.") Prints plates illustrating Vanbrugh's scheme for the hospital's completion, among them several reconstructions of his apparent intentions as "drawn out" by Arthur Bolton. (See also 1927.1.)

1930

1   EATON, WALTER PRICHARD. *The Drama in English.* New York, Chicago, and Boston: Scribner's, pp. 162, 176-177, 179.

Thinks the "Comedy of Manners" is seen "decliningly" in Vanbrugh. The "fun" of *The Provoked Wife* "more often comes from the *situation* than from the words," its best moments stemming from the "opportunities it gives for character acting, and in humor rather than wit." Praises the conversational ease and "comic irony" of Lady Arabella's remarks on marriage in *A Journey to London*.

2   WREN SOCIETY, LONDON. *The Seventh Volume of the Wren Society. 1930. The Royal Palaces of Winchester, Whitehall[,] Kensington, and St. James's[.] Sir Christopher Wren, Architect. . . .* Edited by Arthur Thomas Bolton and Harry Duncan Hendry. Oxford: Printed for the Wren Society at the University Press, pp.5-7, 139, 140-142, 189-195, 199-205, 210-212, 215-223.

Discusses the "close association of Wren and Vanbrugh" at the Board of Works, documents Vanbrugh's attendance at 334 meetings of the Board between May 1715 and June 1724, transcribes minutes recording his participation in Board meetings relating to alterations at Kensington Palace, Hampton Court, and St. James's Palace. Attributes to Vanbrugh the Kensington Water Tower and the "old

Kitchen" at St. James's Palace. Assigns him joint responsibility with Wren for the Orangery at Kensington Palace. Prints and discusses Vanbrugh's 9 November 1704 letter to Godolphin seeking to expel Jackson from his position as Master Mason at the Office of Works (see *Works*, IV, 1928.11). Also prints the Duke of Shrewsbury's 27 March 1713 letter to the Earl of Oxford praising Vanbrugh's performance at the Board of Works.

1931

1 GRAY, CHARLES HAROLD. *Theatrical Criticism in London to 1795.* New York: Columbia University Press, pp. 134, 140, 197, 235, 237, 239.

Includes passing notice of eighteenth-century criticism of Vanbrugh's *Provoked Wife* (e.g., judged "immoral because Vanbrugh allowed the wife to retaliate upon the husband with infidelity instead of rising nobly above the provocation") and *The Relapse* (e.g., a *London Magazine* critic in 1776 "scoffed at the critics of the day who objected to" Vanbrugh's "vulgarisms and coarseness").

2 HISTORICAL MANUSCRIPTS COMMISSION. *Report on the Manuscripts of His Grace the Duke of Portland, K. G., Preserved at Welbeck Abbey.* Vol. 10. Edited by R. F. Isaacson. London: H. M. Stationery Office, pp. 96, 136–142, 144–145, 147–148.

Prints the following documents pertinent to Vanbrugh. (1) William Talman's (1702?) petition to the Board of Works protesting that he was "the only person in that office turned out to make room for Mr. Vanbrooke, who enjoys a very good place in the Office of Arms"; (2) Vanbrugh's 15 June 1711 "estimate for the works at Blenheim" and two letters from Vanbrugh to Robert Harley relating to Blenheim (letters dated 30 September 1710 and 12 February 1710/1711, neither included in Downes's list of Vanbrugh's letters in 1987.4, Appendix B); (3) a Wren/Vanbrugh letter to the Lord High Treasurer relating to Blenheim statuary Marble (dated 29 June 1711); (4) Vanbrugh's 4 November 1712 letter to Marlborough concerning the financing of Blenheim; (5) Vanbrugh's ("1712") "account of what has passed at the Treasury about Blenheim House since the removal of Lord Godolphin" (together with transcriptions of Vanbrugh's 30 September 1710 letters to Lord Pullet and to Harley concerning his intention to make Blenheim a "national monument" as well as a "private habitation"; (6) Vanbrugh's 26 January 1712-13 letter to the Mayor of Woodstock (Webb dates it 25 January in 1928.11) and his 21 February 1712/1713 and 14 April 1713 letters to the Earl of Oxford clarifying the intention of his (misdirected) letter to Woodstock's mayor; (7) a 21 July 1713 letter from "J— S—" to the Earl of Oxford expressing eagerness to "prove" what he had "charge[d]" in his earlier letter "concerning Mr. Vanbrugh."

3 MACMILLAN, DOUGALD, and JONES, HOWARD MUMFORD, eds. Introduction to *The Relapse*, by Sir John Vanbrugh. In *Plays of the Restoration and Eighteenth Century as They Were Acted at the Theatres-Royal by Their Majesties' Servants*. New York: Henry Holt, pp. 349–350.

Introduction to *The Relapse* includes a sketch of the playwright's career, brief remarks on the relationship between Cibber's *Love's Last Shift* and Vanbrugh's sequel, and two paragraphs on Collier's attack and Vanbrugh's reply. Observes that at his death Vanbrugh left "two sons and a reputation as the greatest writer of comedies of his generation, excepting Mr. Congreve, and the best architect after Sir Christopher Wren."

1933

1 TALLMADGE, THOMAS E. "Holographs of Famous Architects." *American Architects* 143, no. 2616 (March):8–12.

Describing it as the "gem" of the Burnham Library's collection of architects' letters and drawings, prints Vanbrugh's letter to Tonson of 25 October 1725 concerning "that B.B.B.B old B. the Duchess of [Marlborough]" (see *Works*, IV, 1928.11). Also reproduces from the Burnham collection Kneller's portrait of Vanbrugh. Vanbrugh is described as "gay, brilliant, and witty, an ex-inhabitant of the Bastille, author of *The Relapse . .*, the most popular member of the Kit-Cat Club." His copy of Palladio is said to have been the tool whereby "he became in the eyes of his admiring friends an architect."

1934

1 MUESCHKE, PAUL, and FLEISHER, JEANETTE. "A Re-Evaluation of Vanbrugh." *PMLA* 49, no. 3 (September): 848–889.

A response to Palmer's (1913.1) and Perry's (1925.7) charge that Vanbrugh's departures from Comedy of Manners formulas are marks of his inferiority to his predecessors. Those expressions of "feeling" with which Vanbrugh endows a number of his characters are genuine, not sentimental. The bulk of the essay is devoted to demonstration, with reference to *The Relapse*, *The Provoked Wife*, and *A Journey to*

London, that Vanbrugh's comedies "derive their vitality from a central corpus of persistent ideas," most significantly (a) the younger brother's plight in consequence of the law of primogeniture, and (b) the causes and consequences of marital incompatibility.

2 SUMMERS, MONTAGUE. *A Bibliography of the Restoration Drama.* London: Fortune Press. Reprint. New York: Russell & Russell, 1970, pp. 121–123. (Annotation and page numbers based on 1970 reprint.)

Includes a list of Vanbrugh's plays indicating dates and venues of premieres and publication history.

1935

1 BENSLEY, EDWARD; HEAL, AMBROSE; and ARDAGH, J. "Vanbrugh's Theatre in the Haymarket." *N & Q*, 13th ser. 169 (December):426–427.

Three replies to 1935.2. Bensley cites documents pertaining to the opening season of Vanbrugh's Queen's Theatre at the Haymarket—all of which agree that the Italian opera *The Triumph of Love* was offered on the occasion of the theatre's opening on 9 April 1705. Heal cites Wheatley's opinion that Dryden's *Indian Emperor* was performed at the Haymarket's 9 April opening, an opinion seconded by Ardagh. (But see 1976.10.)

2 DASENT, ARTHUR. "Vanbrugh's Theatre in the Haymarket." *N & Q*, 13th ser. 169 (November):390.

A query. Unable to "find Vanbrugh's name in the parochial rate-books before 1717," asks if it is "known when Sir John Vanbrugh's theatre in the Haymarket . . . was built."

3 LONDON COUNTY COUNCIL. *Survey of London.* Vol. 16. *Charing Cross (The Parish of St. Martin-in-the-Fields, Part I).* Edited by G. H. Gater and Walter H. Godfrey. London: Published for the London County Council by Country Life, pp. 89, 168–171, 197.

Lockett's Ordinary is described as "the famous 'ordinary' . . . often mentioned in the plays of Cibber and Vanbrugh" (a note cites *The Story of Charing Cross*, pp. 49–50). A discussion of "Vanbrugh House" (Goose-Pie House) quotes from Vanbrugh's petition to build the lodging "upon ye Ground where Mr. Vice Chamberlain's Lodgings stood before the fire." The house is illustrated in an undated drawing. Discussion of a "row of buildings" occupying "nos. 3 to 8, Whitehall Palace" notes that the buildings included "offices of the Surveyor of

Works" in which "Vanbrugh lived . . . as comptroller" until his 1713 dismissal.

4   OSWALD, ARTHUR. *Country Houses of Dorset*. London: Country Life, pp. 72, 83–86.
    Includes discussion of Eastbury House, "third in size among Vanbrugh's great houses, being only exceeded by Blenheim and Castle Howard." Reproduces Vanbrugh's plan for the house, an elevation of the garden front as published in *Vitruvius Britannicus* (1715-1725.1), a contemporary oil painting of the "house in its entirety," and photographs of the "surviving fragment[s]."

5   WREN SOCIETY, LONDON. *The Twelfth Volume of the Wren Society. 1935. Miscellaneous Designs and Drawings by Sir Chr. Wren and others* . . . . Edited by Arthur Thomas Bolton and Harry Duncan Hendry. Oxford: Printed for the Wren Society at the University Press, plate XXX.
    Attributes to Vanbrugh the middle drawing in plate XXX—"Design for Kitchen at St. James's Palace (?) . . . 1715/16."

1936

1   *AGATE, JAMES. Review of revival of *The Provoked Wife*. *The Sunday Times* [London], 11 October.
    Source: Coleman, 1982.2, p. 20; unverified. Review of Embassy Theatre (London) production of *The Provoked Wife*.

2   *B., J. C. Review of revival of *The Provoked Wife*. *Evening News*, 6 October.
    Source: Coleman, 1982.2, p. 20; unverified. Review of Embassy Theatre (London) production of *The Provoked Wife*.

3   *DARLINGTON, W. A. Review of revival of *The Provoked Wife*. *Daily Telegraph*, 6 October.
    Source: Coleman, 1982.2, p. 20; unverified. Review of Embassy Theatre (London) production of *The Provoked Wife*.

4   KELLY, JOHN ALEXANDER. *German Visitors to English Theaters in the Eighteenth Century*. Princeton, N.J.: Princeton University Press, pp. 22, 45, 46–47, 49, 65.
    Remarks on reactions of German visitors to the English theatre include citation of George Lichtenberg's disapproval of the licentiousness of *The Provoked Wife* in the 1776 production he witnessed at

1937

Drury Lane. Lichtenberg's account of the performances of Garrick and Mrs. Abington in that play is mentioned in passing.

5 *Review of revival of *The Provoked Wife*. *The Times* [London], 6 October.
   Source: Coleman, 1982.2, p. 20; unverified. Review of Embassy Theatre (London) production of *The Provoked Wife*.

6 THALER, ALWIN. Introduction to *The Provok'd Wife*, by Sir John Vanbrugh. In *Representative English Comedies*. Vol. 4. *Dryden and His Contemporaries: Cowley to Farquhar*. Edited by Charles Mills Gayley and Alwin Thaler. New York: Macmillan, pp. 409–426.
   A sketch of Vanbrugh's career and evaluation of his comedies. Thinks he "did not develop as a dramatist," his best plays appearing at his career's commencement and at its end (witness *A Journey to London*). With the exception of *The Confederacy,* the products of the intervening years were "second-rate." *The Pilgrim* is called a "rare instance of an adaptation that does not do violence to the original." Ozell's printed version of *Squire Trelooby* is pronounced to be probably "not far removed from the stage version prepared by Walsh, Congreve, and Vanbrugh (cf. 1968.7). *The Relapse* is examined as a "play of ideas." The structure of *The Provoked Wife* is discussed, as is Vanbrugh's expansion of comedy's "dramatis personae" and his extension of the drama's purview from the drawing room to the country (cf. 1973.1).

1937

1 ANTHONY, SISTER ROSE. *The Jeremy Collier Stage Controversy, 1698-1726*. Milwaukee, Wis.: Marquette University Press, pp. 97–102. Reprint. New York: Benjamin Blom, 1966.
   Vanbrugh's *Short Vindication of the Relapse and the Provok'd Wife* is discussed in a chapter examining the "June [1698] Replies" to Jeremy Collier's *Short View of the Immorality and Prophaneness of the English stage* (1698.1). Vanbrugh's reply to Collier's charges is judged to be "feeble," "sarcastic," and "grossly personal."

2 VINCENT, HOWARD P. "Two Unpublished Letters of Vanbrugh." *N & Q*, 13th ser. 173 (August):128–129.
   Prints and annotates a letter of 1708 to Vice Chamberlain Coke concerning payments to performers of an unnamed opera, and a letter of 1713 addressed to Edward Southwell relating to the chimneys at Kings Weston.

1938

1 BYNG, JOHN ("Later Fifth Viscount Torrington"). *The Torrington Diaries, Containing the Tours through England and Wales.* Vol. 4. Edited by C. Bruyn Andrews. New York: Barnes & Noble; London: Methuen, p. 127.

Editor indicates in foreword that vol. 4 prints the second volume of Byng's "recently discovered . . . 'Tour of the Midlands [of 1789].'" Includes Byng's account of a visit to Grimsthorpe, which leaves him unimpressed with "The New Front and Hall . . . built by Sir J. Vanbrugh in all his clumsy Taste." Index lists two other references to Vanbrugh (not seen) in vol. 1, p. 323, and vol. 2, p. 38.

2 EDWARDS, RALPH. Review of Whistler, *Sir John Vanbrugh: Architect and Dramatist* (1938.7). *Burlington Magazine* 73, no. 428 (November):230–231.

Praises Whistler's "grasp of Vanbrugh's essential characteristics, his power of composing in mass, sense of dynamic movement and scenic imagination." Concerning Vanbrugh's return "to favour as an architect after a long eclipse," remarks that Vanbrugh's admirers tend to be members of "circles partial alike to amateurs and the baroque."

3 LICHTENBERG, GEORGE. *Lichtenberg's Visits to England, as Described in his Letters and Diaries.* Translated and Annotated by Margaret L. Mare and W. H. Quarrell. Oxford Studies in Modern Literature. Edited by H. G. Fiedler. Oxford: Clarendon Press. Reprint. New York: Benjamin Blom, 1969, pp. 2, 19. (Annotation and page numbers based on 1969 reprint.)

Includes brief mention of Garrick's performance in the role of Sir John Brute in *The Provoked Wife*, a play the author (writing in 1776 and 1778) thinks it would be "better never to produce." "[A]bominable things" assault "ear and eye" even in the altered version of the play in which Sir John disguises himself as a lady of quality rather than a clergyman. For citation of initial publication, see 1776, 1778.1.

4 STEEGMAN, JOHN. "The Dramatist in Practice." Review of Whistler, *Sir John Vanbrugh: Architect and Dramatist* (1938.7). *AR* 84, no. 502 (September):126–127.

Surveys Vanbrugh's fluctuating reputation as architect. Deprecated by the "wits" of his day, he was praised subsequently by Reynolds (1797.2) and Price (1810.1) and treated respectfully in Seccombe's *DNB* account (1909.3). In "our own day" he has been accorded "less attention . . . than Nicholas Hawksmoor." The comparative neglect is now "admirably rectified" by Whistler, whose account of the architect has "all the gusto and the power to astonish of John Vanbrugh himself."

5 TUNNARD, CHRISTOPHER. "The Case for the Common Garden." *AR* 84, no. 502 (September):109–116.

Lamenting the tendency of housing developers to break up the venerable gardens of "estates such as Claremont," the author advises developers that "with a rational planning of the whole area [to be developed], and the concentration of dwellings in certain parts of it, more people might be housed yet[,] and virtually the whole estate might be left open for the benefit of the residents and public." The baneful effect of developers' "cut[ting] up" of Claremont's venerable garden into small enclosures is illustrated by a photograph in which a "TO BE SOLD" sign stands "cheek by jowl" with the obelisk commemorating "three of the greatest names in English landscape architecture, Sir John Vanbrugh, William Kent, and Lancelot Brown."

6 WEBB, GEOFFREY. "Vanbrugh." Review of Whistler, *Sir John Vanbrugh, Architect and Dramatist* (1938.7). *RIBA Journal* 45 (August):928–929.

Laments Whistler's "relative neglect of Hawksmoor" and his indifference to Vanbrugh's pioneering sponsorship of Italian opera. Speculates that Vanbrugh's familiarity with the "theatrical decor" of Italian opera "may have some bearing on the formation of his style as an architect." Concerning his letters, remarks that Vanbrugh "is not a man who shows us much of his inside."

7 WHISTLER, LAURENCE. *Sir John Vanbrugh, Architect & Dramatist, 1664–1726.* London: Cobden-Sanderson, 327 pp. Reprint. New York: Kraus Reprint, 1978. (Annotation based on 1978 reprint.)

This first full-scale biography of Vanbrugh focuses on the architectural half of his career, painting a portrait of a "sweet-natured gentleman" whose death "was a grief to many, and a delight" only to the Duchess of Marlborough. Among the book's suppositions are (1) that Vanbrugh's "life-long contempt for the Church" (cf. 1984.3) may have its origins in the "superfluity of sermons" to which his energetically anti-Catholic father subjected him "in extreme youth," and (2) that Vanbrugh's birth in the walled city of Chester "introduced him to a style of building that had immense influence on his own." The latter point is illustrated by reference to the recurrent castellar elements of his building style.

8 WILCOX, JOHN. *The Relation of Molière to Restoration Comedy.*
New York: Columbia University Press, pp. 167–175. Reprint. New
York: Benjamin Blom, 1964.

In composing Lord Foppington's dressing scene in *The Relapse*,
Vanbrugh may have been mindful of M. Jourdain in Molière's *Le
Bourgeois Gentilhomme.* Sir Tunbelly and Hoyden may derive from
Sganarelle and Isabelle in *L'Ecole des maris.* Vanbrugh's *The Mistake*,
a scene-for-scene adaptation of Molière's *Le Dépit amoureux,* is "the
first good acting translation of Molière into English." No other debts
to Molière are discernible in Vanbrugh's plays.

1939

1 ACKERMANN, A. S. E. "The Obelisk at Claremont Lodge." *N &
Q*, 13th ser. 177 (October):279.

Transcribes the inscription on the obelisk at Claremont: "Sir John
Vanburg Knight/Owner of this estate 1708/A dramatist and architect/
of celebrity./He built the first mansion/of which the gar[dens] [we]re
laid out/Under Kent. . . ."

2 BARKER, RICHARD HINDRY. *Mr. Cibber of Drury Lane.* New
York: Columbia University Press, pp. 31–32, 141–149. Reprint. New
York: AMS Press, 1966.

Asserts that there is "brutal frankness" in *The Relapse*,
"genial[ity]" in the treatment of character in its predecessor, Cibber's
Love's Last Shift. Examines Cibber's alteration of Vanbrugh's unfinished *Journey to London* (in *The Provoked Husband* Cibber
"pruned away the coarse humanity" of Vanbrugh's warring couple the
Loverules). Also discusses the reception of the play's 1728 premiere,
at which the audience, misdirected by Cibber's prologue, hissed the
Headpiece-Wronghead scenes it assumed were Cibber's, and applauded the Loverule-Townley scenes it imagined Vanbrugh's.

3 HOBSON, M.G., ed. *Oxford Council Acts, 1665–1701.* Oxford:
Clarendon Press, pp. 191, 196.

Includes transcriptions of two Oxford Council actions in which
Vanbrugh's name appears: (1) on 16 September 1687 Vanbrugh and
other members of the retinue of the newly elected High Steward of
Oxford, James Bertie, Earl of Abingdon, were "given the freedom of
the City and bailiff's places"; (2) on 16 February 1688 James II ordered that Vanbrugh and thirty others be "removed and displaced
from their offices and places" at Oxford.

1940

4 KINNE, WILLARD AUSTIN. *Revivals and Importations of French Comedies in England, 1749–1800.* Cincinnati, Ohio (*sic*). [*NUC* indicates this item was a Columbia University diss., 1939, "published also without thesis note"]; New York: Columbia University Press, pp. 32–33, 42–44, 49–50, 250. (Annotation and page references based on Cincinnati edition.)

Includes brief accounts of Vanbrugh's alterations of French comedies in *The Mistake, The Confederacy* (Vanbrugh's dialogue "leaves nothing to the imagination, while Dancourt lets one read between the lines"), *The Country House, Aesop* ("an improvement over Boursault's 'episodic morality' as to wit and humor, but inferior as to sentiment"). Suggests that *The Relapse* borrows from *Le Bourgeois gentilhomme, L'École des femmes,* and *Les Précieuses ridicules.*

5 Review of Whistler, *Sir John Vanbrugh, Architect and Dramatist* (1938.7). *Brooklyn Museum Bulletin* 1 (October):book supplement 2.

Thinks Vanbrugh's "gift" to his century was "scale and heroism."

1940

1 G., F. A. Review of Whistler, *Sir John Vanbrugh, Architect and Dramatist* (1938.7). *Magazine of Art* 33, no. 2 (February):122.

Eight sentences in generalized praise of "the best architectural book of the past few years."

2 "Malvern at Blenheim." *CLife* 87, no. 2246 (February):118–122.

Describes Blenheim's conversion into a school and dormitory for the boys of Malvern public school during wartime.

3 Review of Whistler, *Sir John Vanbrugh, Architect and Dramatist* (1938.7). *Architectural Forum* 72, no. 4 (April):116.

Short notice expressing satisfaction that "one of the great architects of the Renaissance" has at last been accorded a "complete biography."

4 WREN SOCIETY, LONDON. *The Seventeenth Volume of the Wren Society. Designs and Drawings Supplementary to Volume XII. 1935. The Work of Sir Chr. Wren, Sir John Vanbrugh. . . .* Edited by Arthur Thomas Bolton and Harry Duncan Hendry. Oxford: Printed

1942

for the Wren Society at the University Press, pp. 8–11 passim, 80–81, 86.

Discusses several of Vanbrugh's architectural drawings, reproduced in the following plates: XIV—"Design for a Great House by Mr. Vanbrugh," "'Mr. Vanbrugh's House.' Claremont, Surrey"; XV—"Design for Garden Pavilion or Lodge/Sir John Vanbrugh?"; L—"Design for Cupola at Castle Howard. Sir John Vanbrugh, Architect"; LI—"Greenwich Hospital, Design for Chapel. Sir John Vanbrugh, Architect."

1941

1 BORENIUS, TANCRED. "Castle Howard and its Lost Treasures." *Burlington Magazine* 78, no. 454 (January):3–9.

Describes the damage done to the interior of Castle Howard by the fire of November 1940. Suffering damage were Pellegrini's fresco "The Fall of Phaeton" in the dome of the Great Hall as well as a number of pieces of movable furniture and paintings by Tintoretto, Reynolds, and others. Discussion is illustrated by photographs of several of the damaged works in their pre-fire state.

1942

1 ALLEMAN, GELLERT SPENCER. *Matrimonial Law and the Materials of Restoration Comedy.* Wallingford: [University of Pennsylvania Press], pp. 53–54, 120–121.

Notes that Young Fashion would have been subject to statutory penalties (two years' imprisonment) had he taken the presumably pre-sixteen-year-old Hoyden away without her father's consent (or five years of imprisonment had he married or ravished her). "Miss Cross" was about 13 when she appeared in the role of Hoyden in *The Relapse*'s premiere at Drury Lane. Regarding Belinda's reference to the "House of Lords" in response to Lady Brute's proposed adultery (*Provoked Wife* I.i.90–97), Alleman cites the Duchess of Norfolk's defeat of her husband's efforts between 1691 and 1693 to secure a divorce in the House of Lords on the grounds of adultery.

2 PIOZZI, HESTER LYNCH THRALE. *Thraliana: The Diary of Mrs. Hester Lynch Thrale (Later Mrs. Piozzi) 1776–1809.* 2 vols. Edited by Katherine C. Balderston. Published in cooperation with the Huntington Library. Oxford: Clarendon Press.

Source: *NUC*. For annotation of 2d ed., see 1951.3.

1943

1   KIES, PAUL P. "Lessing's Intention in *Der Dorfjunker.*" *Research Studies of the State College of Washington* 11, no. 3 (September):257–263.

Argues that Lessing's *Der Dorfjunker* (1749?), like his similarly plotted *Die Juden* (1749), contains borrowings from Farquhar's *The Beaux' Strategem* and Vanbrugh's *Relapse*. From the latter the alleged borrowing is of the character of Sir Tunbelly Clumsy, whose qualities the author detects in *Der Dorfjunker*'s "crude country gentleman" Von Wahn and the similarly crude Baron in *Die Juden*. Both of the Lessing plays share with *The Relapse* a "country setting" in which "the owner of a country estate . . . tries to marry off a daughter."

2   MAYHEW, EDGAR DE NOAILLES. "English Baroque: Sir John Vanbrugh and the Baroque Country House." Ph.D. dissertation, Johns Hopkins University [t. p. of Library of Congress copy indicates "Submitted . . . 1941"; below that, "Baltimore 1943"], 38 pp.

Includes a sketch of Vanbrugh's life and an account of the development of the early "baroque country house" in England. Vanbrugh is characterized as a practitioner of the "full baroque"—of which Castle Howard is the "first" specimen, Blenheim the "most important." Baroque elements of both houses are discussed. Briefer treatment of Kings Weston, Eastbury Park, and Seaton Delaval ("the last important house of the Full Baroque period"). Four concluding pages discuss Vanbrugh's influence on "Late Baroque" houses (e.g., Holkham Hall and Frampton Court, Gloucestershire).

1944

1   KIMBALL, FISKE. "Romantic Classicism in Architecture." *Gazette des Beaux-Arts*, 6th ser. [25] (February):97–101. (February 1944 cover indicates "Vol. XXVI"—but preceding [January] and succeeding [March] covers indicate "Vol. XXV.")

Vanbrugh is called "the first" landscape architect "to give picturesque treatment to some parts" of the gardens he designed. Cited in evidence are (1) the touches of irregularity he gave to the layout of Castle Howard's Wray Wood and (2) Claremont's "high wooded hill, intruding very close to the house and eccentric to the general scheme." Vanbrugh was also an exponent of romantic classicism in his pioneering use of picturesque garden architecture (e.g., the Belvedere at Castle Howard, the temple at Eastbury, the Rotunda at Stowe).

1945

1 FELL, H. GRANVILLE. "The 'Kit-Cat' Portraits" and "Kneller as Painter." *Connoisseur* 115, no. 496:124–125.

Discussion of Kneller's Kit-Cat portraits is illustrated with photographs of the artist's portraits of Richard Steele and Vanbrugh. Observes that Kneller had a "formula for face painting." "The 'Germanic' expression of the eyes is constant; they are always full and prominent and never set back in shadow. The cheeks are rather 'jowly,' and the features studied are, therefore, seldom strongly characterized." The consequences of this "formula" are discernible in Kneller's rather similar renderings of the countenances of Steele and Vanbrugh.

2 WITTKOWER, RUDOLF. "Pseudo-Palladian Elements in English Neoclassicism." In *England and the Mediterranean Tradition.* Edited by the Warburg and Courtauld Institutes, University of London. London and New York: Oxford University Press. Reprint. In *Palladio and Palladianism.* Compiled by Margot Wittkower. New York: George Braziller, 1974, pp. 159–162, 168–174 passim. (Annotation and page numbers based on 1974 reprint.)

Includes discussion of Vanbrugh's use of Venetian windows at Eastbury, Seaton Delaval, and Grimsthorpe. Records his use of a decorative window and door motif in these houses and others. The motif: "a simple moulded frame which has blocked quoins at regular intervals superimposed on its sides and a compact mass of three or five voussoirs in its lintel."

1946

1 SITWELL, SACHEVERELL. *British Architects and Craftsmen: A Survey of Taste, Design, and Style during Three Centuries, 1600–1830.* New York: Scribner's; London: B. T. Batsford, pp. 82–97. Reprint. London: Pan Books, 1960.

Exuberant, impressionistic descriptions of Castle Howard, The Queen's Theatre at the Haymarket, Blenheim Palace, Seaton Delaval, and Grimsthorpe. British architecture's "most extraordinary genius," Vanbrugh is characterized as "Baroque without the ornament." His medievalisms are averred to have been stimulated by the medieval trappings he observed at Hanover in 1706 in the ceremonial investiture of the future George II with the Order of the Garter.

1947

1 BOYS, RICHARD C. "The Architect Vanbrugh and the Wits." *College Art Journal* 6, no. 1 (Summer):283–290.

A compendium of eighteenth-century criticisms of the architect's buildings, concluding that "not many kind words about Vanbrugh's architecture got into print in his own time." Typical is Pope's criticism of Blenheim Palace: "I never saw so great a thing with so much littleness in it."

2 MIGNON, ELISABETH. "Vanbrugh." In *Crabbed Age and Youth: The Old Men and Women in the Restoration Comedy of Manners.* Durham, N.C.: Duke University Press, pp. 132–159.

In *The Relapse* Vanbrugh added three aged characters—Sir Tunbelly Clumsy, the Nurse, and Coupler—not present in Cibber's *Love's Last Shift*. His substitution of the noisy and irascible Sir Tunbelly for Cibber's less seriously flawed elder character Sir William Wisewou'd is characteristic of Vanbrugh's tendency, particularly evident in the adaptations, to heighten the conflict between young and old. In *Aesop, The False Friend, The Pilgrim* and to a lesser extent in *The Confederacy*, Vanbrugh is shown to have altered the structure and the dialogue of his sources in ways that coarsened or hardened the portraits of aged characters and thereby rendered them contemptible to youth.

3 WEBB, G. F. "Baroque Art." Annual Lecture on Aspects of Art. *Proceedings of the British Academy* 33:130–148 passim.

Notes Vanbrugh's mention of Hugh May's pseudo-medieval remodeling of Windsor Castle apropos of his own medievalisms in the remodeling of Kimbolton Castle. Cites Vanbrugh's "knowledge of up-to-date French examples" of Baroque architecture and his "influence" on the baroque proclivities of the Office of Works during his tenure there. Concerning the relative contributions of Vanbrugh and Hawksmoor to the "new manner of the Office of Works," thinks Hawksmoor supplied "the geometry of architectural forms," Vanbrugh a "romantic and picturesque quality," though each borrowed from the other in his independent designs. Suggests that Salvator Rosa's landscape painting influenced Vanbrugh's picturesque siting of his buildings. His "commendation of the English edition of Pozzo's *Perspective*" is cited as evidence of Vanbrugh's interest as architect in Italian theatrical designers' explorations of perspective.

1948

1 ARKELL, W. J. "The Building-stones of Blenheim Palace, Cornbury Park, Glympton Park and Heythrop House, Oxfordshire." *Oxoniensia* 13:49–54.

Describes the composition and condition of Blenheim's stone—a "cream-colored yellow oolitic freestone," weathered to "a golden yellow on the surface," containing "fragments and whole species of large fossil sea urchins or sand-dollars." The stone's composition is consonant with Vanbrugh's testimony that it was quarried from Cornbury and Glympton. Surmises that the Glympton stone was "a poor variety" which subsequently decayed "where used externally"; hence replaced in the nineteenth century by Bath stone.

2 CLARK, H. F. *The English Landscape Garden*. London: Pleiades, pp. 21, 39, 54–58 passim, plates 32–34, 42–45, 47, 49–50.

Thinks Vanbrugh's "great talent" as a landscape architect "was in the composition of great vistas, and the placing of . . . organized woodlands." Calls Castle Howard's landscape "picturesque in its best and original sense" (a point illustrated in two photographs and an "Engraving from a painting by William Marlowe, 1787"). Notes Vanbrugh's contributions to the landscaping of Claremont (illustrated by an "Engraving from a painting by Geo. Barrett, R.A., 1779") and his garden temples at Stowe (engravings and drawings include the "Witch's House," the Vanbrugh/Bridgeman plan of 1739, a "View from the Brick Temple in Vanbrugh's Garden," and "The Queen's Theatre from the Rotunda by Vanbrugh").

3 RITCHARD, CYRIL. Introduction to *The Relapse*. London: Peter Nevill, pp. 5–10.

The actor very briefly describes *The Relapse*, its stage history, and the personal experiences that preceded his appearance as Lord Foppington in Anthony Quayle's 1948 production at the Phoenix Theatre, London.

4 SMITH, JOHN HARRINGTON. *The Gay Couple in Restoration Comedy*. Cambridge, Mass.: Harvard University Press, 1948, pp. 173–175. Reprint. New York: Farrar, Straus & Giroux, Octagon Books, 1971.

The subplot of *The Relapse* occasionally parodies *Romeo and Juliet*. Chaste Amanda's triumph over libertine Worthy in the main plot is to be taken seriously, *pace* Bernbaum (1925.3). Heartfree and Belinda in *The Provoked Wife* are "gay in the best traditional pattern," *pace* Palmer's assertion (1913.1) that in Vanbrugh "adultery is no longer comic and airy: it is passionate."

5   SWIFT, JONATHAN. *Journal to Stella*. Edited by Harold Williams. Vol. 1. Oxford: At the Clarendon Press, pp. 83–84. Reprint. 1963.
Includes the 7 November 1710 letter (annotated in 1768.1) in which Swift described his "quarrel" with Vanbrugh over his "Verses on his [Goose-Pie] House" (e.g., in 1710.1).

6   WHISTLER, LAURENCE. "Eastbury Park, Dorset: Some Unpublished Designs by Sir John Vanbrugh." *CLife* 104, no. 2711 (December):1386–1389.
Examines a group of Vanbrugh's unpublished designs for Eastbury, comparing them to the "New Design for a Person of Quality in Dorset" published by Campbell in *Vitruvius Britannicus*. Concludes that Vanbrugh "began rather small and arrived at the 'New Design' by expansion." Speculates that George Doddington balked at the cost of executing the "New Design," whereupon Vanbrugh reduced the building's size. (Material is incorporated into 1954.5.)

7   WHISTLER, LAURENCE. "Some Unpublished Drawings of Sir John Vanbrugh. 1.—Vanbrugh's Design for Glympton." *NER* 1, no. 4 (December):250–256.
Announces the discovery of three previously unknown drawings, dating from c. 1714, for Vanbrugh's proposed refacing of Glympton Manor, Oxfordshire. The building, owned by Sir Thomas Wheate, lay four miles North of Blenheim Palace, for which Wheate's quarry supplied stone. Vanbrugh's discovery that Wheate's Glympton stone was of poor quality, together with his quarrel with the Duchess of Marlborough in 1716 (a quarrel that ended his working visits to Woodstock), is proposed as the likely explanation of Vanbrugh's failure to execute his plans for Glympton Manor. (Material is incorporated into 1954.5.)

1949

1   BOYS, RICHARD C. "Sir Joshua Reynolds and the Architect Van Brugh: A Footnote to Boswell." *Papers of the Michigan Academy of Science, Arts and Letters*. 33:323–336.
Argues that the Palladian revival precipitated a decline in Vanbrugh's reputation as an architect that continued until the later eighteenth century. In the last quarter of the century first Robert Adam,

and afterwards William Gilpin, Uvedale Price, and, most influentially, Sir Joshua Reynolds, hailed Vanbrugh's buildings, finding his designs rich in imagination and picturesquely irregular.

2   CARO, RACHEL. "Opera in Haymarket." *CLife* 105, no. 2716 (February):252–253.
    Includes a paragraph describing the theatre as Vanbrugh built it and two paragraphs on the theatre's evolution into a venue for opera performance.

3   GREEN, DAVID, and HUSSEY, CHRISTOPHER. "Blenheim Palace Re-visited: The East Wing." *CLife* 105, no. 2732 (May):1246–1250.
    Discusses the suite of rooms Vanbrugh designed for the private use of the Duke and Duchess of Marlborough. There were seven rooms in the suite, located on the main floor of the east wing, the Duke and Duchess each having "a bedroom, dressing-room, and sitting-room," and the Duke a reception-room in the southeast tower. The Duchess's sitting room, the Bow Window Room with its columns carved by Grinling Gibbons, served as the central unit, though "not . . . entirely assimilated into the vast rectangular composition."

4   GREEN, DAVID, and HUSSEY, CHRISTOPHER. "Blenheim Palace Re-visited: Grinling Gibbons at Blenheim." *CLife* 105, no. 2731 (May):1182–1186.
    Documents and illustrates Grinling Gibbons's work at Blenheim. Examines Gibbons's bills for services rendered, pronouncing that his stone work, most of it on the roof, includes trophies, vases, statues, capitals, and finials. The paucity of wood carvings in the building's interior is attributed to the Duchess of Marlborough's wish "to have things plain and clean" in her residences. Author argues that plans for "the chief chimney pieces" and "finials for the all-important skyline" were dictated by Vanbrugh and his assistant Hawksmoor, with the result that at Blenheim, Gibbons was "transformed . . . to a sculptor of militaristic baroque."

5   HINTON, DENYS. "Architects Built Their Own Stage to Suit Vanbrugh's *Provok'd Wife.* . . ." *Drama: The Quarterly Theatre Review*, n.s. 15 (Winter):25.
    Describes the set constructed for a production of *The Provoked Wife* by the Architectural Association School of Architecture. An altogether free-standing structure, the set was mounted on an aluminum scaffolding, changes of scene being effected by the drawing of sliding flats across a false proscenium opening. The false proscenium "provided a generous apron flanked with the traditional proscenium doors

and [two tiers of] stage boxes . . . filled with costumed playgoers.
. . ."

6 PEVSNER, NIKOLAUS. "Richard Payne Knight." *Art Bulletin*
31:294–295.
Proposes that Vanbrugh Castle (begun in 1717) is the first asym-
metrically designed house of its era—without successor until Walpole
began his gothic castle at Strawberry Hill in 1750. As possible influences on Vanbrugh's "medievalising lack of regularity" at Vanbrugh
Castle, cites "Medieval Chester where Vanbrugh grew up," the towers
he would have seen "everywhere" in France, and Italian-style stage
architecture (e.g., Inigo Jones's "[r]ound towers with machiola-
tions"). (Cf. 1950.11.)

7 [POPE, ALEXANDER]. "A Master Key to Popery." In John Butt,
"'A Master Key to Popery'" (Butt's introduction followed by text
of Pope's "Master Key"). In *Pope and His Contemporaries: Essays
Presented to George Sherburn*. Edited by James L. Clifford and Louis
A. Landa. New York: Oxford University Press, p. 56. Reprinted in
The Poems of Alexander Pope. Edited by John Butt. Vol. 3, Part 2.
Epistles to Several Persons (Moral Essays). Edited by F. W. Bateson.
London: Methuen; New Haven: Yale University Press, 1951, p. 181.
(Annotation based on 1951 reprint.)
Privately circulated but never printed in Pope's day. Includes the
following elucidation of "Timon's Villa" (in Pope's *Epistle to Burling-
ton*, ll. 109–110): "I know that the Building describ'd to be so huge,
so like a Quarry, such a Heap, &c. is the Immortal Castle of Blenheim
(to which the Spite of a Papist may well be imagin'd) and I know
my Lord F——th will be of my opinion. And possibly had not the
Duke of Shrewsbury been once a Papist, he wou'd never have call'd
it a *Quarry of Stone above-ground* [cf. 1956.7]: That well known
saying of his fixes this to Blenheim." Bateson comments (p. 68),
"Although unsigned, there can be no doubt that ["A Master Key"] is
by Pope."

8 WATSON, F. J. B. "Roger Morris and Eastbury." *CLife* 105, Part 1,
no. 2717 (February):317–318.
Reproduces a drawing of Eastbury prepared c. 1733 by Roger
Morris. Depicts Eastbury's garden front with hexagonal pyramids top-
ping the pavilions. At the top of the drawing appears the following

inscription: "This Building was built by Sr John vanbrugh in Dorsetshire for Mr Dodington. I finished the work by a contract for 9,000 [pounds]."

9 WHISTLER, LAURENCE. "Newly Discovered Vanbrugh Designs for Claremont." *CLife* 105, no. 2719 (February):426–427.
    Prints the plan and elevation of Vanbrugh's house at Esher and discusses its transformation into Clarmont House following Vanbrugh's sale of the property to his friend the Duke of Newcastle sometime between 1711 and 1715. The transformation was effected by Vanbrugh's addition of wings to the original house, keeping the "forecourt . . . shallow, the grouping broad so that the original house [might] be as little diminished as possible." Material is incorporated into 1954.5.

10 WHISTLER, LAURENCE. "Three Newly Discovered Designs for Kimbolton Castle Remodelled by Vanbrugh and Hawksmoor, 1707–1709." *NER* 2, no. 5 (May):332–336.
    Discusses three previously unpublished drawings related to Vanbrugh's designs for Kimbolton Castle: (1) an early proposal for the building's fallen south front—drawn perhaps to persuade Lady Manchester of the desirability of having a central door and central saloon two stories in height; (2) an early proposal for the east portico; and (3) a part-elevation of the west front in which the awkwardly unemphatic placement of two rectangular windows above the arches suggests that Vanbrugh was here preserving an earlier feature of the building's design—this apparently in fulfillment of Manchester's wish that "this relatively unimportant front be brought into harmony with the rest as cheaply as possible." (Material is incorporated into 1954.5.)

11 WHISTLER, LAURENCE. "Unpublished Drawings for Castle Howard." *NER* 3, no. 1 (July):27–33.
    Prints and attributes "to Vanbrugh or to Hawksmoor" a previously unpublished bird's-eye-view drawing of Castle Howard, evidently an early version of the bird's-eye engraving published in vol. III of Campbell's *Vitruvius Britannicus* (1715–1725.1). Also printed and discussed is Hawksmoor's drawing for the "West front of the great Cabinet" at Castle Howard, a drawing in which one sees Hawksmoor "translating Vanbrugh's big ideas into detailed instructions." Together with Vanbrugh's 26 March 1724 letter urging Carlisle to complete Castle Howard's garden front, the drawing is said to offer "almost conclusive evidence" that the front in question was indeed "completed by Vanbrugh and afterwards altered by [Sir Thomas] Robinson." (Material is incorporated into 1954.5.)

1950

1   COLVIN, HOWARD. "Fifty New Churches." *AR* 107, no. 639 (March):189–196.

Describes the results of the Act of 1711 whereby a tax on coal was levied for the erection of fifty new churches in London and Westminster. Compares the "shrewd commonsense" of Wren's recommendations for the building project to the "enthusiastic rhetoric" of the "Proposals" Vanbrugh offered. Concludes that Vanbrugh's recommendations prevailed over Wren's. The result: much of the revenue allotted for the project was consumed by the erection of grand porticos and towers for the London churches. More churches might have been built, churches better fitted "to the needs of Protestant worship," had Wren prevailed. (See also 1950.10.)

2   *DARLINGTON, W. A. Review of revival of *The Provoked Wife*. *Daily Telegraph*, 23 March.

Source: Coleman, 1982.2, p. 20; unverified. Coleman cites opinion of reviewer of Arts Theatre Club (London) revival of *The Provoked Wife* that although the play's "wit" is inferior to that of Congreve's comedies, Vanbrugh's play "has two other qualities even more valuable on the stage—gusto and a sense of theatre." Reviewer thinks Myles Eason plays Heartfree with an appropriate "lightness and gaiety."

3   DEAN, C. G. T. *The Royal Hospital, Chelsea*. London, New York, Melbourne, Sydney, Capetown: Hutchinson, pp. 202–205.

Quotes from Vanbrugh's letter to Robert Walpole of 17 October 1715 (1928.11) by way of documenting Vanbrugh's responsibility for carrying out alterations of Walpole's "Treasurer's Lodgings" near the Royal Hospital, Chelsea. Notes that Vanbrugh had been knighted "[t]hrough Walpole's influence" the year before. Attributes to Vanbrugh Walpole's octagonal summer house—Walpole House (which stood "where no. 23 Embankment Gardens now stands") and to Vanbrugh as well the "L-shaped 'Greenhouse,' or Orangery, which overlooks the terrace near the Nurses Home."

4   DUGDALE, GEORGE S. *Whitehall through the Centuries*. London: Phoenix House, pp. 112–113, 153.

Mentions Vanbrugh's Goose-Pie House, built on "the site of the Vice-Chancellor's lodgings, burnt down in 1698." The house is illustrated in an engraving of c. 1810. Also notes Vanbrugh's 1719 plea for the preservation of Whitehall's ancient Holbein Gate, whose narrowness obstructed traffic. Quotes from Vanbrugh's alternative proposal ("carried out" in 1723) that the "wall of the Privy Garden" be "open[ed]."

5 GREEN, DAVID. "Blenheim Column of Victory." *AR* 107, no. 640 (April):271–274.

Describes the building history of the triumphal column Vanbrugh had wished to erect at Blenheim Palace. Following Vanbrugh's dismissal in 1716, the project was executed under Hawksmoor's supervision.

6 GREEN, DAVID. *Blenheim Palace.* Oxford: Alden Press, 35 pp. Reprint. 1951, 1952, and frequently thereafter.

A guidebook for the visitor, offering descriptions (illustrated by photographs) of the building's interior and exterior, its stone and roofs. Discusses Vanbrugh's relations with the Duke and Duchess of Marlborough.

7 GREEN, DAVID. "Visitors to Blenheim." *CLife* 107, no. 2773 (March):648–651.

Records the impressions of early visitors to Blenheim, among them Lady Wentworth, a German tourist (who compared the building to a theatre), and Canon Stratford, who grew so weary of showing the building to guests that he wished to "raze it to the ground." Other of the building's early visitors whose impressions are reported were Peter Wentworth, Thomas Hearne, Daniel Defoe, the Earl of Carlisle, Voltaire, the Adam brothers, Horace Walpole, Samuel Johnson, James Boswell, George III, and Lord Nelson, who visited the building in the company of Sir William and Lady Hamilton.

8 GREEN, DAVID. "The Vogue of Vanbrugh." *CLife* 107, no. 2785 (June):1648–1653.

Impressionistic description of Kings Weston and (in more detail) the interior of Seaton Delaval. Notes the buildings' present conditions—Kings Weston converted to a school, Seaton Delaval gutted by fire in 1822 and occupied for nine years during World War II by soldiers and prisoners of war. Vanbrugh treated the "Men of quality" for whom he built as "jewels to be set" in their houses "with cunning." Author regards the current Vanbrugh vogue as evidence of "enthusiasm for buildings that are less functional than flamboyant"; eight illustrations.

1950

9 LANG, S. "History": "Amongst various drawings for Castle Howard in the British Museum. . . ." *AR* 108, no. 644 (August):129–130.
      Discusses and reproduces a British Museum drawing for the "west
   front of the 'Great Cabinet'" of Castle Howard. Surmises that here
   Hawksmoor drew what Vanbrugh dictated—a bow window and two
   crowning cupolas for one end of Castle Howard's west range. Finds
   in the drawing "proof of the accuracy of the engravings in *Vitruvius
   Britannicus*" (1715–1725.1). Suggests that erection of Castle Howard
   commenced with "the east wing (the office wing) and the east part of
   the south range. . . ."

10 "Mr. Van-Brugg's Proposals." *AR* 107, no. 639 (March):209–210.
      Prints and briefly discusses Vanbrugh's proposals for the building
   of fifty new churches in London and Westminster. (See also 1950.1
   and Appendix E in Downes, 1977.2, where Vanbrugh's proposals are
   also printed.)

11 PEVSNER, NIKOLAUS. "Good King James's Gothic." *AR* 107,
   no. 638 (February):117–122.
      Draws attention to similarities of plan among several Vanbrugh
   houses and several Elizabethan and Jacobean ones. Plans of Chas-
   tleton, Sir John Danvers's house at Chelsea, and Stanton Court are
   compared to those of Vanbrugh's Seaton Delaval, Vanbrugh ("Mince-
   Pie") House, and Vanbrugh Castle respectively. Conclusion: Vanbrugh was "the pioneer of an Elizabethan Revival."

12 *Review of revival of *The Provoked Wife*. *The Times* [London], 23
   March.
      Source: Coleman, 1982.2, p. 20; unverified. Reviewer of Arts
   Theatre Club (London) revival of *The Provoked Wife* suggests that
   "What is needed to bring out [the] diverting quality" of the play's
   conversations "is not an affectation of period style but a respectfully
   close attention to the meaning of [Vanbrugh's] natural and straight-
   forward dialogue."

13 WHISTLER, LAURENCE. "The Authorship of the Stowe Temples."
   CLife 108, no. 2802 (September):1002–1006.
      Prints and discusses a number of drawings, principally of Stowe's
   garden buildings, by James Gibbs. On the basis of those drawings,
   assigns Stowe's "Boycott Pavilions" (and incidentally the stable block
   of Compton Verney) to Gibbs rather than Vanbrugh. After examining
   Bridgeman's (1720–1725) aerial drawing of the Stowe gardens and adducing published eighteenth-century guides to Stowe, concludes that
   Vanbrugh's contributions to Stowe's garden architecture include the

Rotunda, Nelson's Seat, the Keeper's Lodge, the Temple of Sleep, the Great Pyramid, two lake pavilions (attributed to Vanbrugh "with some reserve"), and possibly the "Witch's House." All but the last are illustrated. (See also Seeley's illustrations in 1750.4.) (Material is incorporated into 1954.5.)

1951

1 GREEN, DAVID. *Blenheim Palace*. London: Country Life, 348 pp.
An affectionately detailed history of the building of Blenheim Palace, described by the author as the "Marlborough–Vanbrugh tragicomedy"; profusely illustrated.

2 *HUSSEY, CHRISTOPHER. *English Country Houses Open to the Public*. London: Country Life. Rev. eds. 1953, 1957, 1964.
For annotation, see 1964.5.

3 PIOZZI, HESTER LYNCH THRALE. *Thraliana: The Diary of Mrs. Hester Lynch Thrale (Later Mrs. Piozzi), 1776–1809*. Edited by Katherine C. Balterston. Volume 1, *1776–1784*; Volume 2, *1784–1809*. 2d ed. Oxford: Clarendon Press, 1:349 (& n. 2), 351, 518; 2:986n.1.
Includes the following references to Vanbrugh: (1) quotation of Thrale's poetic "Tale for the Times" is accompanied by "confess[ion]" that her verses are "imitated from Vanbrugh"—whose "wild irregular Measure ['I learnt it in Vanbrugh's Esop'] is a sort of Favourite with me. . ."; (2) quotation of Peter Cox's poem on David Garrick in which the actor's performance in the role of Sir John Brute is mentioned in passing; and (3) passing reference to Sir Francis Wronghead in Vanbrugh and Cibber's *The Provoked Husband*. For citation of 1st ed., see 1942.2.

4 WHISTLER, LAURENCE. "Vanbrugh Buildings at Stowe." *CLife* 109, no. 2817 (January):119.
Adds to the list of Vanbrugh temples at Stowe discussed in 1950.13 two additional Vanbrugh buildings, both demolished: "the Cold Bath, very plain, with a heavily rusticated door," and "Dido's Cave, with a rusticated arch below the scrolled pediment and vase." Offers additional information concerning the Keeper's Lodge, including a photograph showing the building's later accretions. (Material is incorporated into 1954.5.)

1952

1 AVERY, EMMETT L. "The Capacity of the Queen's Theatre in the Haymarket." *PQ* 31, no. 1 (January):85–87.

Estimates the theatre's capacity at 700 in 1710, and more than 1,300 in 1728 (a figure subsequently revised by the author to 900 plus footmen in the upper gallery; see *London Stage*, Part 2, "Introduction," I, xxvi–xxix, and Milhous's estimates in 1984.9).

2 BERKELEY, DAVID S. "The Penitent Rake in Restoration Comedy." *MP* 49, no. 4 (May):223–233 passim.

Worthy's "airy 'platonic'" conversion in *The Relapse* places him among the twenty-three penitent rakes who appear in British comedy of the late seventeenth century.

3 KRONENBERGER, LOUIS. *The Thread of Laughter: Chapters on English Stage Comedy from Jonson to Maugham.* New York: Hill & Wang, pp. 147–165.

Laments that the two plots of *The Relapse* are "unrelated." The Amanda–Loveless plot "lacks the right mixture of urbanity and brutality," Berinthia proving "utterly treacherous," Amanda becoming "almost Victorian." The Fashion–Foppington underplot is "the successful plot, the one that we enjoy," the bearer of "a quite new sort of bustle and joviality." The superiority of *The Provoked Wife* to *The Relapse* lies in its greater unity, though Lady Brute's "moral dilemma" diminishes the play's "fun" without adding a compensating thematic "significance." *The Confederacy*, Vanbrugh's "best play," reveals "in how great a degree he just *was* a playwright rather than a social critic or student of manners."

4 SUMMERSON, JOHN. Review of Donald Green, *Blenheim Palace* (1951.1). *New Statesman and Nation* 43, no. 1101 (April):438–439.

Speculates on the Lord Chamberlain's reasons for issuing a warrant in 1697 authorizing Vanbrugh to build himself a home on the ruins of Whitehall Palace—"Possibly" a reward for Vanbrugh's "Secret missions to France." Thinks the similarity of Vanbrugh's design for Castle Howard to one of Wren's unexecuted plans for Greenwich Hospital suggests that he had "moved in the circle of the Board [of Works] officers" for some time before receiving his 1697 warrant. Finds in Blenheim's "movement" evidence that Vanbrugh devised the building "in opposition to something"—to Wren's classicism, perhaps, which Vanbrugh may have sought to subdue with his own "wild, 'Elizabethan' sense of architectural comedy."

5 WHISTLER, LAURENCE. "Blenheim: An English Palace, with Some Early Designs by Sir John Vanbrugh." *History Today* 2, no. 2 (February):113–125.

Proposes that Vanbrugh's Whig friends Carlisle and Manchester may have recommended Vanbrugh to Marlborough for the Blenheim Palace commission (but cites too the Duchess of Marlborough's testimony that it was James Craggs who did so). Describes Vanbrugh's siting of the building, the evolution of his plans for its execution, and the critique of Vanbrugh's design for the saloon which Marlborough secured from the French artist Louis Sylvester in 1707. (Material is incorporated into 1954.5.)

6 WHISTLER, LAURENCE. "Ordnance Vanbrugh: Military Buildings in the Vanbrugh-Hawksmoor Manner." *AR* 112, no. 672 (December):376–382.

A number of ordnance buildings at Woolwich, Berwick-on-Tweed, and elsewhere may have been designed by Vanbrugh. Examples: the Royal Military Academy in the ordnance depot at Woolwich possesses a bow window reminiscent of one Vanbrugh had deployed at Blenheim; at Chatham the red brick archway of the Royal Naval Dockyard's main gate resembles the archways of the two gates Vanbrugh devised for his family's castellar compound at Greenwich. The presence in the Public Record Office of an elevation and plan of Vanbrugh's Temple of Bacchus at Stowe among a collection of plans and elevations of ordnance buildings drawn by ordnance cadets between 1780 and 1781 increases the likelihood that Vanbrugh had a hand in the buildings in question. (Material is incorporated into *Imagination*, 1954.5.)

7 WHISTLER, LAURENCE. "Talman and Vanbrugh: Episodes in an Architectural Rivalry." *CLife* 112, no. 2914:1648–1652.

Describes the competition between Vanbrugh and Talman for the commission to build Castle Howard for the Earl of Carlisle and rebuild Welbeck for the Duke of Newcastle. Both Vanbrugh and Talman, the established architect, submitted designs for the two projects. Vanbrugh won the Castle Howard commission after Talman quarreled with Carlisle over the bill for his designs. When the quarrel ended in litigation, Vanbrugh advised Newcastle of the matter in a letter of 15 June 1703 in which he sought to discredit his rival for the Welbeck project. Though Newcastle decided against rebuilding Welbeck, he and Vanbrugh remained on cordial terms. (Material is incorporated into 1954.5.)

1953

1 *BERGMANN, FREDERICK LOUIS. "David Garrick, Producer: A Study of Garrick's Alterations of Non-Shakespearean Plays." Ph.D. dissertation, George Washington University.

Source: Coleman, 1982.2, pp. 15, 45n. 23; unverified. Coleman records author's conclusion that Garrick's alterations of Vanbrugh's *Provoked Wife* "trivialise the play's intellectual content."

2 BOAS, FREDERICK S. *An Introduction to Eighteenth-Century Drama, 1700–1780*. Oxford: Clarendon Press, pp. 96–99, 351–352.

Discusses Cibber's transformation of Vanbrugh's fragmentary *Journey to London* into *The Provoked Husband*, noting that the change of title suggests Cibber was more "attracted" to Vanbrugh's Loverule plot than to the Headpiece plot. Suggests that when Cibber published his version of the play he simultaneously published Vanbrugh's fragment in "self-defense"—this to demonstrate to the public that the Wronghead/Headpiece scenes (hissed by his audience on the assumption that they were Cibber's) were in fact Vanbrugh's, while the Townly scenes (applauded because they were assumed to be Vanbrugh's) were the ones Cibber had most extensively altered. Concerning Sheridan's 1776 adaptation of *The Relapse* as *A Trip to Scarborough*, observes that Sheridan's alterations were minimal—some name changes, some cuts in the dialogue, and the omission of the "blank verse passages, a song, and the masque in Sir Tunbelly's house." Sheridan's work "now would be considered sheer plagiarism," his only allusion to his source being the cryptic remark in his prologue that "Some plays most justly call for alteration;/At least to draw some slender covering o'er/That *graceless wit* which was too bare before." The italicized lines are glossed as an "echo of Pope's '[How] Van wants grace who never wanted wit.'"

3 GOTCH, CHRISTOPHER. "Mylne and Kings Weston." *CLife* 113, no. 2923 (January):212–215.

After noting that Vanbrugh's renovations of Kings Weston remained unfinished at his death, describes and illustrates Robert Mylne's "substantial work" on the building "from 1763 onwards."

4 *LYNCH JAMES J. *Box, Pit and Gallery: Stage and Society in Johnson's London*. Berkeley and Los Angeles: University of California Press, p. 41.

Sources: *NUC* and Coleman, 1982.2, pp. 12, 45n. 17; unverified. Coleman quotes Lynch's conclusion that Vanbrugh was the "most frequently revived author" of the eighteenth century. His *The Mistake*,

The Confederacy, *The False Friend*, *Aesop*, *The Provoked Wife*, and *The Relapse* were all revived, *The Relapse* and *The Provoked Wife* "being among the most popular plays of the period." Plays written by Vanbrugh and Farquhar were performed on "15 percent of the evenings devoted to comedy" on the London stage of Samuel Johnson's day.

5 SUMMERSON, JOHN. *Architecture in Britain 1530-1830*. Melbourne, London, and Baltimore: Penguin, pp.164-177, 262, 239. Rev. eds. 1955, 1958, 1963, 1969.

Discusses Vanbrugh's architectural career. It may have commenced with his close-hand observation of (and perhaps participation in) Wren's development of plans for a new Palace of Whitehall in 1699. Examines the "Hawksmoor-Vanbrugh partnership" ("mass became their passion"). Discusses and illustrates with photographs Goose-Pie House, Castle Howard, Blenheim, Kings Weston, Seaton Delaval, and Grimsthorpe. Notes that at Blenheim and elsewhere Vanbrugh "had a feeling, rare at his time, for the qualities of the medieval fortress." Cites Vanbrugh's efforts to save Whitehall's ancient Holbein Gate and the old Manor House at Woodstock from demolition. Notes the influence of Vanbrugh's "movement" on Robert Adam's notions of building. Commentary on Vanbrugh is not altered in later editions.

6 WHISTLER, LAURENCE. "The Evolution of Castle Howard." *CLife* 113, no. 2924 (January):276-279.

Examines Vanbrugh's succession of plans and elevations for Castle Howard. Notes "Hawksmoor's touch" in the "ornaments sketched above the door" in the earliest extant elevation of the north front—evidence that Hawksmoor assisted Vanbrugh in the project even in its earliest stages. (Material is incorporated into 1954.5.)

1954

1 COLVIN, H. M. *A Biographical Dictionary of English Architects, 1660-1840*. Cambridge, Mass.: Harvard University Press, pp. 634-641.

Surveys Vanbrugh's career as soldier, playwright, herald, and architect. Believes that his "baroque" style is inspired neither by Italian nor German models and relies but little on "such conventional baroque devices as the cleft pediment and the use of false perspective." Rather Vanbrugh's buildings achieve their sense of "movement" through "the grouping of masses and the skillful handling of recession and projection," their "chief influences" being the painted landscapes of Claude

Lorrain and Salvator Rosa. Concludes with a list of buildings Vanbrugh is known to have built or altered, followed by citations of pertinent critical commentary. In the revised *Biographical Dictionary* (1980.4) a reference to Vanbrugh's "highly personal" style is deleted, replaced by a reference to his "collaboration" with Hawksmoor.

2 PEDICORD, HARRY WILLIAM. *The Theatrical Public in the Time of Garrick.* New York: King's Crown Press, Columbia University, pp. 198-199, 204-207, 210-213, 216-217, 220-223, 226-227, 230-233.

Includes tabulation of Drury Lane performances of Vanbrugh's original plays and adaptations during the period 1747-1776. *The Provoked Wife* received 95 performances (Garrick playing the part of Sir John 93 times), *The Relapse*—21 performances, *The Mistake*—19, *Aesop*—7, *The Pilgrim*—4, *The False Friend*—1, *The Provoked Husband* (Vanbrugh/Cibber)—51, *The Confederacy*—20.

3 Review of Whistler, *The Imagination of Vanbrugh and His Fellow Artists* (1954.5). *Connoisseur* 134, no. 540 (November):134.

Avers that "from Whistler's exact and informed volume emerges a new vision of Hawksmoor as being nothing less 'than Vanbrugh's equal.'"

4 WEBB, GEOFFREY. "Vanbrugh." Review of Whistler, *The Imagination of Sir John Vanbrugh* (1954.5). *Apollo* 60, no. 355 (September):71-72.

Attempts to distinguish Hawksmoor's manner from Vanbrugh's. Speculates that at Castle Howard and Blenheim, Vanbrugh contributed a "picturesque romantic quality which seems to derive from the scenery of the opera or the heroic play," while Hawksmoor supplied "virtuosity in planning" and an interest in "grandiose composition"— the latter whetted by his reading of Perrault's "French edition of Vitruvius." Further contrasts Hawksmoor's "very plain and massive window dressings" to the more Italian window dressings Vanbrugh deployed in his independent work at Eastbury and elsewhere.

5 WHISTLER, LAURENCE. *The Imagination of Vanbrugh and His Fellow Arists.* London: B. T. Batsford, 323 pp.

Includes chapters (supplemented by 146 illustrations) on Castle Howard, Blenheim Palace, Kimbolton Castle, Claremont, Eastbury, Stowe (whose gardens were Bridgeman and Vanbrugh's joint productions), the smaller "embattled" houses Vanbrugh devised for his own habitation, and the military buildings at Woolwich, Berwick-on-Tweed, and elsewhere that he may have designed between 1716 and 1721. His "Proposals for the Fifty Churches" (1711) are printed in an appendix, as are twenty-three letters not printed in *Works*, IV (1928.11). Vanbrugh's collaborator Hawksmoor is judged to be "more than the assistant and less than the equal partner." (Incorporates material from 1948.6, 1948.7, 1949.9, 1949.10, 1949.11, 1950.13, 1951.4, 1952.5, 1952.6, 1952.7, 1953.6, and 1954.6.)

6   WHISTLER, LAURENCE. "Vanbrugh's Smaller Houses." *AR* 115, no. 686 (February):118–122.

Discusses the "toy castles" Vanbrugh built for himself at Whitehall, Esher, and Maize Hill in Greenwich. (Author incorporates this material into *Imagination*, 1954.5).

1955

1   BERKELEY, DAVID S. "*Préciosité* and the Restoration Comedy of Manners." *HLQ* 18, no. 2 (February):109–128 passim.

Worthy's "Sure there's divinity about her" soliloquy in the last act of *The Relapse* is among the examples cited in evidence of a "vogue" of "préciosité" in later seventeenth-century comedy. ("Préciosité" is defined as "a form of ceremonious social intercourse which derived its attitudes, postures, and special vocabulary from the belief that beautiful and virtuous ladies have a semi-divine status. . . .")

2   HERRICK, GEORGE H. "Vanbrugh's Battle of Blenheim: Sir John's Experience with a Lady Client." *Journal of the American Institute of Architects* 23, no. 3 (March):117–121.

A retelling of the story of Vanbrugh's quarrel with the Duchess over the building of Blenheim Palace.

3   KAUFMANN, EMIL. *Architecture in the Age of Reason: Baroque and Post-Baroque in England, Italy, and France.* Cambridge, Mass.: Harvard University Press. Reprint. New York: Dover, 1968, pp. 5–6, 16–18, 55, 219 n.15. (Annotation and page references based on 1968 reprint.)

"Perfect grouping through concatenation and gradation" characterize Vanbrugh's Baroque "first manner" as he deployed it at Castle Howard and Blenheim. His "second manner" revolts against "inherited modes." Goose-Pie House is cited in evidence, its "dissonances" being among the "first manifestations" of a "momentous movement of artistic reorientation" in the architecture of the later eighteenth century. Other "second manner" dissonances are noted at Kings Weston, Eastbury, and Seaton Delaval, the last illustrated by an engraving from

1955-1956

Campbell (1715-1725.1). Reynolds (1797.2) and Soane (1929.2) are quoted in praise of Vanbrugh.

4 REED, ALAN. Review of Whistler, *The Imagination of Vanbrugh and His Fellow Artists* (1954.5). *RIBA Journal* 62, no. 5 (March):214.
Focuses on Whistler's treatment of the Vanbrugh/Hawksmoor partnership. Finds "somewhat abrupt" the author's "conclusion" that Vanbrugh is "a more limited artist than general opinion has allowed."

5 WHIFFEN, MARCUS. "The Shakespeare of Architects." Review of Whistler, *The Imagination of Vanbrugh and His Fellow Artists* (1954.5). *AR* 118, no. 707 (November):331-332.
Noting that Whistler says little concerning Vanbrugh's "imagination," suggests his book "could more truthfully be called *Sir John Vanbrugh: Addenda and Corrigenda*." Praises Whistler's documentation of Vanbrugh's hand in the remodeling of Cholmondeley and in the design of several ordnance buildings.

6 WHINNEY, MARGARET. Review of Whistler, *The Imagination of Vanbrugh and his Fellow Artists* (1954.5). *Burlington Magazine* 97, no. 625 (April):121.
Believes Whistler's book "makes a reasonable case for still regarding Vanbrugh as the imaginative force and Hawksmoor[,] at first at least[,] as the trained instrument through which this force was given material expression." Who was the superior partner in the Hawksmoor/Vanbrugh collaboration? Thinks the question could be answered definitively only "if the precise dates for the designing of Easton Neston (in which Vanbrugh had no hand) and above all for the elevation of it given by Hawksmoor to Colin Campbell for publication in *Vitruvius Britannicus* could be firmly established." Were it determined that the latter preceded "the domed silhouette of Castle Howard," the relative roles of Hawksmoor and Vanbrugh in the Castle Howard and Blenheim designs "might have to be reversed."

1955-1956

1 *HOOKS, NORMAN. "Sir John Vanbrugh: A Revaluation of His Plays." M.A. thesis, University of Liverpool, 138 pp.
Source: Huseboe, 1976.5, p. 167.

1956

1 BEARD, GEOFFREY W. "Castle Howard: Yorkshire Home of Mr. George and Lady Cecelia Howard." *Connoisseur Year Book, 1956*: 3-12.

A building history of Castle Howard, profusely illustrated with photographs. Discusses the progression of Vanbrugh's proposals for the house, noting, for example, that the cupola was "still absent from the second proposal" and was "not built until 1706." (*Year Book*'s table of contents indicates that an illustration of Castle Howard [painted?] by William Marlowe appeared on the issue's "dust cover.")

2 BRACKENBURY, ANTONY. "The Happy Eastbury Circle." *CLife* 119, no. 3086 (March):422-423.

The circle of artists who congregrated at Bubb Doddington's Eastbury House included on various occasions its builder, Vanbrugh, the painter Sir James Thornhill, the poet James Thomson (1746.1), and neighbor poet-rector Christopher Pitt. Both poets celebrated the house and its owner in verse.

3 GREEN, DAVID. *Gardener to Queen Anne: Henry Wise (1653-1738) and the Formal Garden*. London, New York, and Toronto: Oxford University Press, pp. 32, 37-39, 98-100, 137-138, 144-147, 156, 186-187.

Includes passing discussion of Vanbrugh's contributions to the gardens at Stowe, Castle Howard, and Blenheim Palace (cf. 1954.5). Attributes to soldier Vanbrugh the polygonal shape and other martial effects at Blenheim's gardens. Vanbrugh's role in the Duchess of Marlborough's Blenheim litigation is also briefly discussed, as is his appointment in 1715 to the new post of Surveyor of the Gardens and Waters.

4 HUSSEY, CHRISTOPHER. *English Country Houses: Mid-Georgian, 1760-1800*. London: Country Life, pp. 13, 17, 21, 23, 24, 135, 240.

Includes several glancing references to Vanbrugh's influence on the "picturesque" aspects of mid-Georgian architecture. Robert Adam is credited with discovering "the value of the pictorial element in [Vanbrugh's] work."

5 MANIFOLD, J. S. *The Music in English Drama: From Shakespeare to Purcell*. London: Rockliff, pp. 123, 130, 135.

As documentation of the role played by music in drama of the later seventeenth century, cites the references to "Hautboys" and

1957

"Bagpipes" in the wedding preparations in Vanbrugh's *Relapse* V, v. Thinks the "presence" of "fiddles" is implied in the tavern scene at "the Blue Posts" in *The Provoked Wife* III, ii. As evidence that "the guitar [in Vanbrugh's day] was generally held to be an instrument for girls and foreigners," cites the reference to Corinna and her "guitar-master" in *The Confederacy* II, i.

6   PETERSON, WILLIAM M. "Cibber's *She Wou'd, and She Wou'd Not* and Vanbrugh's *Aesop.*" *PQ*, 35, no. 4 (October):429–435.
    Argues that Vanbrugh adapted *Aesop* with Cibber in mind for the title role. Cibber played the part in the Drury Lane production of 1696, and would later borrow material from Vanbrugh's play in preparing *She Wou'd, and She Wou'd Not*. Cibber's Hypolita, like Vanbrugh's Aesop, "pretends to be a suitor for" a young woman whose father has promised her hand to another man.

7   POPE, ALEXANDER. Letter to unidentified correspondent, "Pope to Mrs. ——— ." In *The Correspondence of Alexander Pope*. Vol. 1. *1704–1718*. Edited by George Sherburn. Oxford: At the Clarendon Press, pp. 431–432.
    Records impressions of a visit to Blenheim, Pope averring that he "never saw so great a thing with so much littleness in it." Finds the building's interior arrangements "inhospitable" and "selfish"—reflecting the character of the Marlboroughs, in "compliance" with whose "taste" the "Architect built it." "[S]ome trifling littleness" is said to "destroy every grandeur" within and without. Endorses the Duke of Shrewsbury's verdict that Blenheim is "a great *Quarry of Stones above ground.*" Ed. Sherburn dates the letter "September 1717?" Brownell (1978.1) thinks 1718 "more likely." (For initial publication, see 1735.1.) Cf. Pope's *Epistle to Burlington*: "Lo, what huge heaps of littleness around!/The whole, a labour'd Quarry above ground" (ll. 109–110 in Bateson, ed., *Poems of Alexander Pope*, Vol. 3, Pt. 2, 1951).

1957

1   BATESON, F. W. "Second Thoughts: II, L. C. Knights and Restoration Comedy." *EIC* 7, no. 1 (January):66.
    A reply to L. C. Knights's dismissal of Restoration Comedy in *Explorations* (1946). Among other "Restoration" comic dramatists, cites Vanbrugh as one whose work merits "defense." Vanbrugh is called "a hit-or-miss dramatist whose best scenes have to be disentangled from much perfunctory stuff."

2 COOKE, ROBERT. *West Country Houses: An Illustrated Account of Some Country Houses and Their Owners, in the Counties of Bristol, Gloucester, Somerset and Wiltshire, Being also a Guide to Domestic Architecture from the Reign of Henry II to Victoria*. Clifton, Bristol: Published by the Author at Litfield House, pp. 110–114.

    Includes discussion of Vanbrugh's alterations of Kings Weston for Edward Southwell beginning in 1710. Eight illustrations.

3 HUSSEY, CHRISTOPHER. "Duncombe Park, Yorkshire—II. The Property of the Earl of Feversham." *CLife* 122, no. 3178 (December):1328–1331.

    Discerns Vanbrugh's hand in the design of Duncombe Park and its grounds. Particularly characteristic of Vanbrugh's style are the entrance front's "great Doric order, the central pedimented attic, and the entrance portal," as well as the Ionic rotunda north of the terrace. Concludes that the house was designed collectively by Vanbrugh and William Wakefield, the latter working from an outline sketch prepared by Vanbrugh.

4 PEVSNER, NIKOLAUS. *The Buildings of England*. Vol. 15, *Northumberland*. Harmondsworth, Middlesex: Penguin, pp. 286–289.

    Includes description of Seaton Delaval, whose plan is termed "Palladian" with the addition of towers and turrets. Similarities are noted between Vanbrugh's elevations and those of Piranesi, who is said to share with Vanbrugh a "scorn for homely comforts" and a "passion for the cyclopic" and the "theatrical." Description is reprinted, from 2d ed., 1974.13, in 1986.2.

5 WAIN, JOHN. "Restoration Comedy and Its Modern Critics." In *Preliminary Essays*. London: Macmillan; New York: St. Martin's, p. 27.

    In discussing the tendency of comic dramatists of the later seventeenth century to introduce "random scraps" of Shakespeare's material into their works, suggests that "the Nurse in Vanbrugh's *Relapse* is a tenth-rate copy of the Nurse in *Romeo and Juliet*."

6 WHINNEY, MARGARET, and MILLAR, OLIVER. *English Art, 1625–1714*. Oxford History of English Art. Edited by T. S. R. Boase. Vol. 8. Oxford: At the Clarendon Press, pp. 327–328, 333–335 (and intermittently elsewhere as indicated in index).

    Describes Greenwich Hospital's King William's Court ("apparently designed by Vanbrugh"), calling it "a rather unhappy attempt to change the scale of the [hospital's] design, and so give it an added grandeur." Thinks Vanbrugh's proposed but unexecuted "new scheme for the whole inner part of the hospital" would have stood as "a baroque monument on the grandest scale." The plan of Castle Howard is discussed and illustrated. Believes that "in both the first drawings and in the final evolution of the great domed block rising over a series of grouped outbuildings," Vanbrugh called on Hawksmoor's "technical experience" to "interpret" his "ideas."

7   WHISTLER, LAURENCE. "Stowe in the Making: Some Original Drawings." *CLife* 122 (July):68–71.

Formerly attributed to William Kent, the portico added to the north front of Stowe, Buckinghamshire in the early eighteenth century is here assigned to Vanbrugh. Like the columns of the north portico at Blenheim Palace, the Stowe portico's outer columns are "doubled so as to assert the solidity of the corners." The resultant "shadowy recessing of the center" likewise resembles Vanbrugh's treatment of the porticos he designed for Blenheim Palace and Kings Weston.

1958

1   DAVIES, JOHN. "Sir John Vanbrugh in Chester." *Cheshire Life* 24, no. 12 (December):55.

Proposes that Vanbrugh's father, Giles, moved from London (where John was born) to the port city of Chester the better to pursue his trade as sugar baker (but see Downes's caveat, 1987.4). Reports that John "probably attended Kings School" in Chester. Avers (without adducing evidence) that "in 1683 Vanbrugh went to France, possibly to learn the family sugar business," and that in the course of his "tempestuous career" he "must often have returned to Chester to visit his brothers and sisters." Laments the destruction of the only house he built in Cheshire, Cholmondeley House, of which only a chapel survives.

2   GREEN, DAVID, and RAYSON, THOMAS. "Restoring Blenheim Palace." *CLife* 124, no. 3230 (December):1400–1401.

Describes the restoration of Blenheim's roof, statues, and masonry under the terms of a Historic Buildings Act grant.

3   HOWARD, GEORGE. *Castle Howard*. York and London: Ben Johnson. Published by Castle Howard Estate, 29 pp. Reprint, apparently with slight revision. *1963, *1965, *1972.

A guidebook for visitors, with maps of Castle Howard's grounds and numerous illustrations of the building and its furnishings.

4 PEVSNER, NIKOLAUS. *The Buildings of England*. Vol. 13, *North Somerset and Bristol*. Harmondsworth, Middlesex: Penguin, pp. 362, 469–470.

Kings Weston is described without relish, characterized as "masculine, somewhat forbidding and certainly entirely graceless." The building's most distinctive feature—the arcaded chimneys—is called a "crazy ornament . . . of no use on the roof."

5 ROSENBERG, ALBERT. "A New Mo[ti]ve for the Censorship of Owen Swiney's *The Quacks*." *N & Q*, n.s. 5, no. 9 (September):393–396.

Avers that Vanbrugh had Swiney's three-act farce *The Quacks* (1705.3) censored because it contained satire directed at himself and other Kit-Cat Club members, including particularly vigorous abuse of his friend and publisher Jacob Tonson. Evidence cited includes Swiney's references to censorship in his Prologue to *The Quacks* and barbed references to Vanbrugh in Act II. The latter have their analogue in lines from *The Diverting Post* of April 1705 in which Vanbrugh is referred to as "the Stage's Reformer, Cla[re]n[c]aux"—this in reference to his appointment as Clarenceux King at Arms in the College of Heralds. Author judges to be a less important factor in the dispute Nicoll's (1925.6) explanation that Vanbrugh sought to stop Swiney's Drury Lane performances of *The Quacks* because his own Queen's Theatre was simultaneously "engaged in a rival adaptation" of the Molière play upon which Swiney's was based.

6 SWIFT, JONATHAN. "The History of Vanbrug's House." In *Poems of Jonathan Swift*. Vol. 1. Edited by Harold Williams. 2d ed. Oxford: At the Clarendon Press, pp. 86–88.

Satirical verses on Vanbrugh's house at Whitehall, first printed in 1710.1. "Van's Genius without Thought or Lecture" is said to have "hugely turn[e]d to Architecture." His inspiration for the Whitehall house is traced to his having watched "Miss" build a house of cards. His "Plan" is said to have been borrowed from that of a mud house he saw constructed by "Boys at play." The editor dates the poem "1706." For Swift's other verses on Vanbrugh's house, see 1711.2 and 1958.7 (an early version of the 1711 poem).

7 SWIFT, JONATHAN. "Vanbrug's House. An. 1703. Built from the burnt Ruins of Whitehall." In *Poems of Jonathan Swift*. Vol. 1. Edited by Harold Williams. 2d ed. Oxford: At the Clarendon Press, pp. 78–81.

Early version of "V———'s House" (1711.2; annotated in 1958.8). In a headnote to the poem the editor records that this "earlier

133

1959

version is here printed for the first time, completely and exactly, from Swift's manuscript." (Cf. 1710.1, annotated in 1958.6.)

8 SWIFT, JONATHAN. "V———'s House[,] Built from the Ruins of Whitehall that was Burnt." In *Poems of Jonathan Swift*. Vol. 1. Edited by Harold Williams. 2d ed. Oxford: At the Clarendon Press, pp. 106–110.

Mock heroic verses (first printed in 1711.2) on Vanbrugh's house at Whitehall. The house is compared, owing to its "motly mingled Style," to a "Goose Py" (an epithet which would stick). Includes satirical remarks on Vanbrugh's career as herald and comic dramatist. (See also 1701.1; cf. Swift's other verses on Vanbrugh's house in 1710.1, annotated in 1958.6.)

1959

1 "Cover Picture [Kings Weston]." *RIBA Journal* 66, no. 12 (October):410.

Glosses the cover picture of Kings Weston, urging that "some use" for the building "be envisaged that will justify keeping the house in proper repair" following the expected vacating of the building by a British Municipal Charities school.

2 "Kings Weston House, Bristol." *RIBA Journal* 67, no. 1 (November):3.

Brief discussion of the history of Kings Weston subsequent to Vanbrugh's alterations of 1713.

3 LOFTIS, JOHN. *Comedy and Society from Congreve to Fielding*. Stanford, Cal.: Stanford University Press, pp. 44–54, 70–72.

Notes an "antimercantile bias" in Vanbrugh's plays—in *The Confederacy* in particular, a play anomalous in its day in its inclusion of major characters "of rank inferior to the gentry." Also examines in passing the economic considerations which inform discussions of marriage in *The Provoked Wife* and *The Relapse*. Thinks Vanbrugh's portrayal of squires (Sir Tunbelly Clumsy, Polidorus Hogstye, Sir Francis Headpiece) "harsher" than Congreve's but "more memorable." Also notes Vanbrugh's exploration of "rural-urban antagonisms" in *Aesop*, *The Country House*, and *A Journey to London*.

4 SUMMERSON, Sir JOHN. "The Classical Country House in 18th-Century England." *Journal of the Royal Society of Arts* 107 (July): 542, 548, 550.

Vanbrugh's Castle Howard, Blenheim Palace, and Kimbolton are briefly discussed as architectural instances of "territorial Whiggery," buildings in which we see "the transfer of authority in architecture from the Court to the landed oligarchs." In contrast to Crown architect Christopher Wren, who built only one country house during his career, Vanbrugh built extensively for private patrons. In Castle Howard, whose "plan and silhouette" evolved from a 1694 Wren scheme for Greenwich hospital, Vanbrugh devised for the third Earl of Carlisle a house that "celebrated the capture of [Court] patronage" by the landed oligarchy.

5   WHISTLER, LAURENCE. "Vanbrugh's Work at Stowe House." *CLife* 125 (February):352–353.

Cites a sentence from the anonymous *Tour of Seats* (1724) testifying that Vanbrugh designed the offices of Lord Cobham's remodeled Stowe House, Buckinghamshire. Speculates that around 1715 Cobham sought Vanbrugh's advice for enlarging his house and further adorning Bridgeman's gardens. Vanbrugh's plans for doing so, only partially carried out in the subsequent remodeling, survive in a perspective drawing by Bridgeman (c. 1723) .

1959–1960

1   KERN, RONALD C. "Documents Relating to Company Management, 1705–1711." *TN* 14, no. 2 (Winter):60–65.

Documents discussed include several pertinent to Vanbrugh's management of the Haymarket Theatre. These include his letter of 1711(?) to Vice-Chamberlain Coke asking that an advertised performance of music at the York Buildings be halted and seeking the Vice-Chamberlain's help in keeping down the salaries of singers and musicians in his employ. Also printed is a set of terms sent to Vanbrugh by the singer Catherine Tofts, and another set included in a letter sent him by the singer Anna Lodi.

1960

1   GREATER LONDON COUNCIL. *Survey of London.* Edited by F. H. W. Sheppard. Vol. 29, *The Parish of St. James Westminster. Part One: South of Piccadilly.* London: Athlone Press, pp. 223–228.

A chapter on "The Haymarket Opera House" includes discussion of the site on which Vanbrugh erected the theatre (1704–1705), his negotiations for purchase of the property and subsequent financial transactions related to the completed building and adjacent properties, his

1960[–1968]

1707–1708 alterations to correct acoustical problems, and what is known or can be conjectured concerning the building's interior and exterior. The "balanced design" of the façade suggests that Vanbrugh had hoped eventually to make the building (which he was obliged to erect on an enclosed site) "entirely free-standing." (See also 1973.10 and 1976.10.)

1960[–1968]

1 LENNEP, WILLIAM VAN. *The London Stage, 1660–1800.* With critical introduction by Lennep, Emmett L. Avery, and Arthur H. Scouten. 11 vols. Carbondale: Southern Illinois University Press, passim.

Includes performance dates, venues, and contemporary testimony concerning London performances of Vanbrugh's plays during the period 1696–1800. Part 2, Vol. 1 (xxvi–xxvii, and intermittently as noted in editor's index) includes discussion of Vanbrugh's management of his Queen's Theatre at the Haymarket.

1961

1 BURNIM, KALMAN A. *David Garrick, Director.* [Pittsburgh (?)]: University of Pittsburgh Press., pp. 178–188.

Notes that Vanbrugh's *Provoked Wife* was "the sixth most frequently played comedy" at Drury Lane in Garrick's day—Garrick himself taking the role of Sir John Brute in all but two of the play's ninety-five performances during his twenty-nine years as manager. The Folger's Drury Lane promptbook is examined in detail for the light it sheds on the company's staging of the play.

2 HARRIS, JOHN. "Vanbrugh at Swinstead." *CLife* 129, no. 767 (January):69–72.

Posits that the turreted pavilion "just beyond" the village of Swinstead was Vanbrugh's creation—designed to serve as "a visual connection between . . . Grimsthorpe Castle to the east" and Swinstead Hall (since demolished) to the west. Discerning a resemblance between the size of old Swinstead Hall's site and a plan (culled from the Ancaster Papers) for an unidentified house of 160 feet by 70 feet, the author proposes that Swinstead Hall was designed by Vanbrugh. The putative elevations of Swinstead's garden and entrance fronts are compared to Kings Weston and to a sketch for Glympton.

On stylistic grounds the Swinstead Hall project is dated c. 1705–1715, the pavilion 1723–1726.

3 HUTCHINSON, ROSS [libretto], and BURNS, WILFRED [music]. "'Virtue in Danger.' A Musical Freely Adapted from 'The Relapse' by Sir John Vanbrugh." Unpublished MS. Typescript in Library of Congress, Music Division.

A musical adaptation of *The Relapse*.

4 LEACROFT, RICHARD. Review of *Survey of London*, vols. 29–30 (1960.1). *TN* 16, no. 1 (Autumn):25–27.

Discusses chapter 8, volume 29 of *Survey of London* (1960.1)— on the siting and interior architecture of Vanbrugh's theatre at the Haymarket. Concludes that "little is known of Vanbrugh's original design" for the theatre (cf. 1973.10).

1962

1 BROWN, T. J. "English Literary Autographs XLI: William Wycherley, 1640?–1716; Sir John Vanbrugh, 1664–1726." *BC* 11, no. 1 (Spring):63.

As a specimen of his handwriting, prints six lines from Vanbrugh's letter of 11 November 1707 to Blenheim Comptroller Edmund Boulter.

2 DAVIES, J. H. V. "Nicholas Hawksmoor." *RIBA Journal* 69, no. 10 (October):370–371.

Includes discussion of Hawksmoor's partnership with Vanbrugh, concluding that "without Hawksmoor, neither Blenheim nor Castle Howard could have been built." Notes affinities between Castle Howard and the 1699 design for Whitehall Palace, in which Hawksmoor had a hand. Finds at Blenheim a "very Hawksmoorian air"—particularly in the "passion for emphasizing the diagonal and using thick pilaster-like elements in the upper stages of towers." Notes further that Vanbrugh appears to have done none of the drawing for either Castle Howard or Blenheim and that the sense of "movement" that characterizes both buildings is absent in Vanbrugh's other buildings but present in Hawksmoor's design for Easton Neston.

3 NAIRN, IAN, and PEVSNER, NIKOLAUS. *The Buildings of England*. Vol. 21. *Surrey*. Harmondsworth, Middlesex: Penguin.

For annotation, see 1971.5.

1963

4 VERNON, P. F. "Marriage of Convenience and The Moral Code of Restoration Comedy." *EIC* 12, no. 4 (October):379–380.

Heartfree's remarks on marriage in *The Provoked Wife* (V.iv) are briefly cited in support of the author's contention that the best plays of the "Restoration" simultaneously criticize the "typical arranged marriage" and celebrate "the rich relationship offered by a freely-chosen marriage."

1963

1 LOFTIS, JOHN. *The Politics of Drama in Augustan England.* Oxford: Clarendon Press, pp. 27–28.

Political references in Vanbrugh's plays include satire of the "Country party's opposition to the four-shilling land tax" in *Aesop*, Part I (1696) and of the "claims made for the militia" in *Aesop*, Part II (1697). The implicit comparison of Sir John Brute's disregard for his marriage vows to James II's violation of his coronation vows is one of several hits at absolutism in *The Provoked Wife* (1697). The Spanish characters and setting of *The False Friend* (1702) capitalize on theatregoers' interest in Marlborough's peninsular campaign.

2 *Review of revival of *The Provoked Wife*. *The Times* [London], 25 July.

*Source: Coleman, 1982.2, p. 20; unverified. Review of Vaudeville Theatre (London) revival of *The Provoked Wife*.

3 *SHULMAN. Review of revival of *The Provoked Wife*. *Evening Standard*, July.

*Source: Coleman, 1982.2, p. 20; unverified. Review of Vaudeville Theatre (London) revival of *The Provoked Wife*.

4 *TYNAN, KENNETH. Review of revival of *The Provoked Wife*. *The Observer*, 28 July.

*Source: Coleman, 1982.2, p. 20; unverified. Review of Vaudeville Theatre (London) production of *The Provoked Wife*.

1964

1 COLLINGWOOD, FRANCES. "Sir John Vanbrugh (1664–1726): The Splendid Amateur." *Builder* [London] 206, no. 6297 (January):189.

Brief survey of Vanbrugh's building career; for the non-specialist.

1964

2 COLVIN, HOWARD, and CRAIG, MAURICE, eds. *Architectural Drawings in the Library of Elton Hall by Sir John Vanbrugh and Sir Edward Lovett Pearce.* Oxford: Printed for the Roxburghe Club by the Oxford University Press, 178 pp.

Includes "between thirty and forty" drawings in Vanbrugh's own hand (plates III–XI, etc.) and fifty or so plans and elevations "connected with" Vanbrugh (plates XIII–XV, XVII–XIX, XXXIII–XXXIV). Most "represent architectural ideas rather than definite projects." The exceptions include drawings for Eastbury and Grimsthorpe and a drawing of the "New White Tower" Vanbrugh would build on his family compound at Greenwich (see Downes 1976.2). Acquired by the Irish architect Sir Edward Lovett Pearce following Vanbrugh's death, the drawings and plans are housed at Elton Hall, Huntingdonshire.

3 FLETCHER, IAN. "The Amateur as Genius." *Listener,* 17 September, pp. 24–26.

In this tercentenary celebration of the year of his birth, Vanbrugh is praised as the author of "problem plays" (*The Relapse, The Provoked Wife, The Confederacy,* and *The Provoked Husband* [*sic*]) that unlike those of Pinero or Jones in the 1890s "remain open-ended," with no solutions proposed. As architect, Vanbrugh is an exponent, with his collaborator Hawksmoor, of the "extreme style," whose characteristics include "a pronounced use of the giant order, deep rustication, and subtly fluent relationships between the various elements of a building." Witness Blenheim, Castle Howard, and the designs in which he may have had a hand for the new Whitehall Palace, c. 1699.

4 GREEN, DAVID. *Grinling Gibbons: His Work as Carver and Statuary, 1648–1721.* London: Country Life, pp. 126–133.

Includes discussion and photographs of wood and stone carvings Gibbons executed under the direction of Vanbrugh and Hawksmoor at Blenheim Palace. Gibbons's design for the eight, thirty-foot-high finials, in which a ducal coronet surmounts an overturned fleur-de-lys, is judged "a typical inspiration of Vanbrugh the Herald," emblematic of "Marlborough's trampling the lilies of France."

5 HUSSEY, CHRISTOPHER, and CORNFORTH, JOHN. *English Country Houses Open to the Public.* 4th ed. London: Country Life, pp. 148–155.

Includes brief descriptions, illustrated with photographs, of Castle Howard, Blenheim Palace, and Seaton Delaval. For citation of 1st ed., see 1951.2.

1965

6 LLOYD, CHRISTOPHER. "Sir John Vanbrugh, 1664–1726." *History Today* 14, no. 11 (November), 765–773.

Brief tercentenary appreciation praises Vanbugh's fidelity to his associates Wren, Hawksmoor, and Congreve, notes his career as playwright and herald. Thinks it was as an architect that he "found the true profession in which he could express his grandiloquent ideas." Concerning his earliest years at the Board of Works, sees in Greenwich Hospital's "vast columns supporting nothing in particular and [in] the crowded effect on the east side . . . the hand of an amateur who was already thinking big." Blenheim is described and illustrated with photographs, the quarrel with the Duchess of Marlborough retold, and the medieval compound he built at Greenwich discussed as evidence of his romantic attachment to the Gothic style.

7 PEVSNER, NIKOLAUS, and HARRIS, JOHN. *The Buildings of England.* Vol. 27, *Lincolnshire.* Harmondsworth, Middlesex: Penguin, pp. 554–558, 691.

Proposes that some years before undertaking the Grimsthorpe project for the first Duke of Ancaster, Vanbrugh built for the same patron a large house at Swinstead. Adduced in evidence are an extant wall and the "mighty doorway of a cottage on the Green with the kind of rustication as at Grimsthorpe." Vanbrugh's alterations of Grimsthorpe between 1722 and 1727 are described and similarities there to his work at Seaton Delaval and Lumley Castle noted. Grimsthorpe's Great Hall is judged Vanbrugh's "finest room—a reflection inside of the outside wall treatment" (i.e., "two storeys of arcading").

1965

1 ASHLEY, LEONARD R. N. *Colley Cibber.* New York: Twayne, pp. 27–28, 39, 43–44, 73–74, 83–84, 91.

Notes Cibber's performance in the roles of Foppington and Brute in Vanbrugh's *Relapse* and *Provoked Wife.* Pronounces Vanbrugh "cynical" in his reluctance as author of *The Relapse* to "accept the end" of Cibber's *Love's Last Shift,* but finds "Vanbrugh's dialogue . . . easily more sparkling" than Cibber's and his "structure [in *The Relapse*] . . . more of a piece." Thinks Cibber's refashioning of Vanbrugh's *Journey to London* into *The Provoked Husband* resulted in a "more moral, more sentimental, more regular, more probable" play than Vanbrugh's. His Queen's Theatre at the Haymarket is described in its unsuccessful first season as an "elaborately decked white elephant."

2 HARRIS, BERNARD. "The Dialect of Those Fanatic Times." In *Restoration Theatre*. Edited by John Russell Brown and Bernard Harris. London: Edward Arnold, pp. 37–39. Reprint. New York: Capricorn, 1967. (Annotation and page references based on 1967 reprint.)

Quoting Cibber's observation (1740.1) on the actor's ease in learning the dialogue of Vanbrugh's plays, the author asserts that Vanbrugh "wrote as he spoke," "put[ting] little store upon words." Sir John Brute's drunken ruminations following Constant's assertion that he "wear[s] a sword" are cited in evidence (*Provoked Wife* [IV.vi]), together with the Headpiece family's expressions of consternation following the cook's report on the loss of a goose pie in *A Journey to London* (I.ii).

3 LANG, S. "Vanbrugh's Theory and Hawksmoor's Buildings." *JSAH* 24, no. 2 (May):127–151.

Argues that Vanbrugh's "Proposals for Building ye new Churches" (1711) influenced Hawksmoor's church designs. Sources of Vanbrugh's own ideas about building are alleged to include Alberti's prescriptions for temple building in *Ten Books of Architecture*. Alberti, Rapin, and de Piles are proposed as sources of Vanbrugh's notions of memorial architecture (Blenheim Palace, for example, having been conceived as a memorial to the Duke of Marlborough and his famous victory). Vanbrugh's notion of "conformity" (fitness or propriety), which he would have found in Fréart, Wotton, and Alberti, are averred to have prompted him to preserve the style of older buildings for which he devised alterations, as witness the Jacobean ceiling he devised above the stairs he built at Audley End. Like Shaftesbury, Vanbrugh favored a "plain and noble," putatively "Grecian," style— a style discernible in "the four so-called Hawksmoor churches."

4 NELSON, DAVID ARTHUR. "The Laughing Comedy of the Eighteenth Century." *DAI* 26 (1965):3347. Cornell University, pp. 53–103.

A chapter devoted to Vanbrugh argues that his three original comedies evince a "breakdown in aesthetic distance"—this because in each of them he created "good-natured" central characters (Lady Brute, Amanda, and Lord Loverule) for whom the audience feels sympathy. In *The Provoked Wife*, *The Relapse*, and *A Journey to London*, Vanbrugh was "too seriously concerned with the problem of marriage to treat both husband and wife with comic detachment."

5 NICHOLSON, NIGEL. *Great Houses of Britain*. New York: Putnam's, pp. 180–189, 211–219.

Chapters describing Castle Howard and Blenheim Palace are illustrated with photographs. The perspective view of Castle Howard that

1966

appeared in *Vitruvius Britannicus* is reproduced prominently in end-papers.

6   SHARMA, R.C. *Themes and Conventions in the Comedy of Manners.* New York: Asia. Reprint. 1977, pp. 56–58, 337–338. (Annotation and page references based on 1977 reprint.)

The female protagonists in *The Relapse* and *The Provoked Wife* are married and their gallants "only seemingly rakish"—facts that rob the plays of their potential for "sparkling wit comedy of the [Restoration] type." The language with which Worthy seeks to seduce Amanda in *The Relapse* betrays "the disturbing influence of emotion and sentiment" discernible in comedy written in the last years of the seventeenth century.

7   WOODS, CHARLES B. "Cibber in Fielding's *Author's Farce.*" *PQ* 44, no. 2 (April):149–151.

The section entitled "Cibber's Bone" recounts the reception given to the 10 January 1728 premiere of *The Provoked Husband*, Cibber's adaptation of Vanbrugh's unfinished *Journey to London.* The "low" Headpiece underplot (which the prologue led the audience to assume had been written by Cibber) was disapproved—particularly that moment in Act IV when Sir Francis Headpiece called for a "broil'd bone" (Vanbrugh's phrase). Applauded was the genteel main plot, assumed to be Vanbrugh's but in fact substantially altered by Cibber. The response testifies both to the continuing strength of Vanbrugh's reputation and to the 1728 audience's diminished appetite for "low" scenes of the kind Vanbrugh had written for his Headpiece family.

1966

1   BARNARD, JOHN. "Sir John Vanbrugh. Two Unpublished Letters." *HLQ* 29, no. 4 (August):347–352.

Prints and annotates Vanbrugh's 28 December 1685 letter to the Earl of Huntingdon requesting his kinsman to "write a line or two to proffer my service to my Lord Lieutenant of Ireland [Henry Hyde, second earl of Clarendon]." Also prints and discusses Vanbrugh's 14 May 1708 letter to Vice-Chamberlain Coke explaining the arrangements he had made for paying singers and dancers at his Queen's Theatre for the 1707–1708 season.

2   BEARD, GEOFFREY. *Georgian Craftsmen and their Work.* London: Country Life, pp. 21, 45, 53, 196.

Front matter includes a photograph of Castle Howard's Great Hall and a dedication to George Howard in which an engraving of

1966

Castle Howard's north front is followed by an excerpt from Horace Walpole's paean: "Nobody . . . had informed me that I should at once see a palace, a town, a fortified city." Elsewhere excerpts from Vanbrugh's epistolary comments on the house-building boom of his day are quoted and the suddenness of his rise to prominence is noted. The wife of Sir William Robinson is quoted in a disparaging remark concerning Vanbrugh's "thick walls."

3 DOWNES, KERRY. *English Baroque Architecture.* London: A. Zwemmer, pp. 73, 75, 76–87, 123–124.
Discusses the inception and execution of Castle Howard and Blenheim Palace—both "product[s] of a partnership" between Vanbrugh and Hawksmoor (the style of both buildings is argued to be "distinct from . . . the independent work" of either architect). Examines the "castle air" of Kimbolton Castle, the painterly quality of Kings Weston, the "Italianate" vocabulary of Seaton Delaval and Grimsthorpe, and Vanbrugh's debt to the "earlier medieval period" in the gates he devised at Eastbury and Chatham.

4 HEARNE, THOMAS. *The Remains of Thomas Hearne: Reliquiae Hearnianae, Being extracts from his MS diaries, compiled by Dr. John [sic]* Bliss; now newly revised by John Buchanan-Brown. Edited by John Buchanan-Brown. Carbondale: Southern Illinois University Press, pp. 154, 185–186.
Based on the 1869 edition (1869.1), "collated with the Oxford Historical Society's monumental edition of the *Collections.* . . ." For annotation, see 1857.3.

5 MALINS, EDWARD. *English Landscaping and Literature, 1660–1840.* London, New York, and Toronto: Oxford University Press, pp. 17–20.
Includes brief description of the landscapes Vanbrugh planned, with the aid of Henry Wise, at Castle Howard and Blenheim. Quotes and discusses Vanbrugh's *Reasons for Preserving Part of the Old Manor at Woodstock* (1709). Notes his collaboration with Bridgeman on Lord Cobham's gardens at Stowe.

6 PATTERSON, FRANK M. "The Achievement of Sir John Vanbrugh." *DAI* 27 (1966):1344A–1345A. University of Iowa, 237 pp.
Discusses Vanbrugh's "intrinsic merit as a dramatist and his success with audiences and readers, primarily those of the eighteenth century." Finds the characters in his original plays "more fully motivated" than their predecessors. In his adaptations Vanbrugh

"invariably improved upon his sources"—a point Patterson pursues in 1976.11.

7   PATTERSON, FRANK M. "The Revised Scenes of *The Provok'd Wife.*" *ELN* 4, no. 1 (September):19–23.

A song appearing in a song book published in 1729 is cited as evidence that the original version of *The Provoked Wife* (IV.i and IV.iii) in which the drunken Sir John Brute robs a passing tailor of his bundle and subsequently disguises himself as a clergyman continued to be "performed as late as the early 1730s." The lyrics of the song in question, published with the subheading "*Sung by* Mr. Harper, *in the* Provok'd Wife," indicate Sir John to be a clergyman rather than the "Woman of Quality" he would become in the revised versions of the scenes, which the author suggests were not performed before c. 1735 (cf. 1982.2, Coleman's Appendix B).

8   PEVSNER, NIKOLAUS. *The Buildings of England.* Vol. 29. *Yorkshire, The North Riding.* Harmondsworth, Middlesex: Penguin, pp. 106–118. Reprint. 1973.

Includes detailed description of Castle Howard's interior and its "massive, violent" north and "festive" south façades. Citing the instance of Seaton Delaval (built without help from Hawksmoor and "in no way inferior to Castle Howard and Blenheim"), the author does not doubt that "brilliant," "resourceful, inventive, witty Vanbrugh" was the principal designer of Castle Howard, and Hawksmoor his "assistant."

9   ROSENBERG, ALBERT. "New Light on Vanbrugh." *PQ* 45, no. 3 (July):603–613.

Prints and annotates Vanbrugh's letter of 1685 to the Earl of Huntingdon requesting patronage; his 1692 letter from the Bastille to Secretary of State Nottingham explaining the cause of his arrest and proposing an exchange of prisoners; his letter of c. 1715 to Peter Le Neve concerning John Anstis's efforts to unseat him in his position as Garter-Principal at Arms in the College of Heralds; and five additional letters relating to Vanbrugh's management of his theatre at the Haymarket.

10   SCOUTEN, A. H. "Notes toward a History of Restoration Comedy." *PQ* 45, no. 1 (January):62–70 passim.

Places *The Relapse* and *The Provoked Wife* in the context of "a second period of the [later seventeenth-century] comedy of manners" commencing in the 1690s. Following the example of Southerne's *The Wives Excuse* in their concern with the problems of married couples, manners comedies of this second period (like those of the first) provide "laughter rather than tears," their protagonists and subordinate characters alike "appear[ing] on stage only to become the objects of ridicule."

1967

1   DOWNES, KERRY. "The Kings Weston Book of Drawings." *Architectural History* 10:7–88.

Probably compiled in the early nineteenth century, the collection catalogued and printed here includes a number of drawings for Kings Weston (devised by Vanbrugh for Edward Southwell c. 1710–1711). Though none of the drawings is in Vanbrugh's hand, some "are apparently from Vanbrugh's office."

2   GREEN, DAVID. *Sarah Duchess of Marlborough*. London: Collins, pp. 145–146, 222–223.

Includes brief discussion of Vanbrugh's deteriorating relations with the Duchess of Marlborough during the building of Blenheim Palace.

3   HARRIS, BERNARD. *Sir John Vanbrugh*. Writers and Their Work, no. 197. London: Longmans, Green, 43 pp.

A rapid sketch of Vanbrugh's achievement, principally as comic dramatist. The language of his comedies is judged to be especially adept at registering "affectation and cant," his art being "manfully resistant" to sentimentalism. He distinguished himself among the Kit-Cats "because his nature proved so eminently capable of entertaining, evoking, and exhibiting his age's tastes for both comedy and [architectural] grandeur."

4   HUSSEY, CHRISTOPHER. *English Gardens and Landscapes 1700–1750*. New York: Funk & Wagnalls, pp. 23–24, 28, 34, 37, 44, 50.

Brief discussion of Vanbrugh's collaboration with Henry Wise in the development of Blenheim Palace's gardens, Vanbrugh's effort to save Woodstock Manor from demolition ("the earliest recorded attempt to preserve an ancient building on scenic grounds"), and his advancement of the career of Charles Bridgeman, whose talents as garden designer Vanbrugh secured first at Stowe and afterwards at Eastbury and Claremont. Fleeting examination of Vanbrugh's "spectacular conception for bridging the valley of the little river Glyme on the grand approach to Blenheim."

1968

5 "The National Trust Bestows an Estate on Its Retiring Chairman." *Connoisseur* 165, no. 664 (June):108–109.

Prints Laurence Whistler's tongue-in-cheek commentary on the "Vanbrugh" house he designed to be engraved on a goblet given by the National Trust to its retiring chairman Lord Crawford and Balcarres. The engraved goblet offers three views of Whistler's pseudo-Vanbrugh house Frocward Carselbar (an acronym for chairman Crawford/Balcarres): the first "between the entrance piers," the second showing the "Vanbrugh front," the third showing "Vanbrugh's asymmetrical Belvedere far off; and the Little Palladian Bridge of 1739.
. . ." Avers that Frocward Carselbar combines Vanbrugh's "two styles, the Heroic (for greater undertakings) and the Embattled (for lesser) in a single façade."

6 WAGNER, SIR ANTHONY. *Heralds of England: A History of the Office and College of Arms.* London: H. M. Stationery Office, pp. 326–341, 350–351.

A chapter on "The Rise of Anstis" offers detailed discussion of Vanbrugh's career as herald. His long rivalry with Anstis is examined, and testimony from manuscript as well as printed sources documents opposition within the College of Heralds to his appointment as Clarenceux in 1704. Though he was "possibly the most distinguished man who has worn the herald's tabard," "poetic justice" was served when Vanbrugh "in his turn was robbed by [Anstis's] intrigue of expected promotion to the office of Garter" in 1714.

1968

1 HARRIS, JOHN. "English Country House Guides, 1740–1780." In *Concerning Architecture: Essays on Architectural Writers and Writing Presented to Nikolaus Pevsner.* Edited by John Summerson. London: Allen Lane, pp. 63–66.

Prefatory discussion includes notice of West's lines on "lamented Vanbrugh" in his poem *Stowe: the Gardens . . . Address'd to Mr. Pope* (1732.1). Also notes West's attribution to Vanbrugh of the Doric Pavilions at Stowe's south entrance. The bibliography proper includes citation of country-house guides published between 1740 and 1840 in which attention is paid to Vanbrugh's work at Blenheim and Stowe.

2 LANG, S. "Richard Payne Knight and the Idea of Modernity." In *Concerning Architecture: Essays on Architectural Writers and Writing*

1968

Presented to Nikolaus Pevsner. Edited by John Summerson. London: Allen Lane, pp. 89-90.

Includes quotation of tributes paid Vanbrugh by Sir Joshua Reynolds (1797.2) and Uvedale Price (1810.1). In both commentaries oblique praise of Vanbrugh's "mixed style" is discerned. Reynolds and Price are quoted by way of demonstrating that "Toward the end of the [18th] century [the] idea of a mixed Grecian-Gothic style is taken up in England on a conscious level . . . in part centring round a reappraisal of Vanbrugh."

3 MAYO, MARIANNE KUNERTH. "John Vanbrugh's *The Relapse*: A Study of Its Meaning." *DAI* 30 (1969):331A-332A. University of Florida, 161 pp.

Argues that *The Relapse* conveys "a consistent view of life," "present[ing] man as constantly beset by temptation and frequently making wrong choices."

4 OSWALD, ARTHUR. "Kimbolton Castle, Huntingdonshire: The Home of Kimbolton School. [Part 1]." *CLife* 144, no. 3745 (December):1584-1587.

Describes Vanbrugh's work on Kimbolton Castle's exterior, work necessitated by the collapse of the castle's garden front in the summer of 1707. Vanbrugh's correspondence with the owner, Lord Manchester, is used to reconstruct the sequence of the architect's restorations.

5 OSWALD, ARTHUR. "Kimbolton Castle, Huntingdonshire: The Home of Kimbolton School. [Part 2]." *CLife* 144, no. 3747 (December):1696-1699.

Includes discussion of the relative claims of Vanbrugh and Alessandro Galilei to the design of the Great Portico on Kimbolton's east front. Supporting the case for Vanbrugh's authorship is his sketch for a portico at Kimbolton showing "a projecting feature, with central doorway and three arched openings above[,] enclosing two pairs of returned flights of stairs"; "battlements take the place of a balustraded parapet." Why does Kimbolton's Great Portico as executed bear so little resemblance to that shown in the Vanbrugh drawing? Perhaps because Lord Manchester, "having been treated [at Kimbolton] to four helpings of Vanbrugh's castle style, jibbed at this extra one"— whereupon Vanbrugh and Hawksmoor obliged him by providing a "great classical portico with a 'colonnade.'"

1968

6 PEVSNER, NIKOLAUS. *Studies in Art, Architecture and Design.* Vol. 2. *Victorian and After.* New York: Walker, p. 261.

Author's "Address Given at the Opening of the Yale School of Art and Architecture 1963" begins by quoting that "great master of fantastic architecture, Sir John Vanbrugh" on the subject of old buildings: they "move lively and pleasant reflections on the persons who have inhabited them, and on the remarkable things that have been transacted in them."

7 SHIPLEY, JOHN B. "The Authorship of *The Cornish Squire.*" *PQ* 47, no. 2 (April):145–156.

Discusses the tangled history of three eighteenth-century adaptations of Molière's *Monsieur de Pourceaugnac*: the collaboration by Vanbrugh, William Walsh, and Congreve entitled *Squire Trelooby* (1704; revised by Vanbrugh for the five Haymarket Theatre productions that began 28 January, 1705/1706); John Ozell's *Squire Trelooby* (1704); and *The Cornish Squire* (1734). Concludes that *The Cornish Squire* represents, as its editor James Ralph maintained, "the state of the Walsh/Congreve/Vanbrugh manuscript following Vanbrugh's revision of the play in 1706. Finds nothing in Ralph's history to justify Hodges's allegation (1928.2) that Ralph's version was a forgery. Notes in support of Ralph's claims that *The Cornish Squire* "differs from the other relevant versions in precisely the two places where John Ozell said the Walsh/Congreve/Vanbrugh *Trelooby* differs from the Molière original." (See also Harley 1970.5.)

8 WAITH, EUGENE. Introduction to *The Relapse*, by John Vanbrugh. In *Restoration Drama*. New York: Grosset & Dunlap, Bantam, pp. 398–401.

Aperçus include the following: some of Vanbrugh's metrically irregular verse may signify "rough drafts which were never corrected"; the Lord Foppington scenes "break down into independent skits"; the play mixes "hard" and "soft" views of human nature, "libertinism and reform" being "left to interact endlessly as in a reversible chemical equation, when the whole problem of Loveless's relapse is put aside to give final emphasis to the success of Young Fashion's trick on his brother."

9 WATKIN, DAVID. *Thomas Hope (1769–1831) and the Neo-Classical Idea.* London: John Murray, pp. 125–133.

Avers that "the picturesque aesthetic was invented in 1709 by Vanbrugh"—this in his 11 June memorandum urging that Woodstock Manor be preserved. Why? Because old buildings interact agreeably with their landscapes and because they "move more lively and pleasing

Reflections (than History without their aid can do) on the Persons who have inhabited them; on the remarkable things which have been transacted in them, or the extraordinary occasions of erecting them." Proposes that Vanbrugh formulated his "Picturesque theory on the spur of the moment as an excuse" for his refurbishing of Woodstock Manor for his own habitation while he worked on the Blenheim Palace project. Discusses the pertinence of Vanbrugh's ad hoc theory to Castle Howard, Vanbrugh Castle, and other of his buildings.

1969

1 BERKOWITZ, GERALD MARTIN. "The Plays of Sir John Vanbrugh and the Comedy of the Late Seventeenth Century." *DAI* 30 (1970):2997A. Indiana University, 307 pp.

Argues that Vanbrugh's drama is critical of comedy of manners conventions, attentive to psychological complexity, hospitable toward characters "from the country, the City and the servant class" (all of whom he treats "with respect"). Author's principal findings are distilled in 1973.1 and later refashioned into a book, 1981.1.

2 *CLARKE, GEORGE. "The History of Stowe—VII, The Vanbrugh-Bridgeman Gardens." *Stoic* 23 (July):257–264 + plates 1–4.

Discusses the state of Stowe gardens both before and after Lord Cobham secured the services of Vanbrugh and Bridgeman in 1719. The Stowe Papers in Huntington Library are examined for evidence of the gardens' pre-1719 state. Bridgeman's "low-oblique" view is said to represent the "projected design" Vanbrugh and Bridgeman prepared for Lord Cobham in 1719–1720 so that "before sinking huge sums of money in improvements," Cobham and his wife would have "a clear idea of the finished result. . . ." In the new design, Bridgeman's "inspired geometry" pulled "together the sprawling limbs of the gardens," while Vanbrugh's Rotunda provided "a vantage point from which the visitor could look inwards over the man-made garden and outwards over the natural countryside."

3 COLEMAN, ANTONY. "Five Notes on 'The Provok'd Wife.'" *N & Q*, n.s. 16, no. 8 (August):298–300.

(1) "[A] great Leap in the Dark" is a phrase attributed by Vanbrugh's contemporaries to Hobbes (with reference to "death"); (2) "Betty Sands" is a prostitute who sold oranges at Drury Lane and became Peter the Great's favorite mistress during his visit to England in 1698; (3) ". . . the Plenipo's, [*sic*] have sign'd the Peace. . ." (III.i) suggests that Vanbrugh prepared his final revisions of the play in

March of 1697; (4) "Blew Posts" (III.i) is a tavern in Spring Gardens. Also examines (5) the significance of several emendations appearing in a pirated 1710 edition of the play printed at The Hague.

4 COLEMAN, ANTONY. "Sir John Brute on the Eighteenth Century Stage." *RECTR* 8, no. 2 (November):41–46.

One of the eighteenth century's "most frequently revived comedies," *The Provoked Wife* attracted some of the principal actors of the day to the part of Sir John Brute. Cites contemporary responses to the performances of Cibber, Ryder, and Garrick, averring that the latter "failed" to fulfill Vanbrugh's intentions for the character, softening the vices of Vanbrugh's "Dirty, cowardly and disorderly" drunkard and thereby weakening Vanbrugh's "deliberate satire on the 'Man of Quality.'"

5 HAMILTON, OLIVE, and HAMILTON, NIGEL. *Royal Greenwich.* . . . London: Greenwich Bookshop, pp. 232, 234, 237, 240.

Notes Vanbrugh's participation in the completion of Greenwich Hospital for Seamen; reproduces Murray's 1718 portrait, captioned "Sir John Vanbrugh, Wren's successor as Surveyor of the Royal Hospital." "[M]uch of his witty correspondance" is said to have "issued" from his Greenwich house, Vanbrugh Castle.

6 VAN NIEL, PIETER JAN. "*The Relapse*—Into Death and Damnation." *Educational Theatre Journal* 21, no. 3 (Oct.):318–332.

A New Critical reading which discovers multiple instances of "irony" and "tension" in *The Relapse* and finds in the religious imagery an "inversion of the Christian ethic." The play depicts "a very present hell" in which "Christian hope is extinguished, even the institution of the church . . . abrogated, overrun by the . . . sexual appetite[s]" of Loveless, Berinthia, Worthy, and Hoyden.

7 ZIMANSKY, CURT A. Introduction to *The Provoked Wife*, by Sir John Vanbrugh. Regents Restoration Drama Series. Lincoln: University of Nebraska Press, pp. xiii–xxii.

Thinks *The Provoked Wife* episodic, "not generously plotted," its "thin story" padded "with gratuitous scenes and set-piece dialogues." Notes the play's debt (for the character of Sir John Brute) to Otway's *Soldier's Fortune* (1681) and to Etherege's *She Would if She Could* (1668). Discusses matrimonial law in relation to Lady Brute. Briefly examines the play's stage history.

1970

1 COLEMAN, ANTONY. *"The Provok'd Wife* and *The Ladies De-fence." N & Q* n.s. 17, no. 3 (March): 88–91.

Examines Lady Mary Chudleigh's borrowing of the name and character of Sir John Brute for her play *The Ladies Defence* (1701). Purportedly written in answer to criticisms of disobedient wives that the Rev. John Sprint had offered in a wedding sermon of 1699, Lady Chudleigh's play assigns to Sir John Brute the attitudes and some of the language of Vanbrugh's Sir John. Instead of the impasse to which Vanbrugh brings Lady Brute in *The Provoked Wife*, however, Lady Chudleigh ends her play sentimentally, offering an eternity of heavenly bliss to wives who, finding their "soft submissions" to be "in vain," nevertheless "bear [their] Fate, and never once complain."

2 COLVIN, HOWARD. "Grimsthorpe Castle, the North Front, Lincolnshire." In *The Country Seat: Studies in the History of the British Country House*. Edited by Howard Colvin and John Harris. London: Penguin, pp. 91–93.

An appreciation of Vanbrugh's "audacity" in extending the center piece of the north front of Grimsthorpe Castle over seven bays. The author compares Vanbrugh's completed design with a plan of the "principal floor" as it existed before the architect began his alterations for the house's owner Robert Bertie, Duke of Ancaster, in the 1720s. Vanbrugh's design for the north front is declared to be a "brilliant improvisation," accomplished with minimal alteration of the original structure.

3 DAVISON, DENNIS, ed. Introduction to *Restoration Comedies*. London, Oxford, and New York: Oxford University Press, xiv.

The introduction to this collection of five "Restoration" comedies (*The Relapse* among them) includes a paragraph on Vanbrugh. His comedies are said to have a "knockabout zest appropriate to their rough-and-ready scene-plotting and hearty characterization." In *The Relapse*, for example, Lord Foppington's town "fopperies" collide with Sir Tunbelly Clumsey's "earthy vulgarities of the country"; "hilarious low comedy and slapstick satire ensue."

4 DOWNES, KERRY. *Hawksmoor*. New York and Washington: Praeger, pp. 46–53, 57–58.

Concerning the sudden commencement of Vanbrugh's building career, the author notes that "in 1699–1700," his friend the Earl of Carlisle having recently granted him the commission to build Castle Howard, Vanbrugh "seems to have had ideas and a patron and little else.'' Hawksmoor stepped in to "provide what [Vanbrugh] lacked: a draughtsman, an administrator, and an expert on detail.'' Castle Howard's "unusual or innovatory features"—the novel interior corridor and the dome—were likely "due to Vanbrugh rather than to Hawksmoor.'' Correspondence between Vanbrugh and his Blenheim assistant Henry Joynes makes it clear that at Blenheim "Vanbrugh was the chief architect and Hawksmoor his recognized subordinate partner rather than his 'ghost.'''

5 HARLEY, GRAHAM D. *"Squire Trelooby* and *The Cornish Squire*: A Reconsideration.'' *PQ* 49, no. 4 (October):520–529.

Challenges Shipley's surmise (1968.7) that James Ralph's *Cornish Squire* (1734) is essentially the Walsh/Congreve/Vanbrugh *Squire Trelooby* as performed on 30 March 1704 or 28 January 1705/1706. Argues that Ralph's play is patchwork plagiarism from Ozell's *Squire Trelooby* (1704) and from *Squire Lubberly*—a literal translation of Molière's *Monsieur de Pourceaugnac* published two years before Ralph's version (cf. 1928.2).

6 LEES-MILNE, JAMES. *English Country Houses: Baroque, 1685–1715.* London: Country Life, pp. 102–111, 148–200.

Compact, lavishly illustrated accounts of Vanbrugh's work at Kimbolton Castle, Castle Howard, Blenheim Palace, Seaton Delaval, and Grimsthorpe Castle. Why so many important building commissions? The author theorizes that Vanbrugh "never lost an opportunity of turning a casual acquaintance to professional advantage.'' Cited as an instance is Vanbrugh's overnight stay at the Duke of Ancaster's seat in 1718, on which occasion the playwright persuaded the Duke to let him rebuild Grimsthorpe Castle.

7 MUIR, KENNETH. *The Comedy of Manners.* London: Hutchinson, pp. 126–141.

Arguing that Vanbrugh had "very little originality,'' Muir finds him borrowing from Cibber more than is generally allowed in his portrait of Lord Foppington in *The Relapse*. The play's "Amanda'' scenes are judged "mawkish,'' their blank verse inept. *The Provoked Wife* is found likewise to be derivative, its characters stock ones, its dialogue, "though natural,'' deficient in "wit and sparkle.''

8 ZIMANSKY, CURT A. Introduction to *The Relapse*, by Sir John Vanbrugh. Regents Restoration Drama Series. Lincoln: University of Nebraska Press, pp. xiii–xxiii.

Discusses the textual history of *The Relapse* and the play's relation to its antecedents—Cibber's *Love's Last Shift* Crowne's *City Poli-*

tiques, Wycherley's *Country Wife*, Otway's *Soldier's Fortune*. Finds Vanbrugh's patches of blank verse "dubious," not written with "satiric intent." Brief discussion of the play's stage history and of Vanbrugh's reply to Collier in his *Short Vindication*.

1971

1 HARRIS, BERNARD. Introduction to *The Relapse, or Virtue in Danger*, by John Vanbrugh. The New Mermaids. London: Ernest Benn, pp xi–xxv.

A sketch of Vanbrugh's career as playwright and architect is followed by an analysis of *The Relapse* in which Collier's moral objections are rebutted. We are told, for example, that "Amanda, though cuckolded, is never ridiculed," and that even in Coupler "there is a magnanimity of nature which reflects the life-affirming quality of the whole play." The patches of blank verse are argued to be functional, skillfully deployed for purposes of "inflation and deflation."

2 *HARRIS, JOHN. *A Country House Index*. London: Pinhorns.
For annotation of 2d ed., see 1979.4.

3 KROPF, C. R. "*The Relapse* and the Sentimental Mask." *JNT* 1, no. 3 (September):193–199.

Sees in the play's abundant religious imagery evidence that Vanbrugh conceived Amanda and Lord Foppington as "Christlike figures" who "preside [in their respective plots] over two opposed orders of reality, both of which are false." Trying to "live in a Sunday school world of ideals," Amanda finds that her "ideal world" crumbles when she moves from the country to the town—a consequence that demonstrates the "inadequacy of sentimentalism in dealing with human problems." In the play's parallel underplot the inadequacy of Lord Foppington's "equally innocent world of appearances" is manifest in Young Fashion's outwitting of his older brother in his scheme to win Hoyden's hand and dowry.

4 LYNCH, KATHLEEN M. *Jacob Tonson: Kit-Cat Publisher*. Knoxville: University of Tennessee Press, pp. 57–61, 154–156, 164–165.

Notes the many building tasks Vanbrugh carried out in association with fellow Kit-Cats. Projects included his Queen's Theatre at the Haymarket and new houses or alterations of existing ones for Carlisle, Manchester, Kneller, Newcastle, Ancaster, and Cobham (for whom he built a number of temples at Stowe). Quotes from Vanbrugh's correspondence with Tonson by way of demonstrating the strong bonds of friendship between the two.

5 NAIRN, IAN, and PEVSNER, NIKOLAUS. *The Buildings of England.* Vol. 21. *Surrey.* 2d ed. Revised by Bridget Cherry. Harmondsworth, Middlesex: Penguin, pp. 160–162.

Revised ed. of 1962.3 includes description of the house Vanbrugh built for himself (Chargate, in Esher) and subsequently sold and enlarged into Claremont House for the Duke of Newcastle. The belvedere Vanbrugh built on the grounds is judged to be "historically of great significance as an early [1717] example of medievalism."

6 SCHNEIDER, BEN ROSS, JR. *The Ethos of Restoration Comedy.* Urbana, Chicago, and London: University of Illinois Press, pp. 10, 73–74, and intermittently as noted in author's index.

Vanbrugh's assertion in his prologue to *The Provoked Wife* that the playwright's task is "To hold to every man a faithful glass/And shew him of what species he's an ass" is said to state "with blazing clarity" the "repeatedly declared" moral intentions of the playwrights of the day. Vanbrugh's *Aesop, The False Friend, The Pilgrim, The Provoked Wife,* and *The Relapse* are among the eighty-three plays used by the author in his statistical investigation of the "ethos" of British comedy of the late seventeenth century.

7 STRATMAN, CARL J.; SPENCER, DAVID G.; and DEVINE, MARY ELIZABETH, eds. *Restoration and Eighteenth Century Theatre Research: A Bibliographical Guide, 1900–1968.* Carbondale and Edwardsville: Southern Illinois University Press; London and Amsterdam: Feffer & Simons, pp. 749–752.

A select annotated bibliography listing principal editions of the plays, biographical studies, and theatre-centered criticism.

8 WHISTLER, LAURENCE. "A Vanbrugh Wemyss?" *CLife* 149, no. 3861 (June):1422–1423.

A prank, the article reports the author's discovery of Vanbrugh's proposal for remodeling Wemyss Castle on the Firth of Forth. Averring that the architect's pencil sketches for Wemyss are "Too slight to be suitable for reproduction," the author provides conjectural constructions of "Vanbrugh's" elevations, among them an "Arrival Front, with no central door." (In a letter of 12 March 1991, Whistler advised me that his "hoax" originated in his being commissioned by the Wemyss family to engrave a window pane for Wemyss Castle. In executing the commission he "invented" for the family's amusement "a previous Vanbrugh house," reproduced as Fig. 5 in the present article.)

1972

1 BREMAN, PAUL, and ADDIS, DENISE. *Guide to "Vitruvius Britannicus": Annotated and Analytic Index to the Plates.* Vol. 4 of facsimile reprint of *Vitruvius Britannicus.* New York: Benjamin Blom, pp. 72–77.

Includes a select bibliography of studies of Vanbrugh's major buildings followed by annotations of the plates in Campbell's *Vitruvius Britannicus* and its successors (1715–1725.1, 1739.1, 1802.1). Annotations include a brief building history of each of the illustrated Vanburgh plans, elevations, and views—of Blenheim Palace, Castle Howard, Cholmondeley Hall, Claremont, Eastbury, Grimsthorpe, Kings Weston, and Seaton Delaval. Authors find it "strange that nobody has yet drawn attention to the existence of different versions of the main ground plans [of Castle Howard] given by Campbell in succeeding issues of" *Vitruvius Britannicus.*

2 FREEMAN, ARTHUR. Preface to *A Short Vindication of the "Relapse" and the "Provok'd Wife,"* by John Vanbrugh. The English Stage: Attack and Defense 1577–1730. New York and London: Garland, p. 5.

Brief preface calls Vanbrugh's *Vindication* "perhaps singly the most important, if oddly one of the least telling replies to Collier" (1698.1). Vanbrugh's "arguments in favor of his comic intent" are said to "lend far too much dignity to his assailant's blunt approach.
. . ."

3 HAYES, JOHN. *Rowlandson: Watercolours and Drawings.* New York: Phaidon, p. 184.

Reproduces (figure 119) Rowlandson's sketch of "Vanbrugh's House in Whitehall Court" (the Goose-Pie House) as it appeared "About 1800–5."

4 NALBACH, DANIEL. *The King's Theatre 1704–1867: London's First Italian Opera House.* London: Society for Theatre Research, pp. 1–11, 18–21, 32.

Includes an account of Vanbrugh's building of his theatre at the Haymarket. Discusses his negotiations for purchase of the site and details of related financial transactions. Reproduces and discusses

1973

William Capon's 1783 drawing of the theatre's entrance and discusses the building's likely dimensions.

5 OLLESON, PHILIP. "Vanbrugh and Opera at the Queen's Theatre, Haymarket." *TN* 26, no. 3 (Spring):94–101.

Discusses and prints documents pertinent to Vanbrugh's efforts to induce the Italian singers Nicolini and Santini to perform opera at his Haymarket Theatre following the genre split decreed by Lord Chamberlain Kent in December 1707. Transcribes Vanbrugh's disappointing box office receipts from 13 January to 6 March 1708.

6 ROGERS, PAT. "An Unpublished Vanbrugh Letter." *Scriblerian* 5, no. 1 (Autumn):42.

In an unaddressed letter dated 1 June 1715, Vanbrugh relays the Duke of Marlborough's wish that 121 felled trees be removed from Whittlewood Forest—the trees being the unused surplus of 248 "formerly cut for the use of Blenheim [Palace]." Editor speculates that Vanbrugh penned the letter "in his quaint official role as Surveyor of the Gardens and Waters, as well as his post at Blenheim."

7 ZIMANSKY, CURT A. "Editing Restoration Comedy: Vanbrugh and Others." In *Editing Seventeenth Century Prose*. Papers Given at the Conference on Editorial Problems, University of Toronto, November 1970. Edited by D. I. B. Smith. Toronto: A. M. Hakkert, 1972.

On the basis of his experience as editor of the Regents Restoration Drama editions of *The Relapse* and *The Provoked Wife*, the author urges future editors of popular editions of comedies of the period to leave punctuation "as light as possible," preserving ambiguities and restoring the long dash. The several patches of quasi-blank verse in *The Relapse* are examined in relation to exigencies of printing in Vanbrugh's day. The importance of inspecting "supposedly derivative editions in Holland and Ireland" is illustrated with reference to Vanbrugh's alteration of Sir John Brute's disguise from that of parson to lady of quality for a 1726 production at Drury Lane—a revision first published in a 1743 Irish edition (cf. 1966.7 and 1982.2).

1973

1 BERKOWITZ, GERALD M. "Sir John Vanbrugh and the Conventions of Restoration Comedy." *Genre* 6, no. 3 (September):346–361.

Examines Vanbrugh's "subversive modifications" of the formulas of Restoration comedy. Vanbrugh modified the "wit-dual," for example, using it in *A Journey to London* not to bury truth "beneath euphemism'' but to show ''how precariously close to dissolution the Loverules' marriage is.'' Vanbrugh also expanded comedy's range of sympathies, treating the problems of post–twenty-year-olds with sympathy, allowing exemplary members of London society to speak favorably of country values, and giving increased prominence to servants and (in *The Confederacy*) to the merchant class. (Material is incorporated into 1981.1.)

2 DIXON, PETER. ''Introduction'' to Vanbrugh and Colley Cibber, *The Provoked Husband*. Regents Restoration Drama Series. Lincoln: University of Nebraska Press, pp. xiii–xxvii.

Includes discussion of the relationship of Vanbrugh's unfinished *Journey to London* to the version Cibber completed and successfully staged as *The Provoked Husband* (1728). Vanbrugh's fragment gave prominence to the provincial Headpiece family and their travails in London. Cibber pruned and subordinated that material to the Loverule plot, renaming Vanbrugh's Loverules the Townlys, foregrounding the quarrels of Lord and Lady Townly, and effecting a final reconciliation between the two that Vanbrugh had not intended.

3 DUCKWORTH, COLIN. ''The Fortunes of Voltaire's Foppington.'' In *Studies in the Eighteenth Century*. Vol. 3. Edited by R. F. Brissenden and J. C. Eade. Toronto and Buffalo: University of Toronto Press, pp. 121–135.

Examines Voltaire's *Le Comte de Boursoufle*, an adaptation of Vanbrugh's *Relapse*. Voltaire owned a copy of Vanbrugh's plays and may well have seen *The Relapse* performed during his 1926–1928 stay in England. In his adaptation, perhaps in response to Jeremy Collier's charge that Vanbrugh's play was under-unified, Voltaire used only the Foppington-Fashion plot, reducing the play to three acts, marrying Hoyden and Fashion in the period elapsing between Acts II and III, and beginning Act II at the gate of Sir Tunbelly's castle. That John Lee, in his own adaptation of *The Relapse* (*The Man of Quality*, 1771), shortened Vanbrugh's play in precisely these ways suggests that Lee had seen Voltaire's adaptation performed in Paris.

4 DURANT, JACK D. ''*The Relapse*, Shakespeare's *Romeo*, and Otway's *Marius*. *RECTR* 12, no. 2 (November), pp. 46–49.

Hoyden in *The Relapse* is an ''inverted Juliet, a Juliet probably freshened in the minds of the contemporary audience by Otway's Lavinia, the heroine of *Caius Marius*'' (1679). Otway's play, reprinted in 1696 and perhaps revived on stage in that year, contains several instances of language (particularly the Nurse's description of Lavinia as an infant) and behavior (e.g., Marius's ''intense eagerness to marry'') that appear to have exerted a more direct influence upon the analogous moments in *The Relapse* than did Shakespeare's play.

5 FIELDING, HENRY. *Tom Jones: An Authoritative Text* [based on 4th ed., 1750.3]. A Norton Critical Edition. Edited by Sheridan Baker. New York: Norton, pp. 567-568.

In Bk. XIV, ch. 1, "An Essay to prove that an Author will write the better, for having some Knowledge of the Subject on which he writes," Fielding opines that "many *English* Writers have totally failed in describing the Manners of upper Life," "possibly" because "they know nothing of it." Exceptions are "*Vanbrugh* and *Congreve*," both of whom "copied Nature." Writers who "copy" Congreve and Vanbrugh are said to "draw as unlike the present age, as *Hogarth* would do if he was to paint a Rout or a Drum in the Dresses of *Titian* and of *Vandyke*" (cf. 1736.1).

6 FISKE, ROGER. *English Theatre Music in the Eighteenth Century.* London: Oxford University Press, pp. 1-2, 33-41, 47, 103.

Quotes Cibber's remarks on the excessively reverberant acoustics of Vanbrugh's theatre at the Haymarket, noting that "in 1709 the resonance was reduced by lowering the ceilings." The acoustics continued to favor singers; hence the theatre became the principal venue for "Italian operas and singers for the rest of the century." By way of explaining the choice of Greber's *Loves of Ergasto* for the Haymarket's April 1705 opening, suggests that Vanbrugh and his partner Congreve, observing the popularity of *Arsinoe* at Drury Lane, approached the Italian soprano Margherita de l'Epine for advice about a suitable Italianate opera with which to open the theater. The latter "might well have suggested a new opera by her lover," Jacob Greber.

7 GIBBON, MICHAEL. "Stowe House, 1680-1779." *Apollo* 97 (June):552-557.

Includes discussion of an undated drawing, here attributed to Stowe's garden designer Charles Bridgeman, in which the south side of the house appears "very like Vanbrugh's work." Although the building in the drawing is laid out in a straight line rather than, as was Vanbrugh's usual practice, "in three parts at right angles to one another," the author detects strong similarities between Vanbrugh's Pyramid Gate at Castle Howard and the "massive end-gateways" with their "pyramid roofs and heavy machiolated cornices" in the Bridgeman drawing. Comparison of the design in the drawing with the completed building leads the author to conclude that Stowe house was "not built quite as [Vanburgh] intended." (Vanbrugh died in 1726, before Lord Cobbham's alterations of his house were completed.)

8 JACKSON-STOPS, GERVASE. "Cholmondeley Castle, Cheshire—
   I. The Home of the Marquess and Marchioness of Cholmondeley."
   CLife 154, no. 3969 (July):154, 155, 157.

   Concludes that William Smith of Warwick was the "architect of
   the 1st Earl's house, built between 1707 and 1715," but "Vanbrugh's
   advice was also sought." Quotes in evidence Vanbrugh's September
   1713 assertion in his letter to Southwell that he had "been a second
   time at Cholmley, and concerted a general Scheme for what is left to
   do." Thinks Campbell's engraving (reproduced here) of Cholmondeley's north front "represents [Vanbrugh's] ideas." Reproduces (as Fig.
   4) a drawing of Cholmondeley's Old Hall before its 1801 demolition
   in which it is evident that Vanbrugh's scheme had not been executed.

9 KENNY, SHIRLEY STRUM. "Theatrical Warfare, 1695-1710." *TN*
   27, no. 4 (Summer): 130-145 passim.

   Includes discussion of competition between Drury Lane and Vanbrugh's Haymarket Theatre between 1705 and 1707. Adduces play
   prologues and records of performance.

10 LEACROFT, RICHARD. *The Development of the English Playhouse*. Ithaca, N.Y.: Cornell University Press, pp. 100, 103-104.

   Discusses and offers hypothetical scale reconstructions (Figs. 68
   and 71) of Vanbrugh's Queen's Theatre at the Haymarket as he origi-
   nally designed it (1704-1705) and after his alterations of 1707-1708.

11 LOFTIS, JOHN. *The Spanish Plays of Neoclassical England*. New
   Haven and London: Yale University Press, pp. 167-172.

   Examines the plot of Vanbrugh's *The False Friend*—an adaptation
   of Le Sage's *Le Traître puni* (itself a translation of the Spanish playwright Zorilla's *La traición busca el castigo*). In comparing Vanbrugh's play to the French and Spanish versions, the author notes that
   Vanbrugh "endows his title character with the attitudes of a long line
   of [Restoration] rake heroes." Because "[w]ithin the Restoration tradition . . . the betrayal of a friend in an attempt to seduce his wife
   could scarcely be viewed with Spanish gravity," the death of the "false
   friend" Don John "could not have the impact of a deserved and inevi-
   table retribution." Vanbrugh's alterations of his source(s) are cited as
   evidence of the English tendency to render "sexual ethics more casually
   than the Spanish did."

12 PRICE, CECIL. Introduction to *A Trip to Scarborough*. In *Dramatic
   Works of Richard Brinsley Sheridan*. Edited by Cecil Price. Vol. 2.
   Oxford: At the Clarendon Press, pp. 553-556.

   Briefly describes the characters in Vanbrugh's *Relapse* and notes
   the play's popularity on the London stage through 1766. Cites John

1973

Lee's reduction of the play to a farce (*The Man of Quality*, 1733). Describes Sheridan's alterations to accommodate the taste of his day in his adaptation of *The Relapse* as *A Trip to Scarborough* (1777), in which "Everything works out morally." Avers that Sheridan's version effectively addressed Collier's criticisms of the structure of *The Relapse*.

13 ROACH, JOSEPH ROGER, JR. "Vanbrugh's English Baroque: Opera and the Opera House in the Haymarket." *DAI* 34 (1974):7376-A. Cornell University, 215 pp.

Examines the Haymarket Theatre as a venue for "English Baroque." Discusses the architecture of Vanburgh's theatre, his sponsorship of *opera serias*, and the satirical assaults to which his experiments in "grandeur" were subjected by such detractors as Pope, Swift, and Addison.

14 ROBERTS, PHILIP. "Vanbrugh's Lost Play: The Prologue." *RECTR* 12, no. 1 (May):57–58.

Prints the prologue, written in an unidentified hand, to Vanbrugh's never-published afterpiece *Sganarell; or, The Cuckold in Conceit*. The play was performed twice—at the Queen's Theatre in the Haymarket on 22 March 1707 and at Drury Lane on 4 June 1709.

15 ROPER, ALAN. "Language and Action in *The Way of the World*, *Love's Last Shift*, and *The Relapse*." *ELH* 40, no. 1 (Spring):44–69.

Vanbrugh's satirical use of religious language in *The Relapse*—e.g., Berinthia's "Virtue is its own reward" in response to Worthy's expressed desire to repay her for aiding him in his scheme to seduce the virtuous Amanda—wittily implies that the "language of virtue" often masks "an actual viciousness." A similar implication is discernible in Parson Bull's casuistical justification of his selfish interest in abetting Young Fashion in his scheme to win Hoyden and her dowry. Vanbrugh's "witty inversion of a traditional [homiletic] language and morality" is the primary vechicle of the play's "morality"—its implicit espousal of "truth and honesty" in the face of social decay.

16 SHERWOOD, IRMA Z. "Vanbrugh's 'Romeo and Juliet': A Note on *The Relapse*." *RECTR* 12, no. 2 (November):41–45.

The Fashion-Hoyden subplot in *The Relapse* bears a relationship to Shakespeare's *Romeo and Juliet* analogous to that of the main plot's relation to Cibber's *Love's Last Shift*. The result: "twin deflations—of [Cibber's] sentimentality in the main plot and of romantic situation and motivation in the subplot." The characters and situations in the subplot are coarsened refashionings of Shakespeare's. The

Fashion/Hoyden relationship is a farcically sordid recasting of Romeo's travails with Juliet.

1974

1 BINGHAM, MADELEINE. *Masks and Facades: Sir John Vanbrugh, the Man in his Setting.* London: George Allen & Unwin, 375 pp.

Addressed to the general reader, this biography does what its title promises, addressing such matters as Vanbrugh's "burgher background," the Kit-Cat milieu, and the institution of the College of Arms. There are no notes.

2 BRUCE, DONALD. *Topics of Restoration Comedy.* New York: St. Martin's, pp. 48–49, 51–55, 129–134, 141–142.

Lively summary of Vanbrugh's career. Concerning the plays we are told that Sir John Brute's drunken impersonation of a parson was "the immediate reason for Jeremy Collier's *Short View.*" There is a lengthy analysis of *The Relapse*'s Lord Foppington, than whom only Congreve's Millamant is judged "more memorable." Elsewhere Belinda and Lady Brute are examined as "she-comrades."

3 CONNOR, TIMOTHY. "Grimsthorpe Castle." *Archaelogical Journal* 131:330–333.

Discussion of Grimsthorpe's alterations under the ownership of the Willoughby family from 1507 onward includes a brief account of the alterations Vanbrugh conceived for the first Duke of Ancaster shortly after 1715. Following the Duke's death in 1723, Vanbrugh's proposed alterations were carried out in part by the first duke's successor—only "in part" because the architect himself died three years later.

4 FALLER, LINCOLN B. "Between Jest and Earnest: The Comedy of Sir John Vanbrugh." *MP* 72, no. 1 (August):17–29.

Praises the complexity of Vanbrugh's portraits of Lord Foppington and Worthy in *The Relapse* and Sir John and Lady Brute in *The Provoked Wife*. In rendering Lady Brute's intractable marital difficulties and in insisting on Amanda's isolation from the "joking celebrants" at the conclusion of *The Relapse*, Vanbrugh shows a "disinclination to dream away the hard facts of the human condition." At odds both with his more cynical predecessors Etherege and Wycherley and with his sentimental contemporaries and successors, Vanbrugh depicts a world that is "neither sad nor ultimately joyful, just somehow tarnished and dull."

1974

5 GLENCROSS, ALAN. *Buildings of Greenwich*. London: Borough of Greenwich, pp. 8, 13 (opposite Fig. 5), 28.

Includes Vanbrugh's name in a list of architects who "contributed to" the "realization " of Greenwich's Royal Hospital for Seaman; reproduces an oil painting of Vanbrugh Castle, c. 1840. Also describes and ascribes to Vanbrugh the Royal Brass Foundry, "completed in 1717."

6 GREENE, DAVID LEWIS. "Sir John Vanbrugh: A Study of his Comedies." *DAI* 36 (1975):311A–312A. University of Pennsylvania, 195 pp.

Examines Vanbrugh's three original comedies, finding them to be "realistic" studies of "marital incompatibility."

7 HOWARD, GEORGE. *Castle Howard*. 2d ed. York and London: Ben Johnson. Published by Castle Howard Estate, 36 pp.

A slightly expanded edition of 1958.3.

8 HUSEBOE, ARTHUR R. "'Lead out' in Vanbrugh's 'The Provoked Wife.'" *N & Q*, n.s. 21, no. 8 (August):295–296.

Constant's phrase "lead out" in *The Provoked Wife* (IV.ii) is glossed as a "reference . . . to the practice of gentlemen ceremoniously escorting ladies from the theatre to the carriage waiting outside."

9 HUSEBOE, ARTHUR R. "Vanbrugh: Additions to the Correspondence." *PQ* 53, no. 1 (January):135–140.

Prints and discusses a letter of 20 January 1708 addressed to Vice Chamberlain Coke relating to salaries to be paid to performers at the Haymarket Theatre. In the letter (previously printed but misdated by Kern, 1959–1960.1), Vanbrugh asks Coke to stop a music concert advertised for performance at York Buildings. Also printed and discussed is a letter concerning renovations of the interior of Kings Weston which Vanbrugh posted to Edward Southwell from Castle Howard on 4 December 1713.

10 JEFFARES, A. NORMAN, ed. Introductions to *The Relapse* and *The Provoked Wife*, by John Vanbrugh. In *Restoration Comedy*. Vol. 3. London: Folio Press; Totowa, N.J.: Rowman and Littlefield, pp. 435–437, 561–562.

Includes a biographical sketch and remarks prefatory to the texts of *The Relapse* and *The Provoked Wife*. Vanbrugh's strengths are said to be his "commonsense," his creation of "diverse individuals," his dramatization of the "struggle between man's animality and desire for reason. . . ."

11 OLSHEN, BARRY N. "The Original and 'Improved' Comedies of Sir John Vanbrugh: Their Nineteenth-Century London Stage History." *RECTR* 13, no. 1 (May):27–52.

A "List of Nineteenth-Century Performances of Vanbrugh's comedies" is preceded by commentary in which one learns that Cibber's sentimental refashioning of Vanbrugh's unfinished *Journey to London* (as *The Provoked Husband*) was "performed with greater regularity than any other comedy of its period." Sheridan's sentimentalization of *The Relapse* (as *A Trip to Scarborough*) was popular in the early decades of the century, and Robert Buchanan's three-act *Miss Tomboy* (a version of *The Relapse* with Hoyden as the principal character) saw 100 performances in the 1890s. In the same decade Thomas King's shortened version of *The Mistake* (as *Lovers' Quarrels*) proved a serviceable "curtain raiser." Among Vanbrugh's plays only *The Confederacy* was performed without substantial alterations during the century. Examination of two promptbooks for the latter play reveals that numerous excisions were made to suit the needs of "decency, morality, and decorum."

12 OLSHEN, BARRY NEIL. "The Reception of Restoration Comedy of Manners in Nineteenth-Century England: An Account of Wycherley, Congereve, Vanbrugh and Farquhar on the Stage and in the Study." *DAI* 34 (1974):5374A–5375A. University of Toronto, n. pag.

Includes discussion of the performance history and critical reputation of Vanbrugh's plays in the nineteenth century. And see 1974.11 for the author's distillation of his principal findings.

13 *PEVSNER, NIKOLAUS. *Northumberland.* With notes on the Roman Antiquities by Ian A. Richmond. 2d ed. of *The Buildings of England.* Vol. 15, *Northumberland.* Middlesex: Penguin.

For annotation of 1st ed., see 1957.4. Discussion of Seaton Delaval is reprinted in 1986.2.

14 ROGAL, SAMUEL J. "John Vanbrugh and the Blenheim Palace Controversy." *JSAH* 33, no. 4 (December):293–303.

Vanbrugh's difficulties in the building of Blenheim are described against the background of declining Whig and rising Tory fortunes. Evidence of various problems—his difficulties in securing stone, for example, and his quarrel with the Duchess of Marlborough over the

1975

building of a grand bridge over the river Glyme—is drawn principally from Vanbrugh's letters.

15 SMITH, JAMES L., ed. Introduction to *The Provoked Wife*, by John Vanbrugh. London and Tonbridge: Ernest Benn, pp. xi–xxviii.

Notes *The Provoked Wife*'s kinship to a group of "marital imprisonment" comedies (commencing with Southerne's *The Wives' Excuse* in 1691) in which alienated spouses contemplating infidelity are treated sympathetically. The theme recurs in *The Relapse* and *A Journey to London*. Sir John Brute's roystering scenes are praised for their celebration of "all the anarchic, filthy, joyous bestiality of man." Lady Brute's dilemma is compared to Nora's in *A Doll's House*. Vanbrugh offered no solution to the Brutes' marital difficulties because "in 1697 no [legal] solutions are available." The play's stage history is reviewed and suggestions for performance are offered.

1975

1 BARNARD, JOHN. *English Drama (Excluding Shakespeare)*. Select Bibliographical Guides. Edited by Stanley Wells. London: Oxford University Press, pp. 187, 197.

Includes a select list of modern texts of Vanbrugh's comedies and five critical studies of his work. A brief survey of critical opinion notes that *The Relapse* simultaneously "satirizes the shift towards sentimentality in Cibber's *Love's Last Shift*" and "broadens the base of the traditional comedy of courtship to include" realistically rendered "marital relationships." Proposes that Vanbrugh's *Vindication* accurately "describes the basis of his realistic mode."

2 BROWNING, REED. *The Duke of Newcastle*. New Haven and London: Yale University Press, pp. 5–7, 12, 36.

Includes brief discussion of Newcastle's relationship with his "political friend" and fellow Kit-Catter John Vanbrugh, who remodeled the young duke's house at Lincoln's Inn Field, built his Claremont House, and arranged his marriage to Lady Harriet Godolphin.

3 HUGHES, LEO, and SCOUTEN, A. H. "The Penzance Promptbook of *The Pilgrim*." *MP* 73, no. 1 (August):33–53.

Detailed examination of the markings of the four prompters whose hands are discernible in an eighteenth-century promptbook of Vanbrugh's adaptation of Fletcher's *The Pilgrim* (1700). Examples: Chetwood's markings for a 1738 revival of the play inconsistently prune some bawdy or blasphemous language and allow other instances to stand. Cross's markings (at Garrick's direction) for a 1750 revival include the notation, "Play not much lik'd. . . ."

4 HUNT, JOHN DIXON, and WILLIS, PETER, eds. *The Genius of the Place: The English Landscape Garden 1620–1820.* New York, Evanston, San Francisco, London: Harper & Row, pp. 119–121.

Prints (from *Works*, IV, 1928.11) the text of the 11 June 1709 letter in which Vanbrugh sought to persuade the Duchess of Marlborough to include Woodstock Manor in the design of a park for Blenheim Palace that would rival that which the "best of Landskip Painters can invent." The editors note the "singularly romantic" siting of the garden buildings Vanbrugh designed for Castle Howard, Stowe, and Claremont, calling him "an important agent in the development of the landscape garden."

5 JACKSON-STOPS, GERVASE. "Eglingham Hall, Northumberland: The Home of Mr. and Mrs. Henry Potts." *CLife* 158, no. 4091 (November):1458–1461.

Includes discussion of the influence of Vanbrugh's Seaton Delaval on the design of Eglingham Hall, Northumberland. The house was "probably built in 1728 by Robert Ogle," and most likely designed by a Yorkshireman, "possibly William Wakefield or William Etty."

6 MILHOUS, JUDITH. "The Date and Import of the Financial Plan for a United Theatre Company in P.R.O. LC 7/3." *Maske und Kothurn* 21, no. 2–3:81–88.

Thinks the document entitled "An Establishm[en]t for ye Company" dates from the spring or summer of 1703 (rather than 1707, as proposed by Nicoll, 1925.1) and "was drawn up in connection with the beginning" of Vanbrugh's Haymarket Theatre project (see 1985.2). Cites in evidence the relatively low salaries offered to singers ("decidedly pre-opera craze") and the inclusion of singers as well as actors in the cast list. A 1707 proposal would have placed actors and musicians in separate companies.

7 SHEPPARD, H. W., ed. *Survey of London.* Vol. 38. *The Museums Area of South Kensington and Westminister.* London: Athlone, pp. 6–7.

Notes the influence of Vanbrugh's manner on gardener Henry Wise's Brompton Park House, which occupied a corner of the site on which the Victoria and Albert Museum now stands. Notes (as a characteristically baroque feature of the Vanbrugh/Hawksmoor style) the "giant arch with a broken pediment" that Vanbrugh deployed at the

1976

"entrance to the Model Room at the Royal Arsenal, Woolwich" (1719).

8 STEWART, IAN. Review of Bingham, *Masks and Facades* (1974.1). *CLife* 157, no. 4045 (January):69.

A two-paragraph review notes that Bingham's Vanbrugh emerges as "the agreeable, versatile and vigorous fellow we have always taken him to be."

9 WILLIAMS, AUBREY. "No Cloistered Virtue: Or, Playwright versus Priest in 1698." *PMLA* 90, no. 2 (March):234–246.

Contests the opinion that Jeremy Collier, "on his own 'moral grounds,' is 'unbeatable.'" Argues that comedies of the later seventeenth century offered valid "representations of marriage pursued and achieved amid the very real hazards and temptations of Restoration London." Gives the last word to Vanbrugh's rejoinder (in his *Vindication*) to Collier's contempt for "a Spark [Worthy in *The Relapse*] that can make no better use of his Mistress [Amanda], than to admire her for her Virtue." Vanbrugh finds Collier's response "so very extraordinary in a Clergyman, that I almost fancy when He and I are fast asleep in our Graves, those who shall read what we both have produc'd, will be apt to conclude there's a Mistake in the Tradition about the Authors; and that 'twas the Reforming Divine writ the Play, and the Scandalous Poet the Remarks upon it."

1976

1 COLVIN, H. M., ed. *The History of the King's Works*. Vol. V. *1660–1782*, edited by H. M. Colvin, J. Mordaunt Crook, Kerry Downes, John Newman. London: H. M. Stationery Office, pp. 56, 58–60, 302–303 (and others).

Includes discussion of Vanbrugh's career at the Board of Works. Examples: "Vanbrugh's repeated assertions that the cost of the King's Works had been 'greatly decreas'd'" during his tenure as Comptroller are dismissed as a "piece of not very scrupulous special pleading." A preservation-minded Vanbrugh was the lone member of the Board who opposed the House of Commons' efforts in 1718–1719 to demolish the ancient gateways that obstructed coach traffic between King Street and Charing Cross.

2 DOWNES, KERRY. "The Little Colony on Greenwich Hill: Vanbrugh's Field at Blackheath." *CLife* 159, no. 4117 (May):1406–1408.

Describes the constellation of pseudo-medieval houses Vanbrugh designed for himself and his brothers at Greenwich in the early 1720s.

The structures included "The Nunnery," "Mince-Pie House," and his own dwelling, Vanbrugh Castle.

3 DOWNES, KERRY. "Vanbrugh and the British Style." *Listener*, 1 April, 407–409.

Suggests that Vanbrugh had privately hoped to carry out the task articulated by Shaftesbury in his *Letter on the Art or Science of Design* (1715) of leading the Board of Works and the nation in a "national style" of building. Publication of Colin Campbell's *Vitruvius Britannicus* (1715) and the subsequent triumph of Palladianism, however, conjoined with popular dissatisfaction with the grandiosity of Blenheim Palace and the installation of Campbell's friend William Benson and thereafter of Hewet at the Board Works, worked against Vanbrugh's aspirations of architectural leadership. Concerning his building style, Downes notes the similarity of Vanbrugh's independently designed buldings to those he produced early in his career in collaboration with Hawksmoor. Suggests that Vanbrugh found Hawksmoor's style "so congenial that it came to form almost the whole of his idea of architecture."

4 HUME, ROBERT D. *The Development of English Drama in the Late Seventeenth Century.* Oxford: Clarendon Press. Reprint. 1977, 1990, pp. 382, 412–415, 419–420, etc. (Annotation and page references based on 1990 reprint.)

References to Vanbrugh's plays include citation of *The Relapse* as an instance of mingled "hard" and "humane" comedy. The notion that in *The Relapse* the playwright was "attacking" Cibber's *Love's Last Shift* is called a "myth." (Both plays were performed by the Drury Lane Company; Cibber himself was "hugely delighted" with Vanbrugh's sequel, and with his plum role as Lord Foppington.) *The Provoked Wife* is called "one of the harshest marital discord plays" of the 'nineties, Vanburgh's comic prose judged "the finest" of its day. The "sensitivity of his perceptions" is praised, as is "the acuteness with which he analyzes his characters' predicaments." *Aesop*'s popularity in its day is noted.

5 HUSEBOE, ARTHUR R. *Sir John Vanbrugh.* Boston: Twayne, 178 pp.

A study of Vanbrugh's career in the theatre. Devotes a chapter each to analysis of *The Relapse* and *The Provoked Wife*, another to the adaptations. A final chapter discusses *A Journey to London* and the critical reception of Vanbrugh's plays from his day to our own. Among the author's critical *aperçus* is the suggestion that "Vanbrugh was not quick to see incongruities that might easily have been corrected" in his plays. In

1976

The Relapse, for example, "Loveless might have been given a motive for going to London . . , or Amanda a reason for inviting Berinthia" to reside in her household.

6 KENNY, SHIRLEY STRUM. "Perennial Favorites: Congreve, Vanbrugh, Cibber, Farquhar, and Steele." *MP* 73, no. 4, P. 2 (May):S4–S11.

Vanbrugh is one of six dramatists whose work between 1695 and 1710 "made an impact on the London theatre and culture far greater than is indicated by the place assigned them in histories of the drama." Of the twenty-five comedies premiering during this fifteen-year period that "became staples in the theatrical repertory," Vanbrugh was the author of the greatest number (6)—his plays seeing 218 performances during the period 1715–1775. The figure would rise to 299 were the Vanbrugh–Cibber *Provoked Husband* added to his total rather than to Cibber's (whose figure of 354 performances includes 81 performances of *The Provoked Husband*).

7 LINK, FREDERICK M., ed. *English Drama 1660–1800: A Guide to Information Sources.* Detroit: Gale Research Co., pp. 314–316.

A select annotated bibliography including editions of Vanbrugh's plays, biographical studies, and criticism of the comedies.

8 LOFTIS, JOHN; SOUTHERN, RICHARD; JONES, MARION; and SCOUTEN, A. H. *The Revels History of Drama in English.* Vol. 5. 1660–1750. Edited by T. W. Craik. London: Methuen, pp. 37–38, 223–224.

Includes intermittent commentary on Vanbrugh. Collier's complaint, for example, that Vanbrugh's portrait of Sir Tunbelly is not an accurate representation of the squirearchy is cited as an instance of the clergyman's failure "to recognize that Vanbrugh had employed broad stage caricature in the service of satire." A three-paragraph appraisal of his achievement discusses *The Relapse* and *The Provoked Wife*, noting that Vanbrugh's other plays "are adaptations, heavily derived from Dancourt and other French writers, and are as well forgotten."

9 MARSDEN, E. "An 18th-Century Dilletante Architect: John Pitt of Encombe." *CLife* 160, no. 4132 (September):662–665.

Describes Vanbrugh's influence on the design of John Pitt's Encombe House in Dorset (c. 1734–1754).

10 MILHOUS, JUDITH. "New Light on Vanbrugh's Haymarket Theatre Project." *ThS* 17, no. 2 (November):143–161.

Identifies the twenty-nine subscribers to Vanbrugh's 1703 proposal to build a new theatre at the Haymarket, noting that fewer than half the subscribers (who included eight dukes and ten earls) were Kit-Cats. Contrary to Cibber's contention, Vanbrugh appears not to have built his theatre for Betterton's Lincoln's Inn Fields players. Instead the evidence indicates that he intended either to unite the Betterton and Drury Lane players into a single company or to "raid" the two companies, taking the best actors from each. It is likely that Vanbrugh opened his theatre before it was "fully rigged and operational"—this in an unsuccessful effort to counter the success of Rich's opera *Arsinoe* with a hasty Italian import, Greber's *Loves of Ergasto*.

11 PATTERSON, FRANK M. "Sir John Vanbrugh as Translator: *The Confederacy*." *RECTR* 15, no. 2 (November):40–46, 60.

Examines the relation of Vanbrugh's *The Confederacy* (1705) to its source, Dancourt's *Les Bourgeosies à la Mode* (1682). Vanbrugh's principal structural changes include (1) creation of an opening scene in which the peddlar Mrs. Amlet excoriates ladies of quality and city wives for their slowness in paying their debts; (2) creation of an initial scene in Act III in which Mrs. Amlet's son Dick steals his mother's necklace from her strong box; and (3) fifty new lines at the beginning of V.ii in which Moneytrap and Gripe and their spouses interact, the husbands unaware that each is being bilked by the other's wife. These and other of Vanbrugh's alterations, many of which sharpen Dancourt's portrait of bourgeois acquisitiveness, give *The Confederacy* a keener satirical edge than Dancourt's play possesses.

12 WHITE, NORVAL. "Vanbrugh, (Sir) John (1664–1726): English Spy, Playwright, and Architect." In *The Architecture Book*. New York: Knopf, pp. 321–322.

A brief entry for Vanbrugh calls Castle Howard and Blenheim Palace "English Baroque, at its best." Adds that Hawksmoor "contributed some of his proto-Cubism" to Blenheim's kitchen wing.

1977

1 ANTHONY, JOHN. *Vanbrugh: an Illustrated Life of Sir John Vanbrugh, 1664–1726*. Aylesbury, Bucks. [England]: Shire, 46 pp.

Four pages are devoted to Vanbrugh's early life and his career as dramatist, the remainder to his architecture. Each of the major buildings is discussed and illustrated.

1977

2 DOWNES, KERRY. *Vanbrugh.* Studies in Architecture. Vol. 16. Edited by Anthony Blunt, John Harris, and Howard Hibbard. London: A. Zwemmer, 385 pp.

The text devotes almost equal attention to Vanbrugh's architectural career and his genealogy. Prints his account book for the period 1715–1726 and concludes with a usefully annotated "List of Works" under the following categories: "Certain works wholly or partly carried out," "Probable attributions," "Ordnance Buildings," "Unexecuted projects for which drawings survive," "Projects known from written sources," and "Attributions rejected as improbable or impossible." Profusely illustrated.

3 *HADFIELD, MILES. *The English Landscape Garden.* Aylesbury: Shire.

Source: LCS. For annotation, see 1988.2.

4 HANSON, N. "Englishmen's Homes in a Castle." *CLife* 161, no. 4162 (April):888.

Sketches Vanbrugh's career as a preliminary to discussing Vanbrugh Castle, in which the architect lived his wedded life from 1719 until his death in 1726. Purchased by Lord Trawley, the building subsequently served first as a girls' and later as a boys' boarding school. In 1977 it was purchased by the Blackheath Preservation Trust with the intention of selling it to a party wishing to restore the building to residential use.

5 JOHANSSON, BERTIL. *The Adapter Adapted: A Study of Sir John Vanbrugh's Comedy "The Mistake," Its Predecessors and Successors.* Stockholm: Almqvist & Wiksell, 75 pp.

The "predecessors" examined are Molière's *Le dépit amoureux* (1656)—of which Vanbrugh's *The Mistake* (1705) was a close adaptation—and Dryden's *An Evening's Love* (1668), to which Vanburgh's play is judged to owe little. The "successors" are two farcical adaptations of Vanbrugh's play—Thomas Ryder's *Like Master Like Man* (premiere 1767 at the Haymarket) and Thomas King's *Lovers' Quarrels* (premiere 1790 at Covent Garden).

6 LOFTIS, JOHN. *Sheridan and the Drama of Georgian England.* Cambridge, Mass.: Harvard University Press, pp. 77–85.

Includes discussion of Sheridan's *A Trip to Scarborough*, an adaptation of Vanbrugh's *The Relapse.* Sheridan deleted Loveless's opening soliloquy—whose resemblance to Horace's (perhaps also ironic) "Integer vitae scelerisque purus" ode is noted. Sheridan was also more attentive than Vanbrugh to the three unities. In replacing

Vanbrugh's frank sexuality with a "muted and at times evasive depiction" of sexual matters, and in "clarif[ying] the moral structure by changes in plot as well as in language," Sheridan removed Vanbrugh's "central and disturbing satirical insights"—among them Vanbrugh's recognition of "the impossiblity of a hardened libertine's abrupt transformation into a devoted husband." (Cf. 1953.2.)

7 MACK, MAYNARD. "'They Have Actually Turned Me Out': Vanbrugh to Marlborough." *Scriblerian* 9, no. 2 (Spring):77–83.

On the (mistaken) assumption that the letter had not previously been noticed, prints and discusses Vanbrugh's communication of 18 March 1712/1713 to the Duke of Marlborough seeking the Duke's help in restoring him to the Comptrollership of the Board of Works. Vanbrugh had been dismissed from the post the day before—this after his letter to the Mayor of Woodstock complaining of the "continual plague and bitter persecution" of the Duke of Marlborough by the Tories had fallen into the hands of Queen Anne's Tory Lord Treasurer Robert Harley. (Cf. Whistler 1954.5.)

8 PODEWELL, BRUCE. "An Identification of the Players in Vanbrugh's *Aesop*, Part II." *RECTR* 16, no. 1 (May):23–26.

Offers the following speculative identifications of players in the 1697 premiere of *Aesop*, Part II: 1st Player, Thomas Betterton; 1st Woman, Mary Betterton; 2nd Woman, Elizabeth Barry. Identifications are offered on the basis of the play's descriptions of the rebelling (Lincoln's Inn Fields) players, who explain their succession to Aesop in the play's initial episode.

9 ROGERS, PHILLIS. "Kings Weston." *Archaeological Journal* 134:324–325.

Brief description of Kings Weston as altered by Vanbrugh and later architects. Notes Vanbrugh's "memorable skyline of colonnaded chimney-stacks"—an arrangement that would be imitated in other houses in the area. Describes the staircase hall, Vanbrugh's only surviving interior at King Weston, and attributes to Vanbrugh three outbuildings—a brew-house and two loggias.

10 WILLIS, PETER. *Charles Bridgeman and the English Landscape Garden.* London: A. Zwemmer, pp. 44–50.

Describes and reproduces plans of the garden designs of those of Vanbrugh's building projects in which Bridgeman had a hand—Blenheim, Eastbury, and Claremont. Vanbrugh's memorandum of 1709 urging the preservation of the Old Manor House at Woodstock is said

1978

to offer "the seeds of thinking about the Picturesque which later in the century were to grow into an elaborate artistic theory."

11 WILLIS, PETER. "'Les Plaisants Paysages': Vanbrugh, Bridgeman et le Ha-Ha." In *Jardins et Paysages: Le Style Anglais*. Vol. 2. Publications de l'Université de Lille [France], III. Edited by André Parreaux et Michèle Plaisant. n.p., pp. 85–95.

Thinks it probable that Stephen Switzer in his *Iconographia Rustica* (1718) had Vanbrugh in mind when he averred that a "man of quality" in the Office of Works introduced the ha-ha into English landscape gardening. Notes the presence of ha-has in those gardens on which Bridgeman and Vanbrugh collaborated—at Blenheim, Eastbury, and Stowe. Stowe's ha-ha is discussed with reference to a drawing by Bridgeman (c. 1720) now in the Bodleian Library. Quotes Lord Perceval's praise of Stowe's ha-ha in a letter of 1704 to his cousin Daniel Dering.

1978

1 BROWNELL, MORRIS R. *Alexander Pope & the Arts of Georgian England*. Oxford: At the Clarendon Press, pp. 198–200, 310–315, 381–382.

Includes discussion of Pope's possible allusion to Vanbrugh's Eastbury House in the *Epistle to Burlington*. Discusses Pope's criticism of Blenheim in personal correspondence (see 1956.7), in the *Master Key . . .* (1949.7), and in the *Epistle to Burlington*. Cites Whistler (1938.3 and 1950.13) concerning Vanbrugh's contributions to Stowe's gardens and garden architecture. Reproduces (with added notations of the locations of Vanbrugh's temples) Rigaud's engraved plan of Stowe's gardens (1739) and his engraving of Vanbrugh's rotunda.

2 MCCORMICK, FRANK GRADY. "The Embattled Career of Sir John Vanbrugh." *DAI* 39 (1978):901A. University of Minnesota, 192 pp.

Offers close readings of *The Relapse, The Provoked Wife, The Confederacy*, and *A Journey to London*. A chapter on the architecture focuses on the recurrent martial features in both the small-scale buildings (such as Vanbrugh's residences at Esher and Whitehall) and the larger ones, especially Blenheim. Martial themes in the architecture are compared to those in the plays. Material is revised into book form, with additional attention to the architecture, in 1991.1.

3 PRICE, CURTIS A. "The Critical Decade for English Music Drama, 1700-1710." *Harvard Library Bulletin* 26, no. 1 (January):38-76 passim.

Includes discussion of Vanbrugh's sponsorship of opera at his Queen's Theatre at the Haymarket. The continuing success of *Arsinoe* at Drury Lane stimulated him to open the new theatre with an opera in April of 1705, Greber's *The Loves of Ergasto*, "probably the first London stage work to be sung completely in Italian." More successful—with a run of twelve nights—was the English dramatic opera Vanbrugh's house mounted in its second season, George Granville's *The British Enchanters*. Vanbrugh's maneuverings in the several theatrical "revolutions" that ensued are noted. In "Revolution I" (which may have had its origins in Vanbrugh's "politicking among his aristocratic acquaintances for 'an agreement between the two playhouses'") the Lord Chamberlain decreed that commencing with the 1706-1707 season, operas were to be performed exclusively at Drury Lane, spoken drama at the Haymarket. In "Revolution II" the Lord Chamberlain (again apparently at Vanbrugh's instigation) reversed the arrangement, granting Vanbrugh's Haymarket Theatre a monopoly on the performance of operas and Rich's Drury Lane a monopoly on the production of plays. Though the "motives" of Vanbrugh and other key players in these events remain largely "hidden from our view," the author argues that it was Vanbrugh the playwright, not Rich the businessman, who was most "responsible for assuring that the foreign opera gained a foothold on the English stage."

4 VAN DER WEELE, STEVEN JOHN. *The Critical Reputation of Restoration Comedy in Modern Times up to 1950*. Vol. 2. Salzburg Studies in English Literature, under the Direction of Professor Erwin A. Stürzl; Poetic Drama & Poetic Theory Editor, Dr. James Hogg. Salzburg: Institut für Englische Sprache und Literatur, Universität Salzburg, pp. 547-574.

A chapter on Vanbrugh includes a biographical sketch followed by summaries of the views of Dametz (1898.1), Mueschke and Fleisher (1934.1), Thaler (1936.6), and Kronenberger (1952.3) concerning Vanbrugh's comedies.

5 WHISTLER, LAURENCE. "Deeds of Partnership." *TLS*, 17 February, p. 205.

Review of Downes, *Vanbrugh* (1977.2). Praises the "exciting illustrations," the transcription of Vanbrugh's account book, and the full delineation of Vanbrugh's family relationships. Questions Downes's attribution of Stowe's north portico to Vanbrugh and the assertion that Vanbrugh and Hawksmoor might have founded a national style of architecture had not Burlingtonian Palladianism intervened. Avers that the style of both men was "too idiosyncratic for general adoption." Distinguishes the Vanbrugh–Hawksmoor style from the style of Vanbrugh's independent buildings.

1979

1 CURL, JAMES STEVENS. Review of Downes, *Vanbrugh* (1977.2). *Town Planning Review* 50, no. 2 (April):243–244.

Characterizes Vanbrugh's "memorandum concerning the building of new churches in London and Westminster" as "one of [his] most interesting contributions to urban reform." Finds especially "farsighted" the proposal that the dead be buried in "Caemitarys provided in the Skirts" of towns rather than within churches. Vanbrugh's Goose-Pie House is described as "symmetrically planned in the most advanced style for its date; hence an object of "the attention of connoisseurs," the "scorn" of "philistines."

2 FLEMING, LAURENCE, and GORE, ALAN. *The English Garden.* London: Michael Joseph, pp. 81, 87–91, 98–99, 101, 118, 122.

Includes several references to Vanbrugh's contributions to garden architecture—among them the "romantic park wall" and Temple of the Four Winds he built for Carlisle Howard, the "lakeside pavilions" he designed for Lord Cobham at Stowe, and the circular temple he designed for Duncombe Park, where he helped Duncombe lay out his gardens; all illustrated with photographs or engravings.

3 GOMME, ANDOR. "Downes v Whistler." Review of Downes, *Vanbrugh* (1977.2). *AR* 165, no. 984 (February):123–124.

Suggests that Downes's discussion of Castle Howard, Blenheim, and Kimbolton "essentially repeats Whistler's account" [1954.5] and that in several instances in which the author "proposes a new hypothesis," as in the account of Eastbury, he does so without adducing "new evidence."

4 HARRIS, JOHN. *A Country House Index: An Index to over 2000 Country Houses Illustrated in 107 Books of Country Views Published between 1715 and 1872 together with a List of British Country House Guides and Country House Art Collection Catalogues for the Period 1726-1880.* Pinhorns Handbooks: 7. 2d ed. London: Pinhorns, pp. 5, 7, 8, 11, 13, 17, 18, 21, 24, 25.

English country houses are listed alphabetically, followed by citations of studies published between 1715 and 1872 in which illustrations of the houses appear. The following houses built or altered by Vanbrugh appear in the index: Blenheim Palace, Castle Howard, Claremont, Eastbury, Grimsthorpe, Kimbolton Castle, Kings Weston, Lumley Castle, Nottingham Castle, Stowe, Seaton Delaval. For citation of 1st ed., see 1971.2; see also 1968.1.

5 HOPKINS, PAUL. "John Vanbrugh's Imprisonment in France 1688–1693." *N & Q*, n.s. 26, no. 6 (December):529–534.
   New information is offered concerning the role played by the exiled Jacobite court in negotiations for Vanbrugh's release. Notes that at the instigation of the Jacobite court, Vanbrugh's mother persuaded the English to propose exchanging a Scottish Jacobite prisoner for her son. When the French refused, Vanbrugh was transferred at his own request to confinement at the castle of Vincennes (May 1691). There he came into contact with the Jacobites at the court of St. Germain, among whom he pretended to be a Jacobite himself, eager by implication to be returned to England so that he might join in the plot against William. (See also 1982.7 and 1982.8.)

6 JORDAN, R. J. "Vanbrugh at Sea." *N & Q*, n.s. 26, no. 6 (December): 526–529.
   Examines the Marquis of Carmarthen's account of the English naval attack on the French at Camaret Bay in 1694, an action in which Vanbrugh participated. Carmarthen's *Journal of the Brest-Expedition* (1694.1) commends Vanbrugh's conduct, noting that he "was extremely serviceable both by his advice and otherwise." Upon Carmarthen's recommendation, Lord Berkeley made Vanbrugh a captain in his Second Marine Regiment in August of the following year.

7 *KAISER, WOLFGANG. "Castle Howard. Studien zu Planungs und Baugeschichte." M. A. thesis, University of Freiburg, 1982.
   Source: Saumarez Smith, 1990.6.

8 LANG, S. Review of Downes, *Vanbrugh* (1977.2). *JSAH* 38, no. 2 (May):208–210.
   Thinks Downes's attention to Vanbrugh's genealogy excessive. Doubts the assertion that Castle Howard's bow window room was "an afterthought . . . copied from a similar room at Blenheim." Notes (*pace* Downes) a "treasury minute" indicating that Vanbrugh revised Hawksmoor's design for the Kensington Orangery.

1979

9 MARSH, EMILIA FIELD CRESSWELL. "The Plays and Architecture of Sir John Vanbrugh." *DAI* 40 (1979):3319A–3320A. Northwestern University, 330 pp.

Argues that the "aesthetic *effects*" of Vanbrugh's "assertive, almost aggressive" buildings have their analogues in his plays. Major and minor characters in the comedies are examined and found to exist "three dimensionally, from all angles, in depth as well as facade in their internal motivations and their relations with their spouses." Architectural qualities are also noted in the structures of the plays, which achieve "variety within an overall harmony of character and structure" through the playwright's "infus[ion]" of "a great deal of physical action to increase pace and movement," and through the introduction of "rhythmic repetitions of motifs in comparison, contrast, or parody."

10 MILHOUS, JUDITH. "Five New Letters by Sir John Vanbrugh." *HLB* 27, no. 4 (October):434–441.

The letters pertain to details of the building of Blenheim Palace and its outworks and to Vanbrugh's duties as Clarenceux King-of-Arms.

11 MILHOUS, JUDITH. *Thomas Betterton and the Management of Lincoln's Inn Fields, 1695–1708.* Carbondale and Edwardsville: Southern Illinois University Press; London and Amsterdam: Feffer & Simons, pp. 189–221.

Chapter 7 describes Vanbrugh's stewardship of the Haymarket Theatre from its inception in 1703 to the Union of 1708. In his efforts to "make a great splash with opera," Vanbrugh was forestalled by Rich, who in *Arsinoe* secured for Drury Lane the opera that Vanbrugh had hoped would open his theatre. Sees Betterton's influence in Vanbrugh's choice of three "English operas" for Haymarket production in spring 1706. Suggests that Vanbrugh chose Owen Swiney to manage his company in that year because Swiney had acquired experience in opera production while working for Rich at Drury Lane.

12 RICHARDS, KENNETH. "A Classical Borrowing in Vanbrugh's 'The Relapse.'" *N & Q*, n.s. 26, no. 6 (December):534–535.

Loveless's confession to Berinthia that he was stricken with love for her upon glimpsing her for the first time at a play (*Relapse* [III.ii]) is claimed to be indebted to Sappho XI or to Catullus Carmen 51 (the latter derived from the Greek poem).

13 "Scribleriana." *Scriblerian* 11, no. 2 (Spring):143.

Includes acknowledgment of a communication from Judith Milhous noting that the Vanbrugh letter printed in 1977.7 had previously been published in Whistler's *Imagination*, 1954.5.

14 STAVES, SUSAN. *Players' Scepters: Fictions of Authority in the Restoration.* Lincoln and London: University of Nebraska Press, pp. 171, 179, 180, 186.

The Provoked Wife is included in a list of plays illustrative of the "marked fashion for female protagonists in 'nineties drama." The same play is cited with Southerne's *Wives Excuse* as one of the "problem comedies . . . which modern critics like better than sentimental comedies."

15 STUART, DAVID C. *Georgian Gardens.* London: Robert Hale, pp. 24, 33, 44, 48, 213, 214, 225.

Notes Vanbrugh's effort to preserve Woodstock Manor "as an eye-catcher," and his 1705 "call for a landscape painter to design the gardens at Blenheim" (illustrated in a photograph). Detects a resemblance between Inigo Jones's use of "'toy fort' gothic buildings in some of his theatre designs" and Vanbrugh's use of "the same style" for Vanbrugh Castle and Castle Howard's garden buildings. His landscaping at Claremont is illustrated in a contemporary painting.

16 WAKEFIELD, SIR HUMPHRY. "Castle Howard: the Majesty of a Great English Country House." *Architectural Digest* 36, no. 4: 150–158.

Scant text, sumptuous photographs of Castle Howard's entrance front, gateway into the east wing court, and interior (especially the Great Hall). The building's present owner, George Howard, leads the tour, explaining that the house "was the joint concept and endeavor of a triumvirate: Vanbrugh, Hawksmoor, and Charles Howard, 3d Earl of Carlisle."

1979–1980

1 CHIAPPELLI, CAROLYN. "The Single-Plot Structure of Vanbrugh's *The Relapse*." *EM* 28–29: 207–225.

The Relapse juxtaposes a "higher" against a "lower" moral level—the "higher" represented by Amanda's persistence in virtue, the "lower" by the vices of Young Fashion and his confederates. Events are so arranged that by the end of the play "the audience begins to be shocked by the increasingly repulsive vices of [Young Fashion's] world" and begins "to understand Worthy's upward impulse toward Amanda." The argument is supported by references to Vanbrugh's *Short Vindication*, in which the playwright evinced "recognition of his own sermonizing" in *The Relapse*.

1980

1 *BARBER, JOHN. Review of revival of *The Provoked Wife*. *Daily Telegraph*, 30 October.

    *Source: Coleman, 1982.2, p. 21; unverified. Review of National Theatre (London) production of *The Provoked Wife* opines, *pace* director Peter Wood, that the play is "essentially . . . a funny satire on marriage." Thinks the "production would be much improved if the wouldn't-it-be-fun-if approach were abandoned with the gratuitous efforts to add significant realism to a merry comedy of manners."

2 *BILLINGTON, MICHAEL. Review of revival of *The Provoked Wife*. *The Guardian*, 30 October.

    *Source: Coleman, 1982.2, p. 22; unverified. Coleman cites observation of reviewer of National Theatre (London) production of *The Provoked Wife* that "Vanbrugh's theme is marital imprisonment." Reviewer calls Lady Brute, "who married [Sir John] for his money," "a captive wretch dreaming of infidelity." Thinks Lady Fancyfull "an affected schemer in love with her own image."

3 CANFIELD, J. DOUGLAS. "Religious Language and Religious Meaning in Restoration Comedy." *SEL* 20, no. 3 (Summer):394–399.

    Includes a providentialist interpretation of Vanbrugh's "witty, ironic use of religious language" in *The Relapse*. "However debased or formulaic" that language may be, Vanbrugh is said to use it "to invoke the very dimensions of [Christian] reality" his characters so "insouciantly flout." In a lengthy note, similarly Christian intentions are discerned in Vanbrugh's deployment of religious imagery in *The Provoked Wife* and in his adaptations.

4 COLVIN, H. M. *Biographical Dictionary of British Architects 1660–1840*. Rev. ed. New York: Facts on File, pp. 849–854.

    In the revised Vanbrugh entry the bibliography is updated and the earlier reference to Vanbrugh's "highly personal" style (1954.1) is replaced by the assertion that his "houses must be seen as a work of collaboration" between Vanbrugh and Hawksmoor.

5 *CUSHMAN, ROBERT. Review of revival of *The Provoked Wife*. *The Observer*, 2 November.

*Source: Coleman, 1982.2, pp. 22–23; unverified. Review of National Theatre (London) production of *The Provoked Wife*. Coleman cites reviewer's commentary on the Brute marriage ("a misalliance from which neither party has the means or the courage to break"), Heartfree and Belinda (who are deliberating "whether to risk their intelligence on a similar venture"), and Sir John (who at one point "analyses his own plight with a masochistic sharpness").

6 DIXON, PETER, and HAYLEY, RODNEY. "*The Provoked Husband* on the Nineteenth-Century Stage." *NCTR* 8, no. 1 (Spring): 1–16.

Purged of all traces of indecency, and altered so that it ended on an "unequivocally pathetic and tender note" with the Townlys' reconciliation, the Vanbrugh–Cibber *Provoked Husband* became a staple on the nineteenth-century London stage.

7 DRURY, P. J. "'No other palace in the kingdom will compare with it': The Evolution of Audley End, 1605–1745." *Architectural History* 23:1–39.

Includes discussion (pp. 24–25) of Vanbrugh's alterations of Audley End for his distant kinsman Henry, Lord Binden, 6th Earl of Suffolk, between 1708 and 1713. Vanbrugh demolished the decayed "north and south ranges of the outer court and the great kitchen . . , leaving intact the western range of the outer court, and the walls extending its west elevation north and south." The result: an "architectural expression of medieval romanticism," the remaining range resembling a "medieval keep" with its gatehouse, towers, bastions, and turrets.

8 *FENTON, JAMES. Review of revival of *The Provoked Wife*. *The Sunday Times*, 2 November.

*Source: Coleman, 1982.2, p. 22; unverified. Review of National Theatre (London) production of *The Provoked Wife*.

9 FLUCHÈRE, MARIE-LOUISE. *L'Oeuvre Dramatique de Sir John Vanbrugh*. n.p.: Ophrys, 971 pp.

Initial chapters examine the historical and theatrical milieu, the principal events of Vanbrugh's life, and the critical reception of his plays. The bulk of the study is devoted to classification and discussion of characters in his three original plays (character types, relationships, and problems with "l'argent" and "l'amour" experienced by the characters). Other chapters examine the structure and comic techniques of

1980

the three original plays. A final chapter discusses Vanbrugh's adaptations and their relationships to their (primarily French) sources.

10 FLUCHÈRE, MARIE-LOUISE. "Sir John Vanbrugh: Bibliographie Selective et Critique." *BSEAA* 17–18 (November):31–54.
    Select annotated bibliography listing editions and collections of Vanbrugh's comedies, biographical studies, and criticism of the plays.

11 *KING, FRANCIS. Review of revival of *The Provoked Wife*. *The Sunday Telegraph*, 2 November.
    *Source: Coleman, 1982.2, p. 23; unverified. Review of National Theatre (London) production of *The Provoked Wife*. Coleman cites reviewer's complaint that parts are miscast—Lady Brute, for example, "who should show a capacity for real feeling, is played by that most artificial of actresses, Geraldine McEwan," while the "narcissistic, posturing Lady Fancyfull is played by an actress, Dorothy Tutin, whose chief strength is an ability to project sincerity."

12 "*The Provok'd Wife* by John Vanbrugh." London: Battley Brothers Printers, 8 pp.
    Program notes for a National Theatre (London) production of *The Provoked Wife*. The sketch of Vanbrugh's character and career is a distillation of the current-traditional view popularized by Dobrée (1925.4) and Whistler (1938.7): Vanbrugh "was a man of dazzling and varied talents" who "moved easily through his times," about whom few "spoke a word of malice." "[F]riendly and clubbable," he "brought to architecture the same gusto which he showed in his plays." A sketch of the stage history of *The Provoked Wife* includes the assertion that David Garrick "never forgot that Sir John was by birth a gentleman. . . ."

13 SALGADO, GAMINI. *English Drama: A Critical Introduction*. New York: St. Martin's, pp. 144, 158–160, 165.
    Vanbrugh's assertion in his prologue to *The Provoked Wife* that the stage portrays "the follies of the age" and "Hold[s] to every man a faithful glass" is cited as an instance of the "fairly standard claim" of realistic portraiture offered by dramatists of the day. *The Provoked Wife*'s "discussions of marriage" are called "serious and occasionally sharp," though their "wit is of a fairly long-winded and predictable kind." Concerning *The Relapse* we are told that "Vanbrugh's skepticism about Loveless's reform is simply the obverse of Cibber's sentimentality [in *Love's Last Shift*] and is treated with no more depth."

14 *WARDLE, IRVING. Review of revival of *The Provoked Wife*. *The Times* [London], 30 October.
     *Source: Coleman, 1982.2, pp. 21–22; unverified. Coleman cites complaint of reviewer of National Theatre (London) production of *The Provoked Wife* that John Wood's performance of the part of Sir John Brute "bears no relationship to the character's name. Instead of the oafish rake he presents a twisted vinegary domestic martyr who changes into a jovial boozing crony once he gets free of the house." Thinks Sir John, Heartfree, and Constant "are much closer relative to the cowards and egoists of reality than the honey-tongued studs who usually strut through the Restoration pleasure garden."

1981

1 BERKOWITZ, GERALD M. *Sir John Vanbrugh and the End of Restoration Comedy*. Amsterdam: Rodopi, 222 pp.
    Proposes that Vanbrugh freed "the comic universe from the limited realism of Etherege." Vanbrugh's drama is said to offer "a larger and more varied population"—a population that includes realistically drawn servants, old men who are allowed to be "wise," and able exponents of country values—than is to be found in Restoration drama. Further, Vanbrugh is "the first" dramatist of his age "to address himself to serious ethical questions [particularly questions concerning marriage and sexuality] within the comic framework," and the first to create characters [witness Lady Brute] deep and complex enough to raise such issues." (Incorporates material from 1969.1 and 1973.1.)

2 BROWN, LAURA. *English Dramatic Form, 1660–1760*. New Haven and London: Yale University Press, pp. 117–123.
    Examines *The Relapse* in a chapter on 1690s "transitional comedy" (comedy in which "social satire and moral action" are uneasily juxtaposed). In "juxtapos[ing] . . . Berinthia's social world and Amanda's moral one" in *The Relapse*, Vanbrugh "experiments with psychological complexity," endowing Amanda, for example, with "a dramatized inner life" in which we observe the "psychological struggle of a moral individual in an amoral world."

3 CAMÉ, JEAN-FRANÇOIS. "Vanbrugh's *The Provoked Wife* and Milton's *Comus*." *CahiersE* 19 (April):89.
    Thinks the Spring Garden seduction scene in *The Provoked Wife* parodies the attempted seduction in Milton's *Comus*. In both instances the imperiled lady is "rescued by outside help"—Lady Brute

by Lady Fancyfull and Mademoiselle, the lady in *Comus* by her two brothers.

4   CORDNER, MICHAEL. "Anti-Clericalism in Vanbrugh's *The Provoked Wife*." *N & Q*, n.s. 28, no. 3 (June):212–214.
   Cites as context for Sir John Brute's antics in the guise of a clergy-man (*Provoked Wife* IV.i and IV.iii) contemporary reports of royster-ing gentlemen and the testimony of the pious that in their drunken carousings such gentlemen "revile or disturbe Ministers." As a possi-ble indirect stimulus for Vanbrugh's account of Sir John's imperson-ation of a clergyman, cites a 1693 account in John Dunton's *The Athe-nian Mercury* of "a Young Man . . . who resolves to put on a Clergymans Habit, and commit all manner of Extravagances therein. . . ."

5   CORDNER, MICHAEL. "Vanbrugh's Lord Rake." *N & Q*, n.s. 28, no. 3 (June):214–216.
   Interprets Lord Rake's assertion that "no penal laws . . . can curb me" in his song in *The Provoked Wife* (III.ii) as an "adroit allusion" to contemporary confusion over the provisions of the Toleration Act of 1689. Particularly germane to Lord Rake's claim was the assump-tion in some quarters of the country that the act freed "the irreligious from the existing legislation which prescribed punishments for non-attendance at divine service." In allowing Lord Rake to promulgate such a misunderstanding of the Toleration Act, Vanbrugh opened him-self to suspicions of impiety.

6   *FLUCHÈRE, MARIE-LOUISE.   Introduction to *The Provok'd Wife*. Paris: Aubier Montaigne.
   Source: *The Scriblerian and the Kit-Cats* 15, no. 1 (Autumn):5–6. Michèle S. Plaisant's *Scriblerian* annotation includes this observation: Fluchère's introduction to her French translation of *The Provoked Wife* "argues that the sinuous course and slow unraveling of the plot are in keeping with Lady Brute's two years' shillyshallying and qualms of conscience. . . ."

7   MILHOUS, JUDITH, and HUME, ROBERT D.   "An Annotated Guide to the Theatrical Documents in PRO LC 7/1, 7/2 and 7/3 (con-tinued), LC 7/2." *TN* 35, no. 2:77–84.
   Lists and summarizes the contents of a number of documents per-tinent to Vanbrugh's management of the Haymarket Theatre—among them his 14 August 1706 agreement to lease his theatre to Swiney "for seven years at 5 [pounds] per acting day." Vanbrugh documents listed

include LC 7/2, nos. 1-9, 50, 52, 55, 73, 74, and 76. (See also 1982.1 and 1982.10.)

8   MILHOUS, JUDITH, and HUME, ROBERT D. "An Annotated Guide to the Theatrical Documents in PRO LC 7/1, 7/2 and 7/3 (continued), Volume 2." *TN* 35, no. 3:122-129.

Vanbrugh agreements listed and summarized include LC 7/2, nos. 103, 104, and 110—the last headed "Vanbrugh's claim that a genre split would not damage Rich." (See also 1982.1 and 1982.10.)

9   SHATTUCK, CHARLES H. "Drama as Promptbook." In *The Stage and the Page: London's "Whole Show" in the Eighteenth-Century Theatre*. Edited by Geo. Winchester Stone, Jr. Berkeley: University of California Press, pp. 163-191.

Includes discussion (pp. 172-178) of a Garrick promptbook for *The Provoked Wife*. Garrick performed the role of Sir John Brute 105 times between 1744 and 1776. He shortened Vanbrugh's text by one-fifth, reducing the number of lines spoken by most of the characters save Sir John Brute, the focal point of his own productions of the play. While he did not "modify one coarse syllable of Sir John's utterance," Garrick played the role in a manner "acceptable to the rising sentimentalism of the age," making Sir John "'an old dandy . . , a joyous agreeable wicked dog.'"

10 SMITH, NANCY GENZMER. "The Darkening Vision of Sir John Vanbrugh, with a Critical Edition of *The Pilgrim*." *DAI* 42 (1982):4012A. University of Maryland, 249 pp.

Early chapters survey the criticism of Vanbrugh's plays and summarize and evaluate each of them. The main body examines *The Pilgrim*'s departures from its source (Fletcher's 1621 *Pilgrim*). Vanbrugh replaces Fletcher's verse with "easy prose," shortens speeches, improves their "force," heightens the contrasts among his characters (cf. 1926.7). The "critical edition" of Vanbrugh's *Pilgrim* is preceded by brief stage and critical histories and followed by an historical collation.

11 WOODBRIDGE, KENNETH. "Iconographic Variations: Classical and Gothic Themes in the English Landscape Garden in the 18th Century." *Lotus International* 30:11-17.

Searching for the theoretical origins of the English landscape garden of the eighteenth century, cites classical Arcadian tradition (which opposed the "natural surroundings of the shepherd's life to the affectations and constraints of the court"), the imaginative Chinese garden as recounted in Temple's *Upon the Gardens of Epicurus* (1692), and Alberti's remarks (in his *Ten Books of Architecture*, first translated into English in 1726) on the siting of one's home and grounds in such a way as to "strike the beholders with surprise." Vanbrugh is named the "first" of two architects (William Kent being the second) to put into practice the "theoretical sources of the 'picturesque' style of landscaping in England." In its "early stages" the picturesque style deployed "architectural features to give character by association, frequently of a nostalgic kind." Cited and illustrated are Vanbrugh's Great Pyramid and the "mock medieval ramparts surrounding the park" at Castle Howard, as well as the "large number of temples, seats, columns, and other memorial structures" he devised at Stowe.

1982

1 COKE, THOMAS. *Vice Chamberlain Coke's Theatrical Papers 1706–1715, Edited from the Manuscripts in the Harvard Theatre Collection and Elsewhere.* Edited by Judith Milhous and Robert D. Hume. Carbondale and Edwardsville: Southern Illinois University Press, pp. 1–225, intermittently as indicated in editors' index.

Includes many documents pertinent to Vanbrugh's management of the Haymarket Theatre. See editors' introduction, 1982.10.

2 COLEMAN, ANTONY, ed. Introduction and Appendixes to *The Provoked Wife*, by Sir John Vanbrugh. Manchester: Manchester University Press, pp. 1–48, 166–192.

The Introduction discusses the printing history, stage history, and critical reception of *The Provoked Wife*. Proposes that the play offers "a consistent moral viewpoint—that of common sense and common decency." Appendixes discuss Vanbrugh's response to the Collier stage controversy, print and discuss *The Provoked Wife*'s songs and revised scenes (here dated c. 1726; cf. 1966.7 and 1961.1), and supply a list of David Garrick's alterations of the play.

3 DOWNES, KERRY. "John Vanbrugh." In *Macmillan Encyclopedia of Architects.* Vol. 4, edited by Adolf K. Placzek. London: Macmillan, The Free Press, pp. 257–269.

A definitive brief survey of Vanbrugh's principal buildings. Synthesizes many of the points made at greater length in other Downes studies listed above and below.

4 DOWNES, KERRY. "Vanbrugh's Heslington Lady." *Burlington Magazine* 124, no. 948 (March):153–155.

Prints and examines a letter Vanbrugh wrote in 1717 to an unidentified correspondent. In the letter Vanbrugh discusses (1) the Earl of

Carlisle's role as mediator in the internecine Whig party strife of 1717; (2) his own role in arranging the Duke of Newcastle's recent marriage to Henrietta Godolphin; and (3) his nascent affection for "your Heslington Lady," whom Downes identifies as Vanbrugh's future wife, Henrietta Maria Yarburgh.

5 HARRIS, JOHN. *William Talman: Maverick Architect.* London, Boston, and Sydney: George Allen and Unwin, pp. 36–39.

Includes brief discussion of Vanbrugh's successful maneuverings to wrest the Castle Howard commission from Talman. The episode is said to show "a nasty side of [Vanbrugh's] nature that conflicts with the usual picture of amicability. . . ."

6 *KAISER, WOLFGANG. "Castle Howard, Ein Englischer Landsitz des Fruhen 18. Jahrhunderts: Studien zu Architektur und Landschaftspark." Ph.D. dissertation, University of Freiburg, 1982.

Source: Saumarez Smith, 1990.6.

7 MCCORMICK, FRANK. "The Jacobite Reference in Vanbrugh's *Relapse* (I.ii.55–57)." *N & Q*, n.s. 29, no. 1 (February):61.

Vanbrugh's reference to Young Fashion as a "Jacobite" is argued to be a private, self-referential joke. In hopes of inducing French authorities to release him from his confinement at Vincennes in 1691, Vanbrugh had sought to pass himself off as a Jacobite. In fact, as his Vincennes captors were unaware, he had been arrested at Calais in 1688 on charges of agitating on behalf of William of Orange's planned invasion of England. (Material is incorporated into 1991.1; and see 1979.5.)

8 MCCORMICK, FRANK. "Vanbrugh's Imprisonment in France: More Light." *N & Q*, n.s. 29, no. 1 (February):57–61.

Describes Vanbrugh's energetic efforts to secure his release from imprisonment in France during the period 1688–1692. Evidence examined includes a letter Vanbrugh wrote from Vincennes exhorting his mother to expose the espionage activities of Pierre du Livier, a French businessman residing in London, if the latter failed to encourage French authorities to release Vanbrugh. This and similarly disingenuous behavior later in his career are adduced as evidence that "Honest Van" was less so than his biographers have generally allowed. (Material is incorporated into 1991.1.)

1982

9 MEEKINS, JEANNE S. "A Manuscript Cast for a 1715 Revival of Vanbrugh's *The Mistake.*" *N & Q*, n.s. 29, no. 6 (December): 527–528.

Author examines names on a manuscript cast list found in a performance copy of the 1706 quarto of *The Mistake* owned by the Pennsylvania State University library. Compares that cast list to casts listed in *The London Stage* for performances in 1705, 1710, 1715, 1726, and 1733–1734. Conclusion: the manuscript in question lists performers in the 1715 revival of the play.

10 MILHOUS, JUDITH, and HUME, ROBERT D. Introduction and Comment[ary] to *Vice Chamberlain Coke's Theatrical Papers 1706–1715, Edited from the Manuscripts in the Harvard Theatre Collection and Elsewhere.* Carbondale and Edwardsville: Southern Illinois University Press, pp. xvii–xxix and 1–225 passim.

Introduction discusses Vanbrugh's management of the Haymarket Theatre. Glosses documents indicating that in April of 1705 and again at the conclusion of the 1705–1706 season, Vanbrugh sought unsuccessfully to unite his new company with Rich's Drury Lane Company. Following "a season and a half of politicking" Vanbrugh persuaded Lord Chamberlain Kent to decree a generic split—the Union of 1708—whereby Vanbrugh was granted a monopoly on the production of opera at the Haymarket that would prove financially ruinous for him. Headnotes and glosses of documents for seasons between 1705 and 1715 contain intermittent commentary on Vanbrugh's activities as manager; usefully indexed.

11 ROSS, J. C. "The Printing of Vanbrugh's *The Provok'd Wife* (1697)." *Library* 4 (December):397–409.

Examination of compositor-patterns discernible in the 1697 edition of *The Provoked Wife* suggests that the play was printed rapidly. During the presumed four-week period following the play's premiere during which it was being printed, the printer James Orme was at work on three other works. "[F]inancially stretched" as a consequence, he perhaps "chose to finish off *The Provok'd Wife* relatively quickly, to get a quick cash return. . . ."

12 *SMITH, CHARLES SAUMAREZ. "Charles Howard, third Earl of Carlisle and the Architecture of Castle Howard." Ph.D. dissertation, University of London, 1986.

Source: Smith, 1990.6.

13 STATHIS, JAMES J. "Those Admirable Devils: The Heroes of Restoration Comedy." In *All the World: Drama Past and Present*. Vol.

2. University of Florida. Department of Classics. Comparative Drama Conference Papers. Edited by Karelisa V. Hartigan. Washington, D.C.: University Press of America, pp. 107–123 passim.

In Vanbrugh's *Relapse* (as in Etherege's *The Man of Mode* and Wycherley's *The Country Wife*) the "Devil" is "transform[ed] into an admirable rake-hero." In his opening soliloquy Loveless, *The Relapse*'s "devil," echoes Milton's Satan (*Paradise Lost* I, ll. 254–255) when he avers that "Our Heaven is seated in our Minds." In a scene with Berinthia in IV.iii, Loveless, "In his role as devil-hero," becomes "a successful tempter and seducer," "consciously free[ing] Berinthia from the sterility of widowhood and unconsciously free[ing] Amanda from a Loveless marriage."

14 WATKIN, DAVID. *The English Vision: the Picturesque in Architecture, Landscape and Garden Design*. London: John Murray, pp. 89–91.

"[T]hat towering imaginative genius of eighteenth-century architecture, Sir John Vanbrugh," is argued to be the progenitor of the "picturesque house." Quotes from Reynolds's encomium (1797.2) proposing that Reynolds wrote with Vanbrugh Castle particularly in mind. Vanbrugh Castle and Seaton Delaval (both illustrated) are said to be "anticipatory of the kind of asymmetrical picturesque architecture produced later in the eighteenth and nineteenth centuries."

1983

1 *BARLOW, GRAHAM F. "From Tennis Court to Opera House." D. Phil. dissertation, University of Glasgow. Vol. 1, Part 3.

Source: Milhous and Hume, 1987.10, p. 99 n.354; unverified. Milhous and Hume note that Barlow's dissertation includes "the best reconstruction of the Haymarket theatre as it existed between 1705 and the alterations of 1709."

2 BROWNELL, MORRIS. "Poetical Villas: English Verse Satire of the Country House 1700–1750." In *Satire in the 18th Century*. Edited by J[ohn] D[udley] Browning. New York: Garland, pp. 11–12, 14–15, 35.

Includes brief discussion of the following poems on houses designed by Vanbrugh: the anonymous "Upon the Duke of Marlborough's House [Blenheim Palace]" (1715.3); Samuel Garth's *Claremont* (1715.2), on the house Vanbrugh built for the Duke of Newcastle; and Swift's "History of Vanbrug's ["Goose Pie"] House" (1710.1), a lampoon on Vanbrugh's own house at Whitehall.

1984

3 MALEK, JAMES S. "Comic Irony in Vanbrugh's *The Relapse*: Worthy's Repentance." *CLAJ* 26, no. 3 (March):353-361.

Argues that "Vanbrugh intends Worthy's repentance to be read ironically." The repentance is undercut both by his aside ("How long this influence may last, heaven knows") and by the "reassert[ion] of the play's dominant amorality and cynical views of love and virtue" in the scene that immediately follows, in which Hoyden's indifference to virtue is made plain. The cynical concluding masque "provides the play's final commentary on . . . love and virtue."

4 MCCORMICK, FRANK. "Vanbrugh and the Duke of Newcastle: The Genesis of the Loverule Plot in *A Journey to London*." *BRH* 86, no. 2 (Summer):216-222.

Suggests 1715-1717 as the likely date of composition of the Loverule plot in Vanbrugh's unfinished *Journey to London*. Adduces in evidence similarities in language and thought between the marriage discussions in the Loverule plot and the discussions Vanbrugh himself conducted with the Duke of Newcastle between 1715 and 1717 in the course of negotiating, at the Duchess of Marlborough's request, a marriage between her granddaughter Harriet Godolphin and Vanbrugh's patron, the Duke of Newcastle. Proposes that Vanbrugh chose not to complete the play because "To have brought the Loverule plot before the public would have been to run the risk . . . of exposing the Newcastles's delicate courtship to public ridicule."

5 "SCRIBLERIANA." *Scriblerian* 16, no. 1 (Autumn):72.

Includes a one-paragraph notice of a 1983 production of *The Provoked Wife*, "adapted by John Retallack for the Actors Touring Company."

1984

1 "Architects as Artists." *RIBA Journal* 91, no. 11 (November):46-47.

A "selection of drawings" from a Royal Institute of British Architects exhibition includes a Vanbrugh/Hawksmoor "preliminary design for the entrance front of Castle Howard, 1699."

2 CAST, DAVID. "Seeing Vanbrugh and Hawksmoor." *JSAH* 43, no. 4 (December):310-327.

Attributes eighteenth- and nineteenth-century criticisms of Vanbrugh's designs to their startling originality. Cites eighteenth-century notions of "effect" ("appearance" as opposed to "fact"), noting that though the parts of Vanbrugh's designs are disparate, their "effect" is one of coherence. Hobbes's notion of "fancy"—the bringing together of dissimilar elements—is invoked to demonstrate the perceptual task demanded of the viewer of Vanburgh's Goose-Pie House, Kimbolton, and Grimsthorpe. Properly to "see" these buildings, the mind must work nimbly to bring together their motley references to the architectural past—principally Roman, medieval, and Jacobean.

3 CORDNER, MICHAEL. "Time, the Churches, and Vanbrugh's Lord Foppington." *DUJ*, 77, no. 1 (December); n.s. 46, no. 1:11–17.
Supplies context for Collier's strictures upon Vanbrugh in his *Short View*. Examines passages in *The Relapse* in which Vanbrugh's "profane wit exploits and inverts the attitudes characteristic of conventional piety" as expressed in contemporary sermons and religious tracts. Draws particular attention to Lord Foppington's fondness for the church at St. James's, Piccadilly—notorious in its day for the "'pride' & Luxury" of its congregation's dress, and associated in the public mind with its first rector, Thomas Tenison. Tenison's subsequent elevation to the position of Archbishop of Canterbury deepened the sting of Vanbrugh's satire on the clergy.

4 FINKE, LAURIE A. "Virtue in Fashion: The Fate of Women in the Comedies of Cibber and Vanbrugh." In *From Renaissance to Restoration: Metamorphoses of the Drama*. Edited by Robert Markley and Laurie Finke. Cleveland: Bellflower, pp. 154–179.
Vanbrugh's heroines (like Cibber's) play "double and duplicitous roles." In *The Provoked Wife* Lady Brute, Belinda, Lady Fancyfull, and Madamoiselle are "safe in their fashionable duplicities," "control[lers] of the play's action" (as witness the "trick" Lady Brute concocts to unite Belinda and Heartfree). In *The Relapse* both Hoyden and Young Fashion are victims of patriarchal society—Hoyden because she is a woman, Fashion because he is a younger son. The casting of Mrs. Kent in the part of Young Fashion in the initial 1696 production "underscores the close relationsip between the victims of a society obsessed with money and property." A patriarchialist himself, Vanbrugh at times endows his heroines with his "own idealized, and distorted, views of women" (e.g., of "Amanda as saint").

5 HUME, ROBERT D. "Opera in London, 1695–1706." In *British Theatre and the Other Arts, 1660–1800*. Edited by Shirley Strum Kenny. Washington, D.C.: The Folger Shakespeare Library; London and Toronto: Associated University Presses, pp. 84–88.
Discusses Vanbrugh's efforts during the period 1705–1708 on behalf of his Queen's Theatre at the Haymarket to best Christopher Rich and his Drury Lane performers in the mounting of operas. Why did

Vanbrugh choose to open his theatre with Greber's *Loves of Ergasto* rather than with Granville's *The British Enchanters*? Because *Ergasto* "made absolutely minimal demands for scenes and machines"—an important consideration given the only partially finished state of Vanbrugh's theatre at its April 1705 opening. Rich's success with *Camille* at Drury Lane "fired Vanbrugh's greed," encouraging him in December of 1707 to secure a monopoly on the performance of opera, which would prove financially ruinous.

6 MARKHAM, SARAH. *John Loveday of Caversham, 1711–1789: The Life and Tours of an Eighteenth-Century Onlooker.* Wilson, Salisbury, Wiltshire [England]: Michael Russell, pp. 296–297.

Includes a lengthy excerpt from an unpublished diary in which Loveday recorded his impressions of Vanbrugh's Eastbury House during a tour of 1737–1738. The house is found to resemble Blenheim (cf. Loveday's 1732 diary, 1890.5). Salient features of Eastbury's entrance front and wings are described; concerning the interior, says "nothing can be greater and there sure nothing can be neater and more elegant throughout."

7 MARTIN, PETER. *Pursuing Innocent Pleasures: The Gardening World of Alexander Pope.* Hamden, Conn.: Shoe String Books, Archon Press, pp. 13–14, 108.

Notes Pope's "always enthusiastic response" to "the results of Bridgman's and Vanbrugh's teamwork" at Stowe's gardens in the 1720s. Says Vanbrugh built an amphitheatre "in Wray Wood at Castle Howard probably . . . in the late 1720s." Ascribes Claremont's amphitheatre to Bridgeman.

8 MCCORMICK, FRANK. "The Unity of Vanbrugh's *A Journey to London*." *DUJ* 76, no. 2 (June); n.s. 45, no. 2:187–194.

Observes that the companionate marriage of the Headpiece family in the main plot is counterpoised against the authoritarian Loverule marriage in the subplot. The resultant interplay of temperaments and expectations dramatizes the vulnerabilities of both companionate and authoritarian marital arrangements. Compares Vanbrugh's rendering of his couples' marital difficulties to Cibber's facile resolution of those difficulties in his completed version of the play (*The Provoked Husband*—in which Lady Townly "ends by becoming a 'convert' to her husband's notions of 'truth'"). Concludes that "Vanbrugh's strength lies in his reluctance to simplify either the personalities or the issues with which he is dealing." (Material is incorporated into 1991.1.)

9 MILHOUS, JUDITH. "The Capacity of Vanbrugh's Theatre in the Haymarket." *THStud* 4, pp. 38–46.

Examining box office reports and other contemporary testimony, and mindful that treasurers did not record attendance by nonpaying footmen and other servants, the author estimates the "comfortable" capacity of Vanbrugh's Haymarket Theatre between 1709 and 1778 to have been 670 persons, its "normal" capacity 763, and its "absolute maximum" 940. (See also 1952.1.)

10 O'CONNELL, JANE. "A Calendar of Plays, Concerts, Farces, Afterpieces, Entertainments and Ridottos together with Commentary: Dublin, 1732 to 1742." *DAI* 46 (1985):432A. St. John's University, 207 pp. passim.

Notes that Vanbrugh was one of seven English dramatists (Rowe, Shadwell, Congreve, Shakespeare, Fielding, and Cibber being the others) "whose plays were in constant demand" on the Dublin stage during the period 1732–1742. The "dominant presence" of works by these English playwrights is said to have "precluded the development of an indigenous Irish [s]tage."

11 PATTERSON, FRANK M. "Lord Fopppington and *Le Bourgeois Gentilhomme*." *N & Q*, n.s. 31, no. 3 (September): 377–378.

Proposes that Lord Foppington's complaint to his shoemaker concerning his ill-fitting shoes is derived from Monsieur Jourdain's similar complaint in Molière's *Le Bourgeois Gentilhomme* (1670).

12 ROBINSON, JOHN MARTIN. "The Art of the Architect: Treasures from the R.I.B.A.'s Collections." *Apollo* [London] 120, no. 274 (December):431.

Among the "treasures" in the Royal Institute of British Architects Drawings Collection is a "Preliminary design for Castle Howard by Sir John Vanbrugh"—here reproduced (as Figure 1) but not discussed.

1985

1 *BARKER, NIGEL PATRICK. "The Architecture of the English Board of Ordnance 1660–1750." Ph. D. dissertation, Reading University, 779 pp. (221 pl.).

Source: Abstract and Downes, 1987.4. Includes (says the Abstract) "a brief reappraisal of the connection between Sir John Vanbrugh and the Ordnance." Downes (p. 513) says the author "returned to the conclusion that the Vanbrugian buildings are so different from

1986

the general run of Ordnance architecture that Vanbrugh must have been concerned in some way."

2 MCCORMICK, FRANK. "Vanbrugh's *Relapse* Reconsidered." *SN* 57, no. 1:53–61.

Argues that *The Relapse* dramatizes, in the careers of Amanda in the main plot and Young Fashion in the subplot, "alternative 'right' ways of behaving, each successful in its own terms, each incompatible with the other." The events of the play are so arranged as to insist that "one cannot . . . possess at the same time Amanda's integrity and Young Fashion's power and wealth." (Material is incorporated into 1991.1.)

3 MILHOUS, JUDITH, and HUME, ROBERT D. "The Drury Lane Actors' Petition of 1705." *TN* 39, no. 2:62–67.

Prints and discusses a petition prepared by Rich's Drury Lane actors sometime between 14 June 1705 and 25 July 1705 protesting against Vanbrugh's proposed uniting of London's two acting companies (see 1975.6). The petition testifies to the actors' fears that the proposed union would leave some of them unemployed. Notes that the union Vanbrugh succeeded in engineering in 1708 "destroyed a healthy competition, put a lot of actors out of work, and bankrupted [Vanbrugh] in the bargain."

4 SINDEN, DONALD. *Laughter in the Second Act*. London, Sydney, Auckland, and Toronto: Hodder and Stoughton, pp. 163–176.

In Chapter 16 the British actor recounts his experiences playing the role of Lord Foppington in Vanbrugh's *Relapse*. He describes his costumes (five of them, "each one topped by a series of wigs that grew in outlandishness as the play progressed"), makeup (glitter, beauty spots, lips "like a well-fitted bra in silhouette"), and the usefulness of the *OED* (from which he learned that "Verole" means "gonorrhea" and "stap me vitals," "constipate me").

1986

1 BEARD, GEOFFREY. *The Work of John Vanbrugh*. London: B. T. Batsford, 176 pp.

A chapter sketching the career of "perhaps the most exciting architect England reared" is followed by two carefully documented chapters in which each of Vanbrugh's principal building projects is discusssed in some detail. Text is followed by Anthony Kearsting's photographs of the buildings, each discursively captioned. Author suggests that Vanbrugh's designs may owe something to his study of such French architectural books as Jean Marot's *L'Architecture françoise* (1652) and Antoine le Pautre's *Oeuvres d'Architecture* (1652).

2 PEVSNER, NIKOLAUS. *The Best Buildings of England: An Anthology.* . . . Edited by Bridget Cherry and John Newman with an introduction by John Newman. New York: Viking, p. 137.
  Reprints Pevsner's description and photograph of Seaton Delaval from 1974.13.

3 STYAN, J. L. *Restoration Comedy in Performance.* Cambridge: Cambridge University Press, pp. 51–54, 62–63, 116–118, 231–233.
  Includes discussion of the use of masks in *The Provoked Wife* and performance possibilities for Lord Foppington's dressing scene in *The Relapse* (I.iii).

4 ZIMBARDO, ROSE A. *A Mirror to Nature: Transformations in Drama and Aesthetics, 1660–1732.* Lexington: University of Kentucky Press, pp. 173–174, 177–182.
  Argues that Jeremy Collier's chiding of the playwright for disregarding "the Rules of the Stage" was a "muddled" critique of Vanbrugh's "delusionist simulation of the real." Endowing his characters with "inner psychological experience" was one means by which he achieved his delusionist effects. Young Fashion's possession of an "'inner' motivation" (as witness his "qualms of conscience") distinguishes him from tricksters of 'seventies comedy. Vanbrugh produces similar effects of interiority in his rendering of Loveless's private ruminations in the opening scene of *The Relapse.*

1986-1987

1 HUGHES, DEREK. "Cibber and Vanbrugh: Language, Place and Social Order in *Love's Last Shift.*" *CompD* 20, no. 4 (Winter):287–304.
  Includes discussion of Vanbrugh's *Aesop*, *The Provoked Wife*, *The Confederacy*, *The Country House*, and *A Journey to London* as dramas "dealing with an unsatisfactory home." Characteristic of Vanbrugh's pessimistic treatment of his theme in each of the plays is the conclusion of *The Confederacy*—in which Dick Amlet's intention to build a new house and raise a family presents us with a prospective recurrence of "the unhomelike residences of the former generation."

1987

1   ANTOINE, FABRICE. "Les fables de l'*Aesop* de Sir John Vanbrugh comme miroir de son art." *BSEAA* 24 (June):7–17.

Detailed examination of the relationship of Vanbrugh's *Aesop*, Part I to its source, Boursault's *Ésope à la ville* (1690), which the author thinks Vanbrugh may have read in the Bastille. No mere translation, Vanbrugh's *Aesop* is judged to be more lively, more interestingly detailed than Boursault's, and keener in characterization.

2   BURNS, EDWARD. *Restoration Comedy: Crises of Desire and Identity.* New York: St. Martin's, pp. 156–182.

Discusses Vanbrugh's comedy in relation to that of Etherege and Cibber. *The Provoked Wife* is seen as "a careful imitation and updating of [Etherege's] *She Would if She Could,*" *The Relapse* as an extension and criticism of the materials of Cibber's *Love's Last Shift.*

3   DOWNES, JOHN. *Roscius Anglicanus, or an Historical Review of the Stage.* Edited by Judith Milhous and Robert D. Hume. London: The Society for Theatre Research, pp. 98–101, 104.

New edition of 1708.1. (See also 1987.10.)

4   DOWNES, KERRY. *Sir John Vanbrugh: A Biography.* New York: St. Martin's, 560 pp.

Devotes 100 pages to Vanbrugh's plays and their context, 300 to his architecture (to which the book's forty plates are chiefly devoted). Hawksmoor is pronounced the "Beethoven" to Vanbrugh's "Toscanini." Family connections—particularly the relations with his mother's kinsmen, the Berties—are shown to have played pivotal roles in Vanbrugh's career. Appendixes include lists of his dramatic and architectural works and of his letters, ten "mostly [previously] unpublished" letters, and the text of an anonymous contemporary verse attack, "A True Character of the Prince of Wales's Poet" (1701.1).

5   HARRIS, FRANCES. "An Unpublished Letter of Sir John Vanbrugh." *HLQ* 50, no. 4 (Autumn):395–396.

In his letter of 28 November 1710, Vanbrugh asks Henry Joynes, Comptroller of the Works at Blenheim, to forward Grinling Gibbons's "last bill" for carved work at Blenheim and to pay the mason Bartholomew Peisley for his recent work on Blenheim's Grand Bridge.

6 HUGHES, DEREK. "Vanbrugh and Cibber: Language, Place, and Social Order in *The Relapse*." *CompD* 21, no. 1 (Spring):62–83.

"Geographical displacement" is argued to be symbolic of the "moral and social condition" of the characters of *The Relapse*. Loveless, for example, achieves his adultery with Berinithia while "pretending . . . that he is away from home." "[S]ocial and moral dislocation" is said to be "reflected" in the "obliquity and disorder" of the language employed in conversations between Worthy and Berinthia in III.ii and between Fashion and Coupler in V.i. In Amanda a division is discerned between "principles and inclinations."

7 JACKSON-STOPS, GERVASE. *The Country House Garden: A Grand Tour*. A New York Graphic Society Book. Boston: Little, Brown, pp. 6, 29, 30, 31, 118, 156–157, 189–191, 195–197.

Asserts that "Vaubon's forts were . . . the decisive influence" on the gardens Vanbrugh designed "in partnership with Charles Bridgeman at Blenheim, Grimsthorpe, and Eastbury." Thinks Vanbrugh's satyr gate at Castle Howard drew inspiration from "the Italian Renaissance and the excesses of Bomarzo." Notes the "military theme" of Vanburgh's walled gardens. Deduces from a passage in an anonymous poem on Castle Howard that the "different styles" of the Temple of the Winds, the Mausoleum, and the Pyramid "were deliberately chosen to represent the civilizations of the past—with Vanbrugh's palace representing the Whig supremacy, greatest of them all." Pronounces Vanbrugh "one of the first to argue for the retention of a genuine ruin"—the Manor House at Woodstock. His monumental bridge at Blenheim, his Temple of the Winds at Castle Howard, and his domed rotunda at Duncombe Park, Yorkshire, are illustrated in photographs.

8 LOWDERBAUGH, THOMAS E. Introduction, etc., to *A Critical Edition of Sir John Vanbrugh's "The Confederacy."* Garland Series, *Satire & Sense: Important texts, for the most part dramatic, from the Restoration and Eighteenth Century*. Edited by Stephen Orgel. New York and London: Garland, pp. 1–85, 200–229.

Introduction avers that *The Confederacy*'s "primary activity" is "the deception of others for one's own profit." Examines the play's image clusters (death, war), departures from its source (Dancourt's *Les Bourgeoises à la mode*), and relationship to Vanbrugh's other comedies. The play's characters and themes are judged to be less tractable, less harmoniously resolved than was generally the case with other plays produced in London in the 1705–1706 season. Other preliminaries include *The Confederacy*'s "Stage History," "Textual History," and "Historical Collation." Editor supplies notes and bibliography following playtext. (See also 1976.1.)

1988

9 MCCORMICK, FRANK. "Sir John Vanbrugh's Architecture: Some Sources of His Style." *JSAH* 46, no. 2 (June):135–144.

Suggests three sources for Vanbrugh's architectural vocabulary: (1) "the interior architecture and scene design of the contemporary theatre"; (2) the encircling walls, the ramparts, and the castle in the city of Chester in which he was raised; and (3) the donjon and court-yards of the Chateau of Vincennes, France, where he was confined in 1691. (Material is incorporated into 1991.1.)

10 MILHOUS, JUDITH, and HUME, ROBERT D. Notes to *Roscius Anglicanus, or an Historical Review of the Stage*, by John Downes. London: The Society for Theatre Research, pp. 98–101, 104.

The notes gloss prompter Downes's account of the early years of Vanbrugh's Queen's Theatre at the Haymarket, commencing with the unsuccessful April 1705 premiere of Greber's Italian opera *Gli Amori D'Ergasto* (*The Loves of Ergasto*). Notes 349–364 comment on the opening season, offering corrections and clarifications of Downes's as-sertions and annotated citations of other pertinent critical commen-tary. Notes 378–379 gloss Downes's account of Vanbrugh's August 1706 agreement "to rent the Haymarket theatre, stock, and license to Owen Swiney for a term of seven years. . . ."

1988

1 ANTOINE, FABRICE. "L'utilisation de l'espace scenique chez Sir John Vanbrugh (1664–1726) et les auteurs comiques contemporains: approche statistique." *BSEAA* 26 (June):37–52.

Compares the number and location (parks, taverns, etc.) of scenes in the comedies of Wycherley, Crowne, Southerne, Behn, Con-greve, Cibber, Farquhar, Steele, and Vanbrugh. Among the author's findings are these: in his two original comedies (*The Relapse* and *The Provoked Wife*), Vanbrugh deployed a greater average number of *scenes* (18) than did the other dramatists in the sample, and he set those scenes in a greater number of *locations* than did all but one of the other dramatists surveyed. In this second category Vanbrugh and Behn led the sample, each using an average of 10 locations. Author believes these findings suggest that among the playwrights of his day Vanbrugh was more than commonly concerned with exploration of "l'espace scenique."

2 HADFIELD, MILES. *The English Landscape Garden*. 2d ed. Shire Garden History Series, no. 3. Haverfordwest, Dyfed [England]: C. I. Thomas, pp. 25–29, 31, 51, 65.

Includes brief mention (and several photographs) of Vanbrugh's contributions to the garden architecture at Castle Howard, Stowe, and

Blenheim Palace. Notes Uvedale Price's "regret" (1810.1) that Vanbrugh "had not been more concerned with garden design." (For citation of 1st edition, see 1977.2.)

3 HUME, ROBERT D. "The Sponsorship of Opera in London, 1704–1720." *MP* 85, no. 4 (May):421–426.

Section II ("The Enforced Genre Division of 1708") examines the sequence of calculations and miscalculations that preceded Vanbrugh's securing of his ruinous opera monopoly in 1708. The "Company Plan" in which he described his intentions for his nascent theatre at the Haymarket (1703) makes it clear that Vanbrugh "intended to emphasize plays, not operas," his hope being to preside over a united company of Rich's and Betterton's players. When Rich balked at ceding his company to Vanbrugh, the latter embarked on an expensive effort to best Rich's company in the performance of opera. In so doing, he overestimated the potential proceeds from the performance of opera, paying extravagant salaries for imported Italian singers, fruitlessly hoping for a royal subsidy of 1,000 pounds to recoup his losses. Concerning the 1708 genre split he engineered, concludes that "To satisfy his own ill-judged ambitions," Vanbrugh "forcibly separated opera from the theater that had always financed and supported it"—an act of "folly" that is "difficult to comprehend."

4 KNUTSON, HAROLD C. *The Triumph of Wit: Molière and Restoration Comedy.* Columbus: Ohio State University Press, pp. 8–9, 52, 53, 54, 83, 106.

Reports Thorndyke's inclusion (1929.3) of Vanbrugh's *Relapse* and *Provoked Wife* in his list of nine "perfect specimens of the comedy of manners." Cites *The Provoked Wife*'s pairing of males (Heartfree and Constant) and females (Belinda and Lady Brute) as an instance of one recurring pattern in manners comedy. Includes Sir John Brute among examples of manners comedy's deployment of the *pharmakos* archetype ("society takes its revenge on nonconformist conduct by humiliation and exclusion").

1989

1 BARIDON, MICHEL. "History, Myth, and the English Garden." In *Studies in the History of Art* 25. Center for Advanced Study in the Visual Arts. Symposium Papers X. *The Fashioning and Functioning of the British Country House.* Edited by Gervase Jackson-Stops, Gordon J. Sohochet, Lena Cowen Orlin, and Elisabeth Blair MacDougall.

National Gallery of Art, Washington. Hanover and London: Distributed by the University Press of New England, pp. 379–380, 383.

Includes discussion of Vanbrugh, who deployed "[Whig-serving] myth with extraordinary success." Henry Nash Smith's definition of myth (an "intellectual construction that fuses concept and emotion into an image") is adduced with reference to Castle Howard—in the design of which Vanbrugh is said to have fused the "concept" of "freedom" with a "feeling" of "pride and elation" over England's overturning of Stuart tyranny (in the 1688 revolution) and her subsequent challenge to French hegemony in Europe. Vanbrugh did so through recourse to "images" evocative of England's "feudal gothic" architecture ("Massive, warlike, irregular"). A photograph of Castle Howard's bastioned park wall is offered in evidence. Thinks Reynolds (1797.2) was the first to identify "the great originality of Vanbrugh" when he noted the "connection [Vanbrugh] established between feudal times, gothic architecture, and the landscape."

2 CORDNER, MICHAEL. Introduction to *Sir John Vanbrugh: Four Comedies*. London: Penguin; New York: Viking Penguin, pp. 9–35.

Doubts that in *The Relapse* Vanbrugh "could have given such comprehensive offense to the reformers without realizing what he was doing," his own father having been a "regular and respectful attender" of the "'Week-day lectures'" in Chester of the dissenting preacher Matthew Henry. Examines the plots of Vanbrugh's "four best plays"—*The Relapse, The Provoked Wife, A Journey to London,* and *The Confederacy.* Focuses on their common concern with "marriages in disarray."

3 DU PREY, PIERRE DE LA RUFFINIERE. "Hawksmoor's 'Basilica after the Primitive Christians': Architecture and Theology." *JSAH* 48, no. 1 (March):43–44.

Vanbrugh's church "Proposals" (see 1950.10) are briefly discussed by way of illustrating the author's contention that Hawksmoor's ideas for "Building Fifty New Churches in London" constituted a sensible "middle ground . . . between Vanbrugh's bombast and Wren's more staid conceptions." Quotes from the rebuttal George Hickes addressed to the church commission entitled "Observation on Mr. Van Brugg's proposals about Buildinge the new Churches." In it Hickes expressed approval of Vanbrugh's wish "not to make churches burying places," but took issue with his failure to insist on a separation of chancels and naves.

4 FOWLER, MARIAN. *Blenheim: Biography of a Palace.* New York: Viking, pp. 23–26, 48–52, 54–63.

Quotes from Vanbrugh's correspondence relating to Blenheim and records his tensions with the Duchess of Marlborough. Characterizes the building's style as "fortified baroque."

5 HARRIS, FRANCES. "Parliament and Blenheim Palace: The House of Lords Appeal of 1721." *Parliamentary History* 8, Pt. 1:43–62 passim.

Includes discussion of Vanbrugh's response to the Duchess of Marlborough's effort—in her May 1721 House of Lords appeal—to have Vanbrugh judged accountable for back wages owed to the Blenheim workers. Examines the preliminary maneuverings of both the Duchess and Vanbrugh, noting the usefulness to Vanbrugh's cause of his experiences as "theatrical entrepreneur, dining companion, and architectural consultant to the Whig aristocracy for twenty years." Vanbrugh's *Justification of What He Depos'd in the Duchess of Marlborough's Late Tryal* (before the Court of Exchequer, which had ordered the Duke of Marlborough to pay the workers' arrears) is judged to have shown "how unwise [the Duchess] had been to choose her scapegoat from among the foremost wits of the age." The Lords voted 43 to 25 in Vanbrugh's favor.

6 JONES, CLYVE. "'To Dispose in Earnest, of a Place I got in Jest': Eight New Letters of Sir John Vanbrugh, 1722–1726." *N & Q* 36, no. 4 (December):461–469.

Prints and annotates eight letters in which Vanbrugh discusses his affairs as Herald. Written between September 1722 and February 1725/1726, the letters offer testimony to in-fighting in the College of Heralds in the 1720s, illuminate the means by which Vanbrugh eventually disposed of his office, and offer glimpses of his cozy domestic circumstances during his years of residence at Vanbrugh Castle.

7 NOKES, DAVID. "Lovers and Brokers." *TLS*, 23–29 June, p. 692.

Review of Jonathan Myerson's Greenwich Theatre production of *The Confederacy*, here given its later-eighteenth-century appellation, *The City Wives' Confederacy*. Stressing the currency of the play's concerns, the production offers sets bearing "conspicuously gentrified façades," housefronts "adorned with Chubb alarms," merchants who figure their profits on handheld calculators, and a teen daughter who listens to Madonna on a Walkman. In the production the play's two merchant husbands are "revealed as pathetic victims of the markets they purport to control," their servants "prov[ing] the real experts at insider-dealing."

8   ROTHSTEIN, ERIC. "Sir John Vanbrugh (January 1664–March 1726)." In *Restoration and Eighteenth-Century Dramatists, First Series.* Edited by Paula R. Backscheider. *Dictionary of Literary Biography.* Volume 80. Detroit: Gale Research, pp. 229–244.

Surveys Vanbrugh's career, singling out *The Provoked Wife, The Relapse,* and *A Short Vindication* for extended analysis. Thinks the edifices of Vanbrugh's buildings "theatrical," tending to subdue their landscapes and "subjugate nature." Finds the buildings' gothic elements evocative of "liberty and property, the old British constitution as against Roman (and Roman Catholic) slavishness." Discerns a three-part structure in *The Provoked Wife,* notes correspondences between the play's two plots, and praises the playwright's creation of "the illusion of emotional complexity." Finds the plot of *The Relapse* loose by comparison, its characters' "interrelations . . . less finely worked out," its "farcical plot less thoughtful."

9   THOMAS, DAVID, ed. Compiled and introduced by David Thomas and Arnold Hare. *Restoration and Georgian England, 1660–1788.* Theatre in Europe: A Documentary History. Cambridge: Cambridge University Press, pp. 21–24, 75–76, 380–382, 414, 422–440.

Among the documents printed are Queen Anne's 14 December 1704 license authorizing Vanbrugh and Congreve to build a new theatre, Christopher Rich's December 1705 complaint concerning Vanbrugh's efforts to lure away several of his Drury Lane performers, the Lord Chamberlain's 13 December 1707 decree granting Vanbrugh a monopoly on the performance of opera at his Queen's Theatre, and contemporary accounts of Garrick's performance in the role of Sir John Brute (*The Provoked Wife*). Also offers speculation concerning Vanbrugh's alterations of his theatre in 1708.

10 TIPPETTS, NANCY LYN. "Sisterhood, Brotherhood, and Equality of the Sexes in the Restoration Comedies of Manners." *DAI* 51 (1990):172A. University of Utah, 211 pp.

Argues that Vanbrugh, Etherege, Wycherley, Congreve, and Farquhar insist in their comedies on the "equality of the sexes." They do so by "acknowledg[ing] and neutraliz[ing]" the "gendered context" of "equality."

1990

1 ALSOP, J. D. "The Quarrel between Sir John Vanbrugh and George Powell." *RECTR,* 2d ser. 5, no. 1 (Summer):28–29.

From an anonymous manuscript newsletter attached to *The Post-Man,* 9–11 April 1706, quotes a report that the actor George Powell "had some words" with Vanbrugh "in a publick house and gave the latter a box in y[e] Ear." Concerning construction of Vanbrugh's Queen's Theatre at the Haymarket, transcribes the following observation, attached to *The Post-Man,* 29–31 August 1704: "Mr. Vanbrookes Play house in y[e] Haymarket is Roofeing and will be finisht by Christmas, being y[e] largest in Europe. [I]t is 60 foot wide, 132 long and 50 foot high. [T]he walles in the foundation 7 foot thick. [I]t is built by subscription and 3000 Guineas already subscribed by y[e] Dukes of Devon, Somerset etc. and it's said the Queen gave 1000 Guineas towards it."

2 BATEY, MAVIS, and LAMBERT, DAVID. *The English Garden Tour: A View into the Past.* London: John Murray, pp. 136, 139–140, 163–164, 167–168, 173.

Includes discussion of Vanbrugh's "predilection for ruins" ("well known to the Kit-Cat Club") and his siting of Blenheim Palace and its "monumental bridge" (illustrated in a reproduction of Turner's painting of "Blenheim House and Park—Oxford," c. 1832). Thinks Reynolds (1797.2) and Price (1810.1) in their celebration of Vanbrugh as "innovator of the picturesque" contributed more than did Mavor in the many editions of his *Description of Blenheim* (1800.1) to the elevation of Vanbrugh's reputation as an architect. Also discussed: Vanbrugh's hand in Stowe's garden buildings, in Castle Howard's garden and approaches, and in the garden on which he and Bridgeman collaborated at Claremont (illustrated in two drawings by John Rocque first published in 1738 and 1754).

3 CLARKE, G. B., ed. *Descriptions of Lord Cobham's Gardens at Stowe (1700–1750).* Buckinghamshire Record Society. No. 26. Dorchester, Dorset: Dorset Press. (See parenthetical page citations below.)

Among the twenty-three eighteenth-century descriptions of Stowe printed in this anthology (several of them never previously published), the following contain references to garden buildings designed by Vanbrugh: (1) author "probably Edward Southwell," *Account of my Journey begun 6 Aug. 1724* (excerpted p. 19) notes "offices ["built by" Vanbrugh] at both ends [of Stowe House]"; (2) Charles, 8th Lord

Cathcart, excerpt from *Diary*, 18 August 1730 mentions Vanbrugh's
Pyramid, Rotunda, and (Vanbrugh's?) "2 Pavillions fort jolie"
(p. 29); (3) Gilbert West, *Stowe, The Gardens* . . . (1732; pp. 39, 42–
43, 47, 49—for annotation, see 1732.1); (4) Jeremiah Milles, excerpt
from *Account, of the Journey that Mr Harndess and I took in July
1735,* mentions Vanbrugh's two doric temples (p. 61), his Pyramid and
its inscription in his memory (p. 62), "Nelson's Pavillion built by Sir
John Vanbrugh" (63), and (to the right of the "Parterre close to the
house") "A Dorick arch with a square Pillaster, and round Pillar on
each side, fluted, built by" Vanbrugh (pp. 63–64); (5) Samuel Richardson, "Appendix" to the third edition of Defoe's *Tour thro' the Whole
Island of Great Britain* (for annotation, see 1742.2); (6) Samuel Boyse,
*The Triumphs of Nature, A Poem, on the magnificent Gardens at
Stowe* . . . (1742—for annotation, see 1742.1); (7) *Some Observations
made in a Journey begun June the 7th, and finish'd July the 9th 1742,*
which includes a rudimentary "Plan of [Vanbrugh's] two Dorick Temples which are adorn'd with a Pedament" (p. 113) and description of
Vanbrugh's Rotunda (p. 115); (8) Benton Seeley, *Description of the
Gardens . . . at Stow* (1744, pp. 126, 129, 131 [Rotunda and "Sleeping
Parlour"]—for annotation, see 1747.1); (9) Benton Seeley, *Views of
the Temples and other ornamental Buildings in the Gardens* (1750;
pp. 147–157—for annotation, see 1750.4); (10) J. d. C., *Les Charmes
de Stow* (1748, pp. 159, 165—for annotation, see 1748.1).

4 CORDNER, MICHAEL. "Marriage Comedy after the 1688 Revolution: Southerne to Vanbrugh." *MLR* 85, pt. 2 (April):282–289.
   Vanbrugh's *Relapse* and *The Provoked Wife* are discussed in relation to three other late-seventeenth-century marriage comedies—
Southerne's *The Wives Excuse*, Crowne's *The Married Beau*, and Cibber's *Love's Last Shift*. Author expresses skepticism about the "tradition" that *The Provoked Wife* was written in the Bastille. Sees link-
ages to *The Wives Excuse* that suggest "the lion's share" of the play
was written "after Vanbrugh's return from France."

5 DUGGAN, MARGARET M. *English Literature and Backgrounds,
1660–1700. A Selective Critical Guide.* Vol. 2. New York and London: Garland, pp. 988–997.
   Includes a select bibliography of works on Vanbrugh.

6 HARRIS, EILEEN. *British Architectural Books and Writers, 1556–
1785.* Cambridge: Cambridge University Press, pp. 91n. 83, 115, 142,
144n.1, 148, 216, 242, 243, 273, 291, 355, 370, 373, 374, 378, 383.
   Vanbrugh references include the following: (1) Carlyle's citation
of James Adam's comments on Blenheim (1860.2); (2) Vanbrugh's

support of John Price's proposed (1719) edition of d'Aviler's *Compleat Course of Architecture*; (3) Campbell's effusive thanks to Vanbrugh for his contribution of designs for *Vitruvius Britannicus* (1715–1725.1); (4) Vanbrugh's approbation of John Sturt's English edition of Pozzo's *Perspectiva*; (5) Langley's account of Vanbrugh's building style in his *Principles of Antient Masonry* (1734.1); (6) James Lewis's tribute to Vanbrugh in his *Original Designs in Architecture* (1780; annotated in 1797.1); (7) Vanbrugh's subscription to Giacomo Leoni's edition of the four books of Palladio's *Architecture.*; (8) Ralph's censure of Vanbrugh's Goose-Pie House in his *Critical Review of the Public Buildings of London* (1734.2).

7 MILHOUS, JUDITH, and HUME, ROBERT D. "John Rich's Covent Garden Account Books for 1735–1736." *ThS* 31, no. 2 (November):226–227.

Includes a table in which Vanbrugh's salary scales for his proposed 1703 "Plan for a United Theatre Company" (see 1975.6) are compared with Rich's later payments to his Covent Garden personnel.

8 SMITH, CHARLES SAUMAREZ. *The Building of Castle Howard.* London & Boston: Faber and Faber, pp. 33–59 and passim.

A chapter devoted to Castle Howard's "Architect" speculates that during the four months that elapsed between his 22 November 1692 release from the Bastille on bond and his April departure for England, Vanbrugh "explore[d] the streets of Paris," during which excursions such buildings as Le Vau's Collège des Quatre Nations and Hardouin-Mansart's château at Marly and his church of Les Invalides "left their mark . . . on Vanbrugh's visual imagination" and were subsquently "echoed in the design of Castle Howard." His "up-to-date knowledge" of French architecture may have induced fellow Kit-Cat Lord Carlisle to offer Vanbrugh the Castle Howard commission after preliminary negotations with Talman soured. The commission secured, Vanbrugh toured the north of England to sharpen his knowledge of current building practice, visiting Nottingham's house at Burley-on-the Hill, Kiveton, and Chatsworth, and perhaps borrowing features from each for his Castle Howard design. Concludes that Vanbrugh "was entirely and exclusively responsible for the first ideas" for Castle Howard. He prepared the initial wooden model and only afterward engaged the experienced Hawksmoor to translate his ideas "into architectural reality." A subsection entitled "Design Analysis" includes praise of Vanbrugh for the ingenuity of his ground plan, in which "maximum visual effects" are wrought from "the minimum number of rooms." (Incorporates material from 1982.12.)

1991

1 MCCORMICK, FRANK. *Sir John Vanbrugh: The Playwright as Architect*. University Park: Pennsylvania State University Press, 196 pp.

A synthesis of Vanbrugh's achievement as dramatist and architect. Includes chapter-length analyses of *The Relapse, The Provoked Wife, The Confederacy*, and *A Journey to London*. Two chapters on the architecture examine the sources of Vanbrugh's building style and argue that the plays and the buildings are linked by their creator's pursuit of the metaphor of the "embattled citadel." (Incorporates material from 1982.7, 1982.8, 1983.4, 1984.4, 1985.1, and 1987.9.)

Index of Authors and Other Sources

Index of Topics and Allusions

Adam, James, praise of V's architecture cited, 1860.2; 1990.6

Adam, Robert, praise of V's arthitecture quoted, 1922.1; 1927.6; 1949.1; 1950.7; 1956.4

Alberti, *Ten Books of Architecture*, 1965.3; 1981.11

Ancaster (Robert Bertie), 1st Duke, 1964.7; 1970.2; 1970.6

Anstis, John, 1967.6

Archer, Thomas, called V's "pupil," 1897.2

Bense, J. F., criticism of V's plays reproved, 1922-1923.1

Bernbaum, Ernest, 1948.4

Bertie family, 1701.1; 1927.13; 1939.3; 1977.2; 1987.4

Bertie, Peregrine, 1701.1; 1927.13

Betterton, Thomas, 1976.10; 1979.11

Beveridge, Colonel William, 1929.4

Bingham, Madeleine, 1974.1 rvd. in 1975.8

Blackmore, Sir Richard, 1791.1

Blaire, Hugh, judgments of V's comedies quoted, 1891.1

Bolton, Arthur, 1929.5

Boswell, James, 1950.7

Boulter, Edmund, 1962.1

Boursault, Edme, *Les Fables d'Ésope*, V preserves its sentimental elements in *Aesop*, Part 1; 1907.2

Bridgeman, Charles, 1948.2; 1959.5; 1966.5; 1969.2; 1973.7; 1977.10; 1990.2

Brownell, Morris R., 1956.7

Brown, Lancelot ("Capability"), 1938.5

Bubb (Doddington), George. *See* Doddington, George Bubb

Burlington, 3rd Earl, 1926.1

Butt, John, 1949.7

Cabanel, Daniel, praises Blenheim Palace in verse, 1815.4

Campbell, Colin, 1924.5; 1926.1; 1926.9; 1935.4; 1948.6; 1949.11; 1965.5; 1972.1; 1973.8; 1976.3; 1990.6

Capon, William, 1972.4

Carlisle, 3rd Earl, 1804.3; 1838 [-1854].1; 1927.11; 1982.12; 1990.8

Carlyle, Thomas, "clothes" philosophy compared to that of V in *Relapse*, 1984.1

Carmarthen, Marquis, comments on V's behavior in naval combat, 1694.1; 1979.6

Chudleigh, Mary, *A Ladies Defence* (1701), 1970.1

Churchill, Sarah, Duchess of Marlborough, 1838.1; 1839.3; 1849.1; 1989.4. *See also* Marlborough, 1st Duke and Duchess.

Cibber, Colley, 1931.2; *She Wou'd, and She Wou'd Not*, 1956.6; 1965.1-2; 1969.4; 1970.8

Clark, George, dines with V, 1901.2

Cobham, Lord, 1959.5

Coke, Thomas, Vice-Chamberlain, 1937.2; 1959-1960.1; 1966.1; 1974.9; 1982.1; 1982.10

Collier, Jeremy, *A Short View of the Immorality, and Profaneness of*

1973.12; 1977.6; stage history, 1974.11; Voltaire's *Le Comte de Boursoufle*, 1862.1; 1862.4; 1973.3; antecedents (*Crowne's City Politiques*, Wycherley's *Country Wife*, Otway's *Soldier's Fortune*), 1970.8; blank verse, 1970.8; 1971.1; 1972.7; criticism of structure, 1698.1; 1893.3; 1952.3; 1989.8; female protagonists, 1984.4; influenced by: Congreve, 1924.2; Molière, 1939.4; 1984.11; influence on, 1943.1 (Lessing's *Der Dorfjunker* and *Die Juden*); interpretation, 1976.5; 1978.2; 1979–1980.1; 1981.2; 1985.2; 1991.1; Lockett's Ordinary, 1935.3; Lord Foppington, 1873.3 (his "dialect"); 1948.3; 1974.2; 1985.4 and 1986.3 (performance possibilities); matrimonial law, 1942.1; mingled "hard"/"humane" comedy, 1976.4; morality of: defended, 1923.2; 1971.1; 1979–1980.1; 1987.6; impugned, 1698.1; 1764.1; penitent rake, 1952.2; préciosité, 1955.1; printing exigencies, 1972.7; rake as "devil" (Milton's *Paradise Lost* infl.), 1982.13; reception, 1704.1; 1931.1 (18th c.); relation to: Cibber's *Love's Last Shift*, 1971.3; 1939.2; 1947.2; 1970.8; 1973.16; Shakespeare's *Romeo and Juliet*, 1948.4; 1957.3; 1973.4 (via Otway's *Caius Marius*); 1973.16; stage history, 1948.3; textual history, 1970.8; themes: "geographical displacement," 1987.6; marital tension, 1974.4; 1978.2; 1989.2; 1991.1; relation to Christian ethic, 1968.3; 1969.6; 1971.3; 1973.15; 1980.3; 1984.3

Squire Trelooby (1704), 1924.4; 1928.2; 1936.6; 1976.5; relation to: *The Cornish Squire*, 1878.1; 1968.7; 1970.5; *Gordian Knot Untied*, said to be source, 1925.1–2; denied, 1925.5

Themes
"antimercantile bias," 1958.3
marital incompatability, 1928.1; 1934.1; 1942.1; 1962.4; 1965.4; 1966.10; 1974.4; 1974.6; 1980.13; 1981.1; 1990.4
politics; 1963.1
primogeniture, 1934.1
"rural-urban antagonisms," 1959.3
"unsatisfactory home," 1986–1987.1

poetry
"To a Lady More Cruel than Fair" (1780), 1780.2
Vanbrugh, Kendrick ["Hendrick"?], 1929.4
Voltaire, adaptation of V's *Relapse* noted, 1862.1; 1862.4; 1950.7

Wakefield, William, 1957.3
Walpole, Horace, 1780.2; 1950.7; 1966.2
Walpole, Robert, 1827.1; 1950.3
Walsh, William, author of *Gordian Knot Untied* (1691), 1925.1
Wentworth, Peter, 1950.1
Wheate, Sir Thomas, 1948.7
Whistler, Laurence, 1938.7 rvd. in 1938.2, 1938.4, 1938.6, 1939.5, 1940.1, 1940.3; 1954.5 rvd. in 1954.3–4, 1955.4–6; 1967.5; 1978.1